A THING OF UNSPEAKABLE HORROR

A THING OF UNSPEAKABLE HORROR

The History of Hammer Films

Sinclair McKay

First published in Great Britain 2007 by
Aurum Press Limited
7 Greenland Street
London NW1 0ND

ISBN-10: 1 84513 249 1
ISBN-13: 978 1 84513 249 1

1 3 5 7 9 10 8 6 4 2
2007 2009 2011 2010 2008

Designed and typeset in Revival Bold by Robert Updegraff
Printed and bound by CPD in Ebbw Vale, Wales

CONTENTS

ACKNOWLEDGEMENTS

With thanks to the British Film Institute, Hammer Films, Lorna Bradbury, Christopher Bray, Michele Cefai, Alex Clark, Toby Clements, Victor Davis, Bryan Forbes, Terry Illott, Martin Jarvis, Victoria Lane, Francis Matthews, Kate O' Mara, Robin Price, Stephen Robinson, Rachel Simhon, John Standing, Sarah Standing and Kate Summerscale.

INTRODUCTION

In 1957, a modest little British film company based in Berkshire and previously best known for quickie melodramas, police thrillers and monochrome science-fiction features, almost accidentally scored an enormous box-office hit with *The Curse of Frankenstein.*

In retrospect, those were innocent days. All it took then was a stolen brain, a dash of gore, an acid bath, and the sight of Peter Cushing nonchalantly wiping a smear of blood on to his lapel and the film critics rose up like a lynch mob, determined to strangle the infant before it was out of the cradle. The sternly socialist *Tribune* described the film as 'Depressing and degrading for anyone who loves the cinema', while in the *Sunday Times* the doyenne of contemporary film critics, Dilys Powell, regretted that such productions left her unable to 'defend the cinema against the charge that it debases'.

The condemnation was predictably counter-productive; across Britain cinema-goers flocked into their local Odeons and ABCs, eager to be outraged. History, too, has taken a more lenient view. Today, cinema grandees such as Martin Scorsese and Tim Burton pay tribute to the influence the movie and its successors had upon their work – and the DVD currently carries a '12' rating. Over the years, moreover, Hammer's careful budget of just under £65,000 has reaped worldwide profits of over £6 million.

It was *The Curse of Frankenstein* that brought the phrase 'Hammer Horror' into the language and kicked off one of the most remarkable commercial success stories of British – and international – cinema. It changed how audiences looked at film. And the studio still casts a long shadow over popular culture today.

Even now, half a century after the release of *The Curse of Frankenstein*, Hammer films remain – in some curious and rather amusing way – hugely influential and quite unrivalled. Clearly we have had countless horror films since the Hammer era. And there were countless horror films before it. None, though, that ever reproduced Hammer's unique only-just-this-side-of-camp appeal.

This is why the phrase 'Hammer Horror' is today greeted by so many people with an affectionate laugh of recognition. Through cinema or television or DVD, the great majority of us are at least familiar with the form. Right from the start, these horrors – the Frankensteins, the Draculas, the mummies – contrived to be both shockingly transgressive and reassuringly familiar; like a slightly disreputable uncle, whose behaviour at social events is certain to be distasteful, yet always contained within careful bounds.

Perhaps you first saw a Hammer Horror when you were a teenager enjoying a Friday night out at the flicks in the 1960s with your mates and your girlfriend or boyfriend, piling into the red-plush-lined ABC cinema auditorium armed with thin, bitter orange squash and cigarettes, ready for a raucous laugh at *The Mummy's Shroud* or *The Kiss of the Vampire*.

More recent generations will have stumbled across Hammer Horror in a different way: for instance, lads and ladettes returning home from the pub of a Friday night, falling on to the sofa, switching the telly on and exclaiming 'Yay!' upon seeing the opening titles of a Hammer, their drink-swilled eyes the same colour as a vampire's. There are circumstances in which *Dracula Has Risen from the Grave* is a huge treat. Quite a few circumstances, actually. Sorry, Christopher Lee, but it's true. That film is the drunk person's *Citizen Kane*.

Or perhaps you are among the art-house crowd who, in recent years, have been enjoying Hammer films in what the programme notes might describe as a 'discrete cultural phenomenon', joining earnest beard-strokers in the subsidised bar before trooping into the cinema to watch (and secretly revel in) the great Hammer film retrospective?

There is the slender chance, perhaps, that you have been to the Yorkshire seaside town of Whitby in the summer and happened across the annual parade of youthful Goths who gather at the town's ruined abbey to celebrate the fact that this is where Dracula, in Bram Stoker's novel, came ashore. The Count didn't in the Hammer version, chiefly because the budget wouldn't stretch to it; but the white (and scarlet) make-up, capes and gowns sported by the Goths are an amusingly elaborate bow to the pervasive aesthetics of these films.

Hammer was an extraordinarily prolific operation, especially for a studio so small, which is why when you see either Peter Cushing or Christopher Lee on your TV screen now, there is still the possibility that you haven't seen the particular Hammer Horror that they are gracing.

There were endless (and endlessly inventive) variations on the Dracula and Frankenstein themes; a multitude of re-matches for mummies and psychos. Intriguing one-offs, including a Gorgon and a snake woman. Even a were-wolf in the guise of Oliver Reed. What was not to enjoy?

As the production team were always pointing out to the newspapers, in a slightly huffy fashion, Hammer didn't just do monsters. In the space of some thirty-odd years, the studio managed to crank out nearly 200 films – searing war dramas, half-term holiday pirate adventures, science fiction, dinosaur epics, vulgar comedies and modish psycho-sexual melodramas. But in truth, enjoyable though these other films were, it is the crypt creepers that we all chiefly return to, with such enjoyment, again and again.

It is a testament to the studio that more recent – and high-budget – productions of *Dracula*, for instance, have fought hard to wrest the story away from that enduring and familiar Hammer iconography. In 1992, direc-tor Francis Ford Coppola sought to realign the Count (Gary Oldman) as a melancholy romantic moving through a disorientating world of dazzling Victorian optical trickery. For Christmas 2006, the BBC reworked the story with Marc Warren, as a parable of sexually transmitted disease, repression – and – unless this is simply imagination – eastern European immigration. What is remarkable is how both productions – lavish, enthusiastic and inventive – none the less swiftly faded from memory in the way that Christopher Lee's blazing-eyed demon somehow never will.

In 1978, Kate Bush sang: 'Hammer Horror – won't leave it alone!' As it happened, production on the films had pretty much ceased by then. But even now, they remain a popular byword for something intrinsically, uniquely and horridly British. We still can't leave it alone.

There was something very British about their production methods too. Hammer films were based for the main part at a country house called Down Place, just outside a pretty village called Bray, in Berkshire. The village is about fifteen miles outside of London, just down the road from Windsor Castle, and it is now rather more famous as the home of two restaurants that boast Michelin stars, Michel Roux's Waterside Inn and Heston Blumenthal's Fat Duck.

Hammer was an independent company, although in time it came to rely on money from all sorts of investors, including American studios such as Warner Brothers. This did not detract from the cottage-industry feel of what it was doing though.

In the production office, you had a gang of executives who remained unchanged for a good part of the company's run. On the set were actors who appeared together so frequently in these films that they formed a sort of gothic repertory company. Then out the films went, to the cinemas, often as double-bills to give audiences an even greater sense of getting their money's worth. The emphasis on getting one's money's worth is a constant theme in the Hammer story, from the budget-scrutinising producers to the running times of the films, which were kept to the bare minimum (celluloid being the price it was). Hammer was always careful with money.

But it was always inventive too. Like many British cultural innovators who came after them, the screenwriters and directors of Hammer were, from 1957 onwards, vehemently interested in pushing the envelope. They were determined to show more blood, more gore, than had ever been seen on the screen before. They were determined to get more sex up there – more heaving embonpoint, more seduction, more sauce. Quite where this full-throated ferocity came from in the 1950s is something we shall be investigating. Could this really be the same nation that had produced *Genevieve* and *Doctor in the House* just a few years earlier?

And by God, Hammer was determined to conquer America. This tiny company was set on cracking those Stateside audiences. Extraordinarily, right from the start, Hammer succeeded. Throughout the late 1950s and much of the 60s, the studio largely beat off the US domestic competition in the horror market. And this conquest was perhaps ultimately more cultural than commercial.

In fact, it is no exaggeration to say that during a period when Britain's influence and power was starting to wane sharply, we did at least have the scant consolation of dominating not just America but in fact the world when it came to horror. From Japan to the continent, there was a time when Hammer Horrors were not only enjoyed by countless millions, but imitated widely by scores of film-makers. The only way to do horror was the Hammer way.

The British have always had an especial affinity for tales of macabre violence. As well as the authors of *Frankenstein* and *Dracula*, Mary Shelley and Bram Stoker, Britain also nurtured other dark influences, such as the eighteenth-century rise of the Gothick (and who isn't allergick to that superfluous 'k'?), and the Victorian taste for wild and bloody stage melodrama. Hammer was the 1950s flowering of many generations' worth of influence – as peculiarly British as municipal floral clocks.

So there's spookiness and sexiness but underneath all that, there is still something else going on. It's not just the incredibly sincere acting; or the occasional surprising beauty of the camerawork; or the power of the music. It's something more difficult to pinpoint – intangible. But something which is still there today when you see these films once more. You may start off laughing but you don't laugh for long. What were the Hammers really all about? What was it that my ten-year-old self, furtively creeping down the stairs to watch the late-night Hammer on TV in the 1970s, enjoyed so much? And to be utterly truthful, still blushingly enjoys today?

Why is it that the DVDs continue to sell so ridiculously well both here and in the States? Why do Hollywood directors such as Martin Scorsese, Roman Polanski, Quentin Tarantino and Tim Burton cite Hammer films as formative influences? How did they come to inspire the artist Andy Warhol?

More recently, why did a consortium of businessmen, including Charles Saatchi, buy the studio name and the archive? Why has the normally snooty British Film Institute painstakingly restored and reissued the first three Hammer Horrors for the art-house DVD market? Why, in other words, some twenty-five years after it ceased production, does Hammer remain a byword for a very particular form of screen entertainment?

The Hammer phenomenon also leads us to ask other, wider questions about British culture then and now. For instance, the rise of Hammer Horror was very swift. Its fall, when it came some twenty years after, was equally vertiginous. What does this tale tell us about the British film industry as a whole? How does the decline of Hammer fit in with the general sickliness of a domestic industry? How did the studio manage to retain its cheerfully inventive spark when all around it was sinking into gloom? And more especially, what do Hammer's prodigious years of success tell us?

Today's British film industry appears to be dominated by downbeat small-scale dramas, flashy and savage gangster romps and – yes – the occasional horror film, such as *28 Days Later* (2002) and *Dog Soldiers* (2002). The question is: is there anything that anyone can learn from Hammer's story and is the success of this studio the kind that could be repeated today were the same principles applied?

One thing can be said with iron certainty. Hammer represents something a little more resonant than just a series of lurid and ultimately silly horror films. With a distance of fifty years, is it possible that they can now tell us something about modern British culture, and about ourselves?

Chapter One

WHAT IS A HAMMER FILM?

 Before getting into history and culture; and before asking questions about form, structure and identity – or indeed, before simply overlooking such questions altogether – we could begin by writing out a little visual checklist of all the best-loved Hammer leitmotifs still recognised the world over. Of course, many different studios made horror movies at this time but these are elements which remained unique to Hammer. I think you will be taken aback at how many of them you can give an enthusiastic tick of recognition to.

1) Christopher Lee's blood-red contact lenses. Actually, you don't see these as often as you would think but they are a treat when you do. They are popped in for special dramatic moments – including throat biting and expressing rage – and always look frightfully uncomfortable. Rather like that businesswoman in the Acuvue TV ad. There were two varieties of lens that were custom-made for Lee throughout the course of the films: 'veined' and 'completely red'. 'Veined' was for when the Count was just thinking about it. Lee said of his Dracula films, 'I was constantly crashing into people and falling over things.'

2) Peter Cushing's eyeball, as seen through a magnifying glass, when he is peering at a disembodied brain; this particular image (sans brain) has been lifted and used now in so many films and TV shows that the people at Hammer must rue the day they didn't copyright it. It was turned into a very nice jokey homage in the film comedy *Top Secret* (1984), when Cushing in a cameo role lowers the magnifying glass to reveal that his eyeball really *is* that huge.

3) Countless plunging necklines; the Transylvania that Hammer consistently seeks to portray is a land where the manufacture of semi-saucy silky nightwear must be one of the chief bedrocks of the economy. Certainly rare is the Hammer actress who is not required, at some point, to run through a pine forest (allegedly nocturnal – we shall return to this issue) in a white nightie, displaying heaving décolletage, being closely pursued by a horse-drawn hearse. Among those who received this honour were Jenny Hanley, Veronica Carlson, Barbara Ewing and – remarkably – the fashionable hotel owner Anouska Hempel, who now does not care to be reminded of the Dracula film in which she played Dracula's girlfriend. Actress Kate O'Mara says she has not been able to face watching her own flimsy-nightie Hammer roles. 'But I did, thank goodness, have a no-nudity contract,' she says firmly.

4) That inn (always slightly over-lit) at the centre of the all-purpose studio-built middle-European village. The actor Michael Ripper is always the landlord, although the length of his sideburns changes between films, presumably to give the illusion that he is another, quite different, Transylvanian landlord. But contrary to the popular view, strangers *are* generally welcome at his bar. In the early days of his stewardship, the stranger is usually flinty Van Helsing, turning up late in the evening with a Gladstone bag full of crucifixes and stakes and asking for food even though it is perfectly plain that the kitchen is shut. As the inn progresses from film to film, it increasingly becomes a place of sanctuary for beleaguered romantic leads and alcoholic priests at the mercy of resurrected vampires. Though in one film – *Dracula Has Risen from the Grave* (1968) – the screenwriter spots this flaw and has Dracula infiltrate the inn itself, an act of such awesome desecration that not one of the characters suspects until it is too late.

5) Home counties woodlands masquerading as Transylvania. To be slightly more specific, Black Park near Slough in Berkshire, which has also doubled as Switzerland in *Goldfinger* and the planet Alzarius in *Doctor Who*. But Black Park is the ne plus ultra of Hammer locations. Occasionally, we see it in daylight – when, say, a party of peasants and a priest are trudging along for a woodland burial, signifying that the *evil has returned*. The sun is also present when the English travellers are attempting to make their way to the castle after the coachman has refused to take them a step further. But then night – allegedly – falls. And those woods of pine trees take on a whole new existence. The thunderous clip-clop of speeded up horses' hooves and the satanic crack of whips; the rustle of daring silky nightwear as the heroine attempts to make a dash for it in impractical high heels through the

trees; the pale blue of the alleged night sky; and the shadows thrown by the protagonists, despite it being well past midnight. Of all the Hammer enthusiasts around the world, the French (oh yes, the French adored them) would probably have found this perfectly easy to swallow. *Le fantastique* and all that. More on the French – and the Italians and the Germans – later.

6) Dracula's scarlet-lined cloak. No, but it's a beauty though, a genuine touch of Transylvanian class. It's iconic. Always at the corner of your eye when the Count is presenting himself at the French windows of the young heroine's bedroom. Always very much to the fore when the Count has been defeated, and is crumbling to dust. It is always against this scarlet silky lining that Dracula meets his (temporarily) final moments.

7) The scene-stealing character-actor manservants, among them Phillip Latham and Patrick Troughton; doubtless mindful that the role of faithful castle retainer can be hugely unrewarding, these veterans mug and camp for all that they are worth, driving their vampiric master into quite understandable paroxysms of fury.

8) Peter Cushing's nostrils flaring with suppressed rage; they are always doing this, whether he is being Van Helsing and people are not taking his garlic-based precautionary measures seriously enough, or whether he is Baron Frankenstein and the local gendarmerie have come round and have had the impertinence to ask what all that commotion in his attic was about. Cushing was probably the finest of Hammer's actors. The utterly believable icy malice that he brought to the role of Frankenstein was precisely the opposite of his gentle, considerate, softly-spoken real-life personality. You do sense, though, that those nostrils saw some real-life provocation in their time.

9) Virile young protagonists unable to plunge the stake in at the crucial moment; surprisingly, given the familiarity of the scenario, this is a unique element of Hammer suspense, the moment when the coffin and its dreadful occupant are discovered in the cellar, and the hero – be it Barry Andrews, Dennis Waterman, Martin Jarvis or Anthony Higgins, who later went on to be the star of *The Draughtsman's Contract* – has it within his power to destroy the monster. Key elements in this scene include: uncertain handling of the stake and mallet; fatal dithering as the vampire sleeps; and then the need to escape when the vampire *very suddenly* wakes up. Incidentally, you never see a vampire woozily waking up and then deciding to get ten more minutes' shut-eye.

10) Heavily breathing, extravagantly bosomed vampire ladies seducing virile young protagonists; this, of course, a further element of sauce that the audiences would have been after, whether it's a bare-chested Edward da Souza at the mercy of a tooth-flashing temptress in *The Kiss of the Vampire* (1964) or, in the studio's original *Dracula* (1958), Jonathan van Eyssen being given the glad-fang by Valerie Gaunt.

11) Gobbets of blood with an occasional milkshake-like texture; Hammer itself sometimes self-deprecatingly referred to its special-effects blood as 'Kensington gore' and it seems to have been one of the small unspoken conspiracies between production team and audiences that the blood on show would never be realistic and, at worst, be howlingly absurd. At the time of *Dracula AD 1972*, the studio was apparently having the stuff made by a small factory in Cornwall, at a price of £28 a gallon, which actually seems rather steep. Some of the silliest sanguinary efforts are to be found in *Taste the Blood of Dracula* (1970) – the fluid alluded to in the title, sloshed around in goblets by Ralph Bates, begins as a Nesquik-style powder and becomes something with the look of runny raspberry jam. The aesthetic reasoning seems to have been this: the screenplay and strength of the acting would convey sufficient quantities of horror of themselves – and to make the blood realistic would have damaged the carefully contrived fantasy world in which these stories took place.

12) Peter Cushing pursing his lips while holding a surgical saw; again, a crucial part of the 'dare' element in Hammer films are the scenes when Baron Frankenstein is about to embark upon some gruesome surgery – usually involving a brain transplant – and the director is challenging the audience not to flinch or bury their faces in their hands. The signal for such a moment is when Cushing holds up a sinister-looking surgical saw and compresses his lips with a sort of ghoulish determination. The camera will *always* cut away just before the Baron makes that first incision – we just hear the sound effects instead – but those who hide their eyes won't know that. Again, there is a faint element of conspiracy here between producers and audience, the knowledge that some moments of horror can actually produce laughter. And it isn't at all a bad thing; in fact, it's rather healthy. This ability to subtly lighten the tone is again what marks Hammer out against so many of its contemporaries.

13) Those vast, pearly teeth; throughout the course of these films, an estimated 140 pairs of fangs were used by Christopher Lee and his vampiric cohorts and Hammer fangs were always particularly handsome examples, never bettered even to this day. There was

something about the proportions they got just right – long, but not too long, sharp but not sabre-toothed. Indeed, by the 1970s, they had got a fraction smaller; actors would have them specially fitted – at a sinister dentist in Belsize Park, says actor Martin Jarvis (who incidentally tells me that he kept his fangs as a souvenir of his role in *Taste the Blood of Dracula* but then lost them). The shorter fangs allowed slightly more variety of facial expression. And when the teeth were not being used, they would be kept carefully on special shelves. Hammer was the first studio not to fade to black when the teeth closed in on the neck, although only continental and Japanese audiences actually saw them go in. Then there would be the shot of the victim gasping, and then closing their eyes in a moment of para-sexual ecstasy. What Hammer started in that pioneering *Dracula* they then felt duty bound to continue up until the Count's final hurrah in 1973.

None of the above is meant to make Hammer sound risible. Quite the reverse. It takes a colossal amount of creative energy to invent new clichés. When *The Curse of Frankenstein* opened in May 1957, cinema audiences were used to certain conventions. The first was that blood was never shown. The second was that horror films would have an expressionist element; the sets would be subtly distorted, the camera angles and the lighting very slightly off-kilter to drive home to audiences that these were invented worlds that they were watching. These worlds were filled with cobwebs, candelabras and crypts, and inhabited by people and creatures with a taste for formal dress.

But then there was also the flavour of these earlier films, particularly the Universal pictures monster cycle – the star turns from Boris Karloff, Bela Lugosi, Lon Chaney Jr – of the 1930s and 40s. The point about them – and also about the careful and rather brilliant Val Lewton chillers from RKO – is that the monsters were always defeated by the redemptive force of love, as well as the unquestioned moral worth of the leads.

In the space of the initial twenty minutes of its first gothic horror, Hammer did away with all that. And what marks a Hammer film out now is not so much amorality as simply an impatient shovelling of the young protagonists into the background as the monsters, supernatural or otherwise, take full centre stage. Any remaining romantic element is darkened considerably, entirely lacking the rather sweet innocence of Universal days. Be it the hapless juveniles who cross Baron Frankenstein's path – none perhaps more so than Simon Ward and Veronica Carlson in *Frankenstein Must be Destroyed* (1969) – or the love-struck youngsters who have to fight off Christopher Lee's attentions as in *The Scars of Dracula* (1970) there is little room for redemption, still less the comfort of a clinch in the closing frames. Another

Hammer trademark is that the films almost always end with a shot of the (ambiguous) demise of the monster.

So there was a harshness in the Hammer universe from the start, an unforgiving Manichean quality. Between the icy sadism of Christopher Lee's Count and the grave efficiency of Peter Cushing's Van Helsing, the juvenile leads find themselves in a world without any form of reassurance, a world in which they are on their own. Sometimes (given that this was supposed to be the permissive age) they get to couple; but even then there are other obstacles to their love, such as the heroine's guardian being a strict monsignor, or the hero's honest poverty.

That was the background against which the horrors were played out. Yet as the films progressed, from the 1950s to the 60s and the 70s, other tropes and leitmotifs, doubtless initially unconsciously, began to seep through. At first sight, there might be nothing simpler and more straightforward than a good old Hammer film. Look a little closer, though, and you will see something more interesting than just horror going on there. From questions of class conflict to the burgeoning feminist movement to the faltering, shambolic state of post-war, post-colonial Britain, there are strange, distant, distorting echoes to be heard.

It is worth asking where the notion to have welters of gore sprang from in the first place. What made a previously respectable, if slightly hard-up, studio suddenly transform into this slavering beast?

The truth is that Grand Guignol was a taste that had long lurked in British culture. Since the very beginning of cinema at the turn of the century, domestic film audiences had demonstrated a taste for strong meat. In 1902, for instance, when short silent films were still shown in fairgrounds as opposed to specially built cinemas, queues formed round the tents to see a production called *A Fight with Sledgehammers*.

Later, as more film production companies sprang up, the supernatural, with all its opportunities for dazzling visual trickery, proved hugely popular. These early silent audiences saw endless highly primitive versions of *Faust and Marguerite* (a big favourite at the time), *Maria Marten* (killer caught by accusing ghost), *The Face at the Window* (killer caught by galvanised corpse) and even a two-minute version of *The Mummy*, where an Egyptian disrobes to reveal naught but a skeleton.

Hammer's earliest productions, which were made in 1934, were a little less exotic. The studio had been started by Enrique Carreras, a cinema owner, and William Hinds, a man who managed to combine the professions of jewellery salesman and music-hall comedian.

Enrique (or Henry) Carreras was related to the Spanish family that made popular cigarettes – the Carreras brands, including Black Cat, remained a tobacconists' staple up until the 1960s. Seeing the growing popularity – and potential – of film, Enrique created the Blue Hall chain of cinemas. The word 'blue', incidentally, did not then carry the connotations that it did later.

When Carreras and Hinds went into partnership, they pooled their knowledge of film and variety audiences to concoct straightforward (and mostly cheap) romances and crime dramas. There was no element of the supernatural in these early Hammer films, although one of their most prestigious productions at that time was *Mystery of the Marie Celeste* (1936) starring Bela Lugosi. Given the coup of landing this star – the screen's first Dracula, all the way from Hollywood – it was clear that in this version of the spooky ship story, the macabre disappearances had to be in some way Lugosi's fault.

For another genre, they managed in 1936 to secure the services of the black singer Paul Robeson for the drama *The Song of Freedom*. This was, for its time, a remarkable film. Robeson plays a London dockworker who is given the chance to develop his skill for opera singing, and who subsequently discovers he is descended from royalty. What made the film so notable was the effort to portray a black leading man without stereotyping. Hammer was ahead of its time; another big cinema hit that year was *Sanders of the River*, the title of which is now used as shorthand for casual, unthinking imperialist racism. *The Song of Freedom* is not perfect but does lead us to question whether historical attitudes to race really were as polarised as we assume.

And why the highly distinctive – and aggressive – name Hammer? Hinds, in his youth, had performed a comic theatrical act with a partner. On being hired to make their stage debut, they were still lacking a proper name, so in some desperation – for they were to go on that night – they called the act Hammer and Smith, after the London borough in which it originated. This theatrical act did not last but William Hinds liked the sound of his stage name 'Will Hammer'. In forming a film company with the same name in 1934, he granted it a form of immortality.

By the latter part of the 1930s, with the coming of war – and also the all-conquering rise of superior, glossier Hollywood productions – the British film industry slumped, and the fledgling Hammer, also sometimes operating as Exclusive Films, was forced to suspend its operations.

Two years after the war, in 1947, Carreras and Hinds resumed, but this time with the help of Enrique's son James and William's son Anthony, both young men having served in the war and now being demobilised.

In fact, the extrovert James Carreras had had a most distinguished war, rising to the rank of Lieutenant Colonel. This was a very senior rank – and hugely impressive given that Carreras had joined up only a few years previously as a humble gunner. On top of this, he was given the promotion at an astonishingly young age, in his mid-thirties.

Prior to the war, Carreras had made his first steps into the family business by working as a cinema manager. As a young chap, he was noted by his friends as a hugely competitive and all-round sportsman. The war brought another attractive facet of his character to the fore: his enthusiastic ability to lead other men.

Anthony Hinds, meanwhile, had served in the RAF, in a marginally quieter role, as part of a photography unit in combat zones. So, what was more natural in those drab post-war years than that the two sons should join their fathers in one of the very few British industries to have any sense of excitement about it?

This cosy family arrangement – made all the cosier when Carreras's grandson Michael also joined them shortly afterwards – set about making what were called 'quota quickies', cheap features that cinemas were more or less forced to show because the Labour government, in an effort to protect the British film industry, had placed limits upon the number of foreign productions that could be shown on British screens. In 1948, Hammer scored a big hit with an adaptation of a popular BBC radio serial – *Dick Barton, Special Agent*. The studio got a couple of sequels out of it too before the star was sadly killed in a car crash.

In 1951, Hammer set up base in what was to become the house thereafter associated with it – Down Place in Bray, Berkshire. The idea behind this move was really prudence – it was simpler and cheaper from the production point of view for a small film company to operate out of a country house. A scene requiring a bedroom, for instance, could be filmed in a real bedroom. Down Place came to pay for itself many times over.

The house itself was a pleasant, though broken down late-eighteenth/early-nineteenth-century mansion, white-stuccoed, with a strikingly large bay window. Over the years, as the studio gradually settled in and the original owners, who for a while held on to a part of the house, moved out, the property underwent some intriguing changes. Within the building were both sets and offices. Round by the side of the house could be found a specially built extension, rather like a lean-to, for the set designers and props men to use for construction purposes. Then, across the courtyard, several small sound stages were built, structures that resembled vast agricultural sheds. Surrounding the house and the sound stages were many acres of lush Thameside woodland, a Stanley Spencer idyll of mossy birch and clear flowing water. By the late 1950s, around the back of Down Place, and just a few steps from the sound stages, one could find the ramparts and imposing front door of Castle Dracula; by the early 1960s, they had been joined by a purpose-built middle-European style village square, with higgledy-piggledy roofs, archways leading nowhere, shop fronts, an inn and a bridge. Over the years this little village square would prove to be extraordinarily versatile.

For even when Hammer hit the big money with its gothic horrors, the studio never lost sight of the importance of frugality, sometimes filming the horrors back to back on the same sets, and then releasing these films months apart so that no one would notice.

The actors, too, although better paid than by many of the more rackety independent studios, were still not rich. Indeed, as Hammer's success grew, only studio bosses really seemed to betray the trappings of it.

By the mid-1950s, as well as continuing with domestic melodramas and crime quickies, Hammer branched out with a couple of nondescript science-fiction dramas – *Spaceways* (1953) and *Four Sided Triangle* (1953), the latter involving a convoluted mix of robotics and a romantic threesome.

At the time, a small concern like Hammer was up against relative giants in the form of Rank and London Films. The younger James Carreras and Anthony Hinds had shrewd noses for what could make a big popular hit though. And when BBC TV transmitted Nigel Kneale's groundbreaking science-fiction drama *The Quatermass Experiment* in 1953 – to street-emptying effect, as the public lapped up this serial concerning an astronaut returning to earth infected with a murderous alien plant monster – Hinds and Carreras leapt in to snap up the rights.

As a result of a deal they had with an American production company, Lippert – which guaranteed their films would be screened in the US – Hammer productions at this stage were each rather unhappily required to feature an American star. Doubly unhappily when the star in question, Brian Donlevy, portrayed the brilliant and sensitive scientist Bernard Quatermass as a shouty Brooklyn bully with a rather strange walk.

None the less, *The Quatermass X-periment* – the title a sly challenge to the censors to grant an adult 'X' certificate – was a success and the sequel swiftly followed.

Bryan Forbes – who was later to become a much-lauded director, producer, screenwriter and general éminence grise of British cinema – had a supporting acting role in 1957's *Quatermass II*, in which a refinery on a bleak shoreline is infiltrated by sinister gas aliens with toxic pods. The memory of his glamorous location work at an oil refinery on the gusty Essex coast still makes Forbes laugh. 'I was one of the people attacked by the alien pods,' he said. 'This pod exploded and I ended up with what was supposed to be a terrible alien growth on my face. Come lunchtime and we all went off to the pub. Of course, I couldn't take this stuff off, the make-up was too complex; the landlord refused to serve me.'

He also had a rather startling recollection of the film's butch star. 'Brian Donlevy made a pass at me,' Forbes said. 'Obviously to no avail. It was all very strange. And the location was incredibly windy and his wig often went sailing off into the air.'

Elsewhere, the young writer Nigel Kneale was so appalled by the alcoholic bewigged Donlevy and his inexplicable performance that he withheld the rights to his third serial for a good ten years. (Happily, when Hammer did make *Quatermass and the Pit* in 1967, they did so with a brilliant Quatermass, in the shape of Andrew Keir, and a muscular script from Kneale – the result was one of the most fondly remembered of the studio's films.)

So was science fiction to be the way forward then? Another American, Dean Stockwell, took Donlevy's place in the Quatermass rip-off *X – The Unknown*, featuring sinister alien radioactive slime in the Scottish Highlands. Then came *The Abominable Snowmen* (1957), this time featuring Forrest Tucker and a clutch of other-worldly yetis in the Himalayas. But something more was needed.

It came in the form of a script from an American film-maker, Milton Subotsky, reviving the old story of Frankenstein. Called, a little baldly, *Frankenstein and the Monster*, it was treated with great scepticism at the studio. This was not merely because Subotsky had only one film credit to his name, or because it lacked any of the detail required for a proper shooting script, but also because Hinds and Carreras felt it contained too many elements in common with the Universal Pictures series of Frankenstein films, which had been hugely popular in the 1930s and 1940s. Many of these elements, they realised, would still be within Universal's copyright, including the iconic monster make-up of square skull and bolted neck.

The producers instead turned to their young screenwriter Jimmy Sangster, who had penned some noirish thrillers for the company, and asked him to ditch anything about Mary Shelley's story that might seem familiar from the old Universal sagas. Sangster did so with apparent glee and the resulting screenplay, now called *The Curse of Frankenstein*, was so pungently strong that when it was submitted to the censors for a read-through, as films of this type always were, the comments back suggested that it would be too unpleasant even for an adult 'X' certificate. With a cheery blitheness that was to become something of a trait, Carreras and Hinds put these views to one side and carried on with the screenplay unchanged, in full colour, with an unflinching emphasis on bright gore that had never been seen on the cinema screen before.

In truth, even at the start, Hammer owed less to literary antecedents, be they Shelley or Stoker, than it did to that old British tradition of barnstorming bloodthirsty melodrama.

And this, really, is how Hammer's golden gothic era started. Why did those original *Curse* audiences respond so enthusiastically to such unprecedented levels of on-screen brutality? And why then did they continue to respond to the slew of blood-soaked films that were to follow? Hammer was clearly tapping some kind of cathartic nerve that had not been touched since the war.

In the midst of a febrile period in British culture and politics, stretching from the late 1950s to the mid-70s, when a sense of prosperity mingled with a feeling of seemingly unstoppable decline, it seems that Hammer films – bright, violent, titillating – were somehow calculated to insinuate their way into the murkier corners of the national subconscious.

We can see now that these gothic melodramas hold a mirror up to the times in which they were made; from the initial attempts to maintain some degree of surface, elegance and gloss to the markedly sexier, nipple-flashing efforts that signalled the dying days of these films in the 1970s.

And (gratuitous outbreaks of sex aside) there is a sense of unease running through every Hammer film, not to do with graveyards or coffins, but a sense that the world itself is a dark, unforgiving place. Look at the pessimism and cruelty of the pre-credits sequence of *Frankenstein Created Woman* (1967). On some bleak heath land, a drunken prisoner is being led to a rusted old guillotine, apparently unbothered by his forthcoming execution. Then, a few yards off, his young son appears. The prisoner suddenly spots him and is desperate for his boy not to witness his death; but the guards don't listen, his head is forced into position, the blade falls and the stricken boy sees his father decapitated. In the first few minutes, Terence Fisher has laid down the rules very firmly for the audience: this is a world of arbitrary evil luck, without pity, and especially weighted against the working classes.

A Hammer film is also notable for being a very brisk thing – usually eighty-four minutes on the dot. Obviously this was to do with careful budgeting, but the time constraints also meant that Hammer had to introduce new structures for old stories. They did not hang around, which is why most Hammers will kick off with a good solid fright delivered within the first three minutes or so. In the opening scene of *The Evil of Frankenstein* (1964), the theft of a corpse from a peasants' cabin and a girl's terrified run through the woods, only to bump into Peter Cushing, takes about fifty seconds. And you can forget about a leisurely build-up of tension. There is a sort of exuberance to a Hammer film that renders all that rather unnecessary. In *Frankenstein Must be Destroyed* (1969), there is a terrific fight between the Baron and a house thief, who makes the dreadful mistake of breaking into Frankenstein's infernal laboratory and encounters, amongst other things, a corpse in a glass cabinet which falls on top of him. That takes place within about five minutes of the opening credits, and the unpleasantness is sustained pretty much all the way through from there.

The camerawork and editing are, as implied, possibly as far from the old Universal Pictures as one could get. In the 1930s and 40s, Hollywood horrors often had a dream-like, ethereal quality; whatever else Hammer was, it was certainly not ethereal. The Eastman colour and the lighting were bright; the camera was jumpy rather than fluid; and the editing was sharp and kinetic.

And there is one other absolutely crucial ingredient, the thing that makes a Hammer film instantly recognisable as such even if you are not looking at the screen: the scores of composer James Bernard. Whether it's the heavy three-note signature used throughout the Dracula films or the nervier, shriller, more staccato music used throughout the Frankensteins, Bernard disproved the old theory that if a film score is noticed, then it has failed. Part of the great pleasure of these films was being worked into an (occasionally unnecessary) state of anxiety by these brilliantly calculated scores. With the exception of John Barry and James Bond, no other composer created such a distinctive and effective soundscape for a series of films.

So that's the thing about Hammer. Everyone – but everyone – will have seen at least one of their films. And no matter how hazy one may be about the more – shall we say – populist end of the cinematic market, you would certainly know a Hammer film if you were not only to see it but hear it. Of course you would. These films left a print on our culture, a great deal deeper than has previously been acknowledged. They had more influence than anyone may care to think about.

Yes, it is the case that they could scarcely be described as hugely frightening anymore. Early Hammers, once considered instantaneous adult 'X' certificate material, now slope on to DVD with a cursory 'PG' or '12'. The films, however, have grown more powerful in different ways over the years. The story of the studio – and of its films and stars – is also the story of how we as a nation watched films and grew up.

Chapter Two

BLOOD AND THUNDER

 In one sense, you can now see where the censors were coming from. *The Curse of Frankenstein*, the film that kick-started Hammer's fortunes, does not make for genteel viewing, even now. Christopher Lee's hideously scarred monster is brutish and lacking the studied pathos of Boris Karloff's celebrated 1930s Hollywood version; the violence, far from being tastefully suggested, is shown full screen and in full colour; of the original romantic sub-plot, there is no remnant – instead, Baron Frankenstein has a chilly affair with the parlourmaid, Justine, who ends up as one of the monster's victims. Then there is the Baron himself, a frosty, psychotic figure many light years away from the tortured romantic sensibility of Mary Shelley's original. Yet Hammer's Frankenstein is still intriguingly closer in spirit to that very British sense of the gothic.

For the critics, everything about this film – from the unsparing use of blood to the sight of human organs pickled in jars to the strategic use of an acid bath to the unflinching close-ups of gruesome detail, including the monster being shot in the face – was beyond the pale. C. A. Lejeune, for the *Observer*, denounced it as 'one of the half-dozen most repulsive things I have ever seen on the screen'. In *Time* magazine, she went on to make this prissy pronouncement: 'I feel inclined to apologise to all decent Americans for sending them such sickening bad taste.'[1] Other critics were just as vaporous. 'A sickening and nauseating way to make a living' was the *Sunday Express*'s tautologous verdict on its producers. Such notices obviously proved irresistible bait for apparently degenerate young audiences.

So this, very briefly, was how Hammer was to define its style for the next twenty years or so. Youngish Baron Frankenstein (Peter Cushing) inherits his late father's estate, a tutor in the shape of Paul Krempe (Robert Urquhart) and a match-made fiancée in the shape of Elizabeth (Hazel Court). But master Frankenstein has been reading too deeply into the mysteries of the universe and enlists Krempe to help him in his growing obsession with using the revitalising properties of static electricity (or something – the science is never entirely clear). When this becomes a compulsion to create a living man, Krempe, horrified by this madness, tries to withdraw. But the Creature – containing a damaged brain that had belonged to Frankenstein's old professor, murdered by his former pupil – escapes, and Krempe reluctantly helps Frankenstein track it down. At the climax, the Creature escapes once more from its bonds, targets Elizabeth, then the Baron; then, having been shot again, the Creature accidentally topples backwards into an acid bath. But who would expect the Transylvanian police force to believe such a story? So, at the end, it is the Baron who finds himself facing the guillotine, having been convicted of murder.

Good thunderous stuff, and quite a lot to pack into a lickety-split eighty-four minutes. But we have to put this film into context to see both how Hammer grabbed the popular imagination, and also how this spectacular outbreak of unpleasantness didn't simply arrive out of nowhere. In particular, we have to place this film next to the all-dominating Rank Studios that at that time held the domestic industry in a sort of cultural stranglehold.

Our collective memory of the British cinema of the 1950s is a sort of collage in washed-out colour of Dirk Bogarde, Dinah Sheridan, Kenneth More, John Mills, Diana Dors and Virginia McKenna. And actually, as collective memories go, it's reasonably accurate.

The British film industry by the start of that decade was in a terrible state. Alexander Korda's British Lion was faltering, as was the formerly superlative Ealing, which throughout the late 1940s had reinvented the terms of screen comedy but which, after 1955 and the triumph of *The Ladykillers*, seemed abruptly to run out of steam.

The company that dominated all – Rank – was suffering the most. It wasn't just that audience numbers in those immediate post-war years were starting to decline. It was that the films themselves were somehow just failing to find the mass markets that they needed. In a way, there is an echo here of the situation in the 1930s: when competing against the lushness of Hollywood, British films must have just looked terribly parochial. And this is key at the start of a decade when the younger generation of Britons were looking increasingly to America for cultural inspiration right across the board.

Rank Films, as well as dominating the British industry, also defined all the stereotypes about British films at that time: its productions were twee, coy and safe. When one looks a little closer, one sees how Hammer's spirit of wilful nastiness had an element of almost child-like anarchic delight about it. It was as though the smaller studio was deliberately kicking out against the stifling moralising of Rank.

At the beginning of the 1950s, Rank's managing director, John Davis, who had been brought in to save the company from collapse, instituted a number of ruthless cuts. These included closing the Gainsborough Studios in Hoxton and Shepherd's Bush. The company had a co-financing deal with Ealing Studios, which came to an end in 1955. And Davis also started to exert the most extraordinary creative control over every single aspect of Rank's operation.

From 1955, the studio produced twenty films a year. Some were made independently, although that term was loose at best: all elements of any Rank production, from script to casting, had to be approved by a committee called the Rank Board before they were given the go-ahead.

The actors were kept on reins that seem not only unthinkable but also laugh-out-loud funny today. Ingénues such as Joan Collins and Diana Dors attended the Rank Charm School, which trained them in everything from deportment to elocution. Control was exerted over male leads in a less subtle way. Harper and Porter cite the story of Dirk Bogarde, then famous for the Richard Gordon *Doctor* films, who was handed a note from David Lean, telling him not to walk through the studio restaurant as though he owned the place.[2]

J. Arthur Rank himself was famously a strict Methodist and John Davis was adamant that any Rank film would portray moral certainties. His stated intention was to make 'clean' films that would be successful at the box office. Added to this, he felt that these films should all be 'healthy entertainment for all members of the family'.

Nor would he indulge what he saw as working-class vulgarity. One screenplay, by the talented comedy writer Norman Hudis, was rejected on the grounds that 'it appealed to the stalls and the Rank Organisation caters to the Dress Circle'.[3] It is not really so difficult now to see why Rank foundered.

Also consider the views of Ealing's head, Michael Balcon, who was interviewed in the mid-1950s: 'We were middle-class people brought up with middle-class backgrounds and rather conventional educations,' he said. 'Though we were radical in our points of view, we did not want to tear down institutions ... we were people of the immediate post-war generation and we voted Labour for the first time after the war; this was our mild revolution.'[4]

In order to put that first Hammer Horror in sharper perspective, look at the other British films released around that time: they included *Battle of the River Plate* (1956), *Bridge Over the River Kwai* (1957), *Ill Met by Moonlight* (1957), *Doctor at Large* (1957), Norman Wisdom – the 'lovable gump' – in *Up in the World* (1957) and the Boulting Brothers adaptation of Kingsley Amis's *Lucky Jim* (1957). All perfectly good in themselves even if it couldn't really be described as a vintage year (excepting *Kwai*) and the cinema-going public were not given a great deal of variety – either war or middlebrow comedy. One might see that such a selection was lacking a certain sort of energy. In other words, the domestic cinema was working within very firm parameters of taste and of morality, with little room for ambiguity.

Even Ealing, which could always previously boast outstandingly inventive scripting, was beginning to falter in the mid-1950s. Studio head Michael Balcon was forced, after the split with Rank, to go to MGM with a begging bowl; the result was a six-film deal and none of those films were any good.

But what of the more raucous, exploitative end of the film market at this time? What, in other words, were the fledgling Hammer's real competitors getting up to? In fact, by 1957, the horror film, previously such a staple of cinema-going, was in a bit of a trough.

British (and indeed other) cinema audiences would have been used to several different kinds of monster movies: creepy ghost stories filmed in stark black and white (for example, Ealing's *Dead of Night* [1945] or the sublimely unsettling *The Uninvited* [1944]); then from the generation before – but still seen in regular reissues in the 1950s – there were the glossy Hollywood horrors, with Boris Karloff and Bela Lugosi. There were efforts such as *Frankenstein Meets the Wolf Man* and *Son of Dracula*. These Universal entertainments, quaint even when they were first made in the 1930s, had run out of steam by 1945.

The chills that audiences of 1957 would have been most familiar with were those of the Creature Feature, heir to Hollywood Horror. This genre, always science-fictional in inspiration yet stubbornly gothic in tone and execution, was kicked off by the still-effective *Creature from the Black Lagoon* (1953), Universal's rather brilliant 3-D telling of the story of a prehistoric half-man, half-amphibian surviving in the distant depths of the Amazon rainforest. Following this was a spectacular called *Them!* (1954). This time, in the wastes of the Arizona desert, H-Bomb testing has produced some seriously eerie results – a strange high note to be heard on the sirocco winds, and people in isolated trailers and shacks being slaughtered by nameless monsters, their deaths the result of a massive injection of formic acid. The death-dealers turn out to be giant ants. Snigger if you must but, if you haven't already, see the film for yourself – you will be surprised at just how creepy a giant ant can be, especially if left unseen for the best part of the film's duration.

So once Hollywood had hit on the idea that the biggest monster of all was uncontrolled nuclear power (*The Incredible Shrinking Man!* [1957] and *Tarantula!* [1955] being two other great examples of the genre) or the fear of Communist infiltration (*Invasion of the Body Snatchers* [1956]), the spectacle of Lon Chaney Jr turning into a human yak started to look a little passé.

And by the time Hammer decided to branch into gothic, the American branch of the genre had completely faded out, fit only to be parodied by Abbott and Costello. But the horrors that Hammer wanted to launch actually came from quite a different cultural stream; one that would have held resonance even for the youngest audience members.

The studio's founding fathers, Enrique Carreras and William Hinds, and their heirs would certainly have been highly familiar with an earlier strain of British Grand Guignol, that of the ripe-as-stilton melodrama.

They would have known of the late Victorian penny dreadfuls – cheap periodicals aimed at teenage boys filled with gothic serials such as *The String of Pearls*. There would still be memories of the notorious penny gaffs: makeshift theatres to be found in the poorer districts that would entice audiences in – again, mostly young men – first with a display like a freak show, followed by rather perfunctory and violent dramas involving people being strangled, bludgeoned or having their throats cut.

Some have suggested that the famous – though actually rather tedious – gothic novels written by Mrs Radcliffe in the late eighteenth century were key influences. *The Castle of Otranto* and *The Mysteries of Udolpho* were the first narratives to feature haunted European settings, helpless heroines, sinister villains and secret labyrinths of dungeons and crypts. In other words, all the requisite paraphernalia of the genre, although clumsily assembled. Also oft-cited is Matthew Lewis, author of the similarly meandering *The Monk*, which pushed the genre a little further with sado-masochistic descriptions of baroque tortures.

There were popular serials published in pamphlet form too, such as the early nineteenth century effort *Varney the Vampire*. Incidentally, both the young Jane Austen and Thomas Love Peacock were to satirise and indirectly pay tribute to this new and rumbustious form: Austen's *Northanger Abbey* features a heroine who imagines herself to be living in a gothic romance; Peacock's *Nightmare Abbey* parodies Byron and Shelley, showing the characters' dark preoccupations to be manifestations of the fevered Romantic imagination. Although there is never any hint of self-parody in the Hammer films, they did have a certain sense of glee about them – an enthusiastic tonal quality that recalls Peacock rather than Radcliffe. But the studio had other macabre precursors too.

On stage, for instance, in the full pomp of the Victorian age, melodrama became an ever more lavish spectacle: thunderstorms were summoned, trapdoors deployed, villains declaimed and heroines quailed, while the mechanical conjuring effects used to convey supernatural manifestations became increasingly inventive. The influence of this particular form of entertainment on the studio was arguably strong.

One might be tempted to reach back a little further than that and protest that there was nothing new under the sun; one could go back to the early seventeenth century to the plays of John Webster (who could forget that line in *The White Devil*: 'I'll make Italian cut-work in your gut' or the conceit of a portrait daubed with poison, so that when its painted lips are kissed ... ?). One might be tempted to cite the climaxes of Jacobean tragedies such as *The Revenger's Tragedy* or *Women Beware Women* where practically every-one on stage meets a gruesome and highly baroque death. Why not go back a little further, to Elizabethan theatre? We have Lavinia being raped, then her tongue cut out and her hands cut off, prior to Tamora's sons being baked and served at table as means of revenge – thanks there, of course, to William Shakespeare's *Titus Andronicus*. There is scarcely any need to mention the murder of Duncan, or the blinding of Gloucester, or the serial butchery of *Richard III*. A little further back yet and we have the novel theatrical sensation of watching a man beat his own brains out against the bars of his prison cage. In some historical accounts, audiences gasped at the sight of offal used as brain matter. This was the character Bajazeth in Christopher Marlowe's *Tamburlaine the Great*. Animal offal being used as 'brains', incidentally, was a trick that Hammer would employ some 400 years later. Oh, and while we're at it, let's not forget Marlowe's Dr Faustus being dragged down into the fiery regions of Hell by the Devil to whom he has sold his soul.

All of which is a simplistic way of saying that the British taste for ghoulish excess has been a mainstay of the culture ever since *Beowulf.* Nor does it make it any more highbrow. But in terms of context, it has been assumed by many that Hammer represented a sudden grim descent into savagery. It did no such thing.

Even in the 1930s, when the fledgling censors were at their most twittering and nervous, British audiences were transfixed by the stunningly hammy anti-heroes portrayed by the splendidly named Tod Slaughter in films such as *Murder in the Red Barn*, *Sweeney Todd* (for which Slaughter was most famous) and *Crimes in the Dark House*. Throats were cut, heads were bludgeoned, trapdoors opened and various heroines were stalked and menaced by this portly, crinkly-haired figure, with his extravagant moustache and even more extravagant acting style. It is more than possible that screenwriter Jimmy Sangster was drawing on these gruesome and hugely popular melodramas in his attempt to get away from the more forgiving and morally rigid Universal films.

Melodrama, in its stage and film form, was a rather classier style of entertainment compared to that offered up in the penny gaffs. As a form, it seemed to have several consistent ingredients, among them a relish for acts of rather inventive violence, the victimisation of pretty young women and the doing-down by a villainous aristocracy of the honest working man. It carried faint echoes of more respectable literature. What else is Thomas Hardy's *Tess of the D'Urbervilles* (1897) but middlebrow melodrama – the honest girl of the soil seduced by the wicked squire and then, many trials and tribulations later, hanged for that squire's murder? Incidentally, Hammer executives would have particularly relished the passage where Mrs Brooks, looking up at the hotel ceiling, sees a patch of blood appear then slowly widen and grow as, upstairs, Alec bleeds to death.

One of the most popular melodramas of all was *Maria Marten: or the Murder in the Red Barn*. This production, loosely based on a real-life crime, featured as its dramatic crux the disclosure in a dream of the murderer and the whereabouts of the corpse by the ghost of the victim. Not only was it a perpetual favourite on stage, it was filmed many times.

So when it came to the idea of *Frankenstein,* the young Jimmy Sangster and seasoned director Terence Fisher knew that they had a heritage of ghoulishness to draw on. We might see how their treatment of Frankenstein's laboratory was slightly closer to Mary Shelley's 'workshop of filthy creation' than the thunderstorm-harnessing electrical wonders of the Universal version (although they also had a miniature budget). In all other respects, though, Sangster and Fisher were delving, consciously or not, directly into the blood-red history of the British stage.

The Curse of Frankenstein opens with titles against a crimson background, which would have signalled an instant treat to British audiences more used to the dour black and white of domestic films. Also, bear in mind that this was the first horror film in colour. James Bernard's music is weird, atonal, doomy, with none of the customary romantic motifs normally offered in the titles of monster films. We dissolve immediately to a painted middle-European landscape of mountains and purple sky, and thence to a studio-bound prison, where we find Peter Cushing, and learn to our confusion that he is the incarcerated Baron Frankenstein.

For contemporary audiences, the confusion would have been twofold, because somehow people had come to associate the name 'Frankenstein' not with the monster's creator but with the monster itself. And so, with that sorted out, just what was Baron Frankenstein doing in this straw-filled dungeon? Again, in all previous films, the Baron had always been portrayed as a little misguided and perhaps fixated but he was always a hero of sorts in the end. So just what was mild-mannered Peter Cushing doing in jail?

All of this is terribly shrewd stuff, nicely wrong-footing an audience that would have taken its seats expecting lurching brutes in asphalt-spreading boots. And within minutes we are in flashback, as Baron Cushing, awaiting execution, tells the weird story of his life and of his calamitous downfall. We see him as a young chap (Melvyn Hayes, who somehow contrives to look older than Cushing) inheriting his father's wealth; his friendship with tutor Paul (Robert Urquhart); his painfully contrived romance with Elizabeth (Hazel Court). And we also see it going terribly wrong.

Having revived a cute dog from the dead (and if only he had stopped there – the torch-bearing mobs would have been 'ooh-ing' and 'aahing' and demanding that he *continue* his experiments, perhaps even with kittens and goldfish), Frankenstein makes the creepy leap and decides that he wants to bring life to dead human tissue and, for reasons not wholly explained, his mentor and tutor Paul Krempe goes along with him.

It all starts to go wrong fairly swiftly. He gets the body, swinging from a gibbet, fine; the brain, as tradition demands, is stolen from a morgue and placed in a glass jar which is smashed during the course of a struggle. Bits of glass are embedded in brain, certain to result in a *wrong 'un*. And then the creation of the wrong 'un itself, with intriguing test tubes and strings of fairy lights as opposed to Universal's power-station display.

Terence Fisher's colour schemes for Frankenstein's laboratory, all sickly greens and yellows, certainly echo Mary Shelley's intriguing phrase about 'filthy creation', and the Baron is repositioned more as a sinister alchemist than hi-tech scientist, again closer to Mary Shelley's original. Where he differs, however, is in the sheer stunning ruthlessness of his actions, including the cold-blooded murder of his old professor in order to obtain his (at that point) very fine brain.

As the monster, Christopher Lee attempts to give it some soul – certainly there is a look of suffering to be seen in his one good eye. But he is not given many opportunities to use it. We see him first, in a dazzlingly fast close-up, as the bandages around his face are unwrapped. Then he makes his bolt for it and after some lurking in the countryside, we see him again, being shot full in the face in the middle of an autumnal wood. After this, a possibly understandable rampage begins. The bodies pile up.

At no point does his vile creator acknowledge his suffering in any way and when, at the end, the Creature ends up toppling down into an acid bath, we cannot feel any corresponding rush of relief for Frankenstein; quite the reverse. It seems clear that he has escaped natural justice.

Human justice catches up with him in the end, though, and in the film's final scenes, Cushing, sounding increasingly demented, fails to convince a priest that his gruesome and strange story is true, and so faces the guillotine at dawn.

All of which sounds reasonably intriguing but, in some ways, the film is heavy-handed. First, the structure is wonky: a cracking opening is followed by a good half an hour of ennui before even the dead dog is revived. And there is nowhere for the audience's sympathy to go: the monster is too repulsive, Frankenstein too horrid, and alleged good guys, Paul and Elizabeth, too tedious to give a monkey's about. Terence Fisher's direction, for much of the time, errs on the side of staid (although this, apparently, was deliberate – he didn't want any flash gimmicks to get in the way of the story). Only when the Creature is unveiled do we get a moment of real shock and verve.

'We refused to have anything mechanical,' said Fisher in an interview with *Films and Filming* in 1964.

> Our monster, with his do-it-yourself stitches, is very different from Karloff's nuts and bolts. We wanted the monster to fit Chris Lee's melancholy personality. We wanted a thing that looked like some wandering, forlorn minstrel of monstrosity, a thing of shreds and patches but in flesh and blood and organs.[5]

And monster aside, Hammer had succeeded in putting something on screen that no one had ever got across before: not merely the startling scarlet of the blood wiped casually on to Peter Cushing's lab coat; not merely the squishy looking organs swilling around in background jars; not even the eyebrow-raising notion of dear sweet Peter Cushing having a wild affair with a parlourmaid.

The vital thing – the really new thing – was that Jimmy Sangster and Terence Fisher portrayed a world in which violence was met with no answering sense of redemption. That, rather than the (now minimal-seeming) gore alone, would have been the element that deep down upset the critics more than anything.

This goes for the censors too; they passed the film for an 'X' but there had been muttered talk about imposing even stronger viewing restrictions. Incidentally, *The Curse of Frankenstein* today carries a '12' certificate, putting it in the same category as *Pirates of the Caribbean* and the new *Doctor Who*. Innocent days!

So who were these monsters Jimmy Sangster and Terence Fisher, these pitiless corruptors of the moral good? Director Fisher was in fact a cheerful be-cardiganed middle-aged veteran of the British film industry. After a youthful spell in the Navy, he had broken into film as a runner, then worked his way up, being present at the editing of Will Hay films amongst others. Fisher got on to a directing course with the Rank Organisation and then, in the 1940s, he started making melodramas for Gaumont.

One film is sometimes cited as the precursor of Fisher's chief thematic concerns at Hammer: *So Long at the Fair* (1950). In this period thriller, a brother and sister travel to the turn-of-the-century Paris World Fair. The sister wakes one morning to find that not only has her brother gone missing, but so too apparently has the hotel room in which he was staying. The conspiracy deepens as other characters flatly deny to the heroine that she was travelling with anybody else. As ever with these cork-screwy kind of thrillers, the explanation at the end – involving a localised outbreak of plague – is a bit of a let-down. But the increasingly oppressive atmosphere is good.

In the 1950s, Fisher found himself directing for Hammer; one effort was the low-budget *Metropolis* knock-off *Four Sided Triangle*, which nicked Fritz Lang's conceit of an idealised woman being duplicated in robot form. Even here though, in this winningly low-tech science-fiction melodrama, there are no great signs of what was to come. And when *The Curse of Frankenstein* project lumbered into view in 1956, Fisher was assigned to it largely for reasons of contract fulfilment.

Jimmy Sangster was a different matter though: a young man, in his late twenties when he wrote *Curse*; he was bullish, sparkily intelligent and breezily unconcerned about the process of reinventing an entire genre. Sangster had actually been called up after the war ended, serving some time in the RAF. This was frequently the case with young men at this time, enabling the troops overseas to be demobilised and brought home faster. Following this spell of military experience, Sangster too had worked his way up through the film rungs, from runner to first assistant director. His first screen credit came for the faux-Quatermass thriller *X – The Unknown* (1956), which fulfilled his ambition of becoming a screenwriter. He had done such a good job on that that Hinds and Carreras knew that he would be just the youthful iconoclast needed for a completely fresh telling of *Frankenstein*. There was one other terrifically important factor: in age terms, Sangster was reasonably close to Hammer's target audiences. If anyone knew how to go for the jugulars of this 'New Elizabethan' generation, it would be him.

By May 1957, Britain had already been through the moral panic kicked off by *Rock around the Clock*; this film featured the portly singer Bill Hailey and – although it is now difficult to imagine quite why – it inspired outbreaks of rowdiness in cinemas, including seat slashing. Popular culture was becoming rapidly dominated by the emergence of the teenager as a social and economic force. The older generation was worked into a lather of indignation by the perceived menace of yobbish Teddy boys and rock and roll. Middle-class newspapers such as the *Daily Express* were piercingly shrill with disapproval. But others in the entertainment business – music, television and film – instantly saw past the sense of superficial threat and divined that this new generation of young people had far greater spending power than its forebears, however unattractive a prospect these young people seemed.

There is a wonderfully telling photograph of an East End audience queuing for the 1963 Hammer double-bill of *The Evil of Frankenstein* and *Paranoiac*. For the most part, the queue is composed of young men, in pork-pie hats, wearing surpassingly grim expressions. Anyone in twin-set and pearls would have run a mile from that scenario.

'It's true that the films weren't really seen as respectable when they kicked off,' recalls actor Martin Jarvis, who has fond memories of his (non-thuggish) teenage years in the 1950s, going off to see Hammer films himself. 'We were all aware of Hammer at that time as being something with not that great a reputation. I went to the Croydon Odeon to see Hammers like *Camp on Blood Island*,' he says with a laugh. This, it should be pointed out, was one of Hammer's early, fierce, war dramas, concerning a Japanese POW camp. 'I also saw Hammer's first Dracula,' Jarvis says. 'It actually was a pretty good film – and Christopher Lee made the most wonderful Dracula.' Finally, in 1970, Jarvis got to meet the Count on set when he took the role of Jeremy Secker in *Taste the Blood of Dracula*. By that stage, the reputation of the studio – certainly from a young actor's point of view – had changed quite a bit.

In America, the audience for *The Curse of Frankenstein* was a shade more wide-ranging, simply because children were allowed to see the film as well as the grown-ups. It is one of those small cultural curiosities, that unless things really were exceptionally gruesome, sadistic and sexual in nature, the horror genre was considered by Americans to be a perfectly natural and reasonably harmless one for youngsters to enjoy. '*Curse* was the first British film to take advantage of the changing nature of the (American) cinema audience,' noted Sarah Street, 'exploiting its appeal to the young people who frequented Drive-In theatres.'[6]

One other factor in domestic success was that *Curse* opened to a Britain not long emerged from the scrimping hardship and tedium of rationing. A Britain that, in the years after the war, was still struggling to see how Empire would work, and what the future held for a nation depleted by the conflict. A Britain that had only just begun to look in on itself with a critical eye. And of course, a Britain that just months beforehand had been through the Suez crisis, the crucial moment when it became clear that, despite wartime victory ten years beforehand, Britain's place in the world was no longer as assured as it had been. The mood engendered by the Coronation in 1953, that high point of optimism about the new world, and Britain's role within it, was already sinking into something more realistic.

In cultural terms, the country had seen the emergence of the 'Angry Young Man' (although historian Dominic Sandbrook argues convincingly that there was never any such movement – the writers concerned, from Kingsley Amis to John Osborne to Colin Wilson, were simply too disparate – and that it was all the invention of an over-excitable press[7]). A spy had been born in 1953, by the name of James Bond, whose ruthlessness and perceived amorality were both intriguing and repulsive to an older generation brought up on Buchan and Dornford Yates.

And one might argue in psychological terms that the war itself would have rendered the nation immune to the sorts of chills that Universal had purveyed; having seen and lived through so much, surely a histrionic figure like Bela Lugosi would have seemed plain silly? Interviewed in the early 1960s, Christopher Lee, now inextricably identified with the horror genre, defended the films he was in against accusations of ghoulishness and sadism, citing the things he had seen during his war service and asserting that, next to that, Hammer films were little more than fairy tales.

There was also a patriotic element in reclaiming our native monsters from the clutches of Hollywood. This became explicitly the case as Carreras and Hinds went through all the complex negotiations with Universal to make their own Frankenstein. They even went to the length of sending Universal the proposed screenplay. Universal dismissed it, on the intriguing grounds that no finished film ever resembled a script.[8]

Screenwriter Jimmy Sangster saw very little in the way of romance in any of it, though. The prime motivation – to him and indeed to his employers – was the making of money. 'If Anthony Hinds had asked me to write a Carry On film,' he said modestly of his own work, 'I would have done. Then I would have been known as a comedy writer.'[9]

Incidentally, I had a convivial lunch with Jimmy Sangster some time ago at Kensington Place; he talked of the range of things he had written throughout his long career, emphasising that gothic horror only accounted for a very small portion of his working life. But the titles he returned to with greatest enthusiasm throughout the course of this lunch were not only his early Hammer Horrors but also full-blooded (non-Hammer) melodramas like *The Hellfire Club* (1960) and the Burke and Hare thriller *The Flesh and the Fiends* (1959). It was the recollection of these productions that made him snort with fond laughter.

And Sangster has acknowledged elsewhere that at Hammer there was a gleeful process of pushing things as far as they could go. 'We had the "pass the marmalade" moments,' he said.

> For instance, there was one scene in *The Curse of Frankenstein*
> where the parlourmaid discovers the secret room containing the
> chained-up Creature, and as she goes in, the Creature breaks free of
> its chains and, suddenly, Frankenstein slams the door behind her and
> locks her in with the monster. We don't see what happens behind
> that door but we hear the most terrible, terrible screams. We then
> cut immediately to a breakfast scene with Frankenstein and
> Elizabeth sitting at a breakfast table and Frankenstein saying:
> 'Could you pass the marmalade?'[10]

The point of this was twofold: a moment of dramatic relief after the horror and the tension, and also a spark of black comedy that the audience could respond to with a sense of delighted complicity. As the years wore on, Hammer became the master of that invisible, unspoken relationship.

The film was not ideal for all those concerned. Among them was the young Christopher Lee. The least of his ordeals was having to spend hours in the make-up chair with Phil Leakey making him look like something that a small woodland animal had been chewing on. Add to that the discomfort of having to take in fluids and liquidised food through a straw during those long studio days. Minor setbacks when held up against the far larger consideration of his film career but the indignity must surely have rankled with this most dignified of men.

Lee had been brought up at the heart of the establishment – a family background of Italian aristocracy, said to be distantly descended from Charlemagne, and educated at Wellington College. He had fought a highly distinguished war in Special Services. And when he was demobilised, he determined that acting was to be his career.

Before *Curse*, Lee had already appeared in several British films, including *Moulin Rouge* (1952), but never in any leading role and, understandably, this young chap was ambitious. So this Frankenstein vehicle must have seemed something of a disappointment, even though he was polite enough never to have said so. On top of this, the exuberantly horrible script left little chance for the sort of brilliant heart-breaking pathos that Boris Karloff had brought to the part a generation ago. Lee's ever-kind co-star Peter Cushing thought otherwise, however, and always crossed the street in interviews to pour praise on Lee's performance. The two men formed a strong friendship on that set which was to last across the years. Cushing recalled:

> The first time we [Lee] met, he was wearing the grotesque make-up conceived by Phil Leakey and a story was put about that when it was all removed at the end of the day and he and I came face-to-face in the corridor – well, then I screamed![11]

Nor indeed this time was the monster the star of the picture. That honour fell to the then forty-year-old Peter Cushing. Producer Anthony Hinds and Terence Fisher quite deliberately wanted a young(ish) Baron: he was there so that the young audience they wished to attract would find a point of identification.

In fact, the first ever idea of how to do the film was in black and white and starring a, by that stage, rather elderly Boris Karloff. Thank the heavens that was one point at which Universal Studios stepped in to say no. Another quite spectacularly horrifying idea was that the part of the monster could go to the young Bernard Bresslaw. Horrifying because, in fact, it doesn't take that much imagination to see it.[12]

It is clear then that Jimmy Sangster (who became fondly known at Bray Studios as 'The Nasty') was the essential motor for flicking a 'V' sign at the tastefulness of the Rank ethos, and at the biddyish twitterings of the censors. His favoured genre (like so many of his generation) was gangster thrillers, suggesting that he was a keen student of Hollywood 'B' movies – all the shooting, the violence, the lax sexual morality. It is possible that Sangster was unwitting in applying this violence and immorality to the horror film – not being a fan of this genre, he may not have realised just how delicately it had trod before. It would have seemed a natural thing to him, to present a world of monsters in which the humans are the biggest monsters.

Also perhaps to set that world of monsters in a middle Europe obviously very much removed from real life and yet perhaps still carrying echoes of the slaughter and conflict of real life. Did the French and German audiences of the time perhaps see this cunningly contrived world as an escapist fantasy infinitely preferable to the world that had recently been smashed to pieces around them?

The influences on director Terence Fisher are a little more obscure. Like Sangster, though, it is possible in moments to detect lightning flashes of surprising anger in Fisher's work. The early scenes of *The Curse of Frankenstein* are presented flat as a pancake, the camera utterly unmoving. But when the Creature is unleashed, so too is a large amount of energy in the editing. It was as though the film was unleashing a hitherto unseen side to Fisher. Perhaps after years as a journeyman director, plodding along without any real critical attention, as so many directors did, he recognised that for good or for ill (and most probably ill), this was the film with which he would make his mark. Certainly his name and that of Hammer were to become inextricably intertwined.

But just as powerful as either of these two men was dear old Peter Cushing himself, who brought a unique neurotic force to the role of the psychopathic Baron. While taking the role entirely seriously, he also entices the audiences into relishing his cold-bloodedness. In the absence of any engaging good guys, we, in the end, have to fix on the Baron as a point of identification. Whether unwrapping some filthy cloth containing two severed hands, speaking coldly to parlourmaid Justine or recoiling from the monster he has conjured, Cushing's Frankenstein is a wondrously vile creation, all the more vile for not being fully the villain of the piece.

In the final scenes, as the guillotine looms, Cushing conveys the sense of the character starting to lose his mind, while at the same time remaining wholly, non-comprehendingly remorseless. And part of the thrill for the young audience would have been the notion of a tremendously posh, well-spoken character behaving in this way. In fact, Jimmy Sangster's original conception had been to have the Baron as a younger man yet – a strutting dandy. The fact that he became the slightly older, icier, more calculating Peter Cushing was the seal of genius, and the start of an acting job that Cushing wouldn't better.

It is funny to watch the film now. It is not that it is quaint so much – but it just somehow doesn't feel like a product of the 1950s or indeed identifiably of any decade. This is something to do with the combination of lurid, primitive colour washes, the period costumes, the style of acting and the music. In other words, the whole thing is such a collision of styles and genres that you simply cannot tell where you are. It doesn't look at all as a traditional horror film is understood to look. The world it depicts is largely studio-bound and largely empty – apart from the key players, there is nobody there. The loopy script structure is in itself unsettling – the normal emotional forces that pull us through a film are absent here as the story slows, then speeds, then double-backs, and we are unable to find anyone to latch on to to guide us through it.

All of this is mainly because the people who made the film had never really paid attention to the horrors that came before it, and so came to it genuinely fresh and genuinely original. But now, at the end, as you shake your head and wonder quite what it was all about, you can feel a stir of what those original audiences must have felt; a sense of some visceral response, more complex than simple horror, almost like the feeling you get when you have been pulled into a particularly rancorous and unpleasant argument. It leaves you feeling a little soiled but at the same time leaves you feeling relieved of the burden of decorum.

The staggering success of the film meant naturally that a sequel had to be whisked into production, just as the sound stages were clear of the studio's next film, *Dracula* (see next chapter). Originally entitled *I, Frankenstein*, *The Revenge of Frankenstein* (1958) picked up at exactly the moment where the original stopped, with the Baron about to have his head cut off.

Following an inexplicable sleight-of-hand trick involving the priest ending up decapitated instead, Frankenstein is back in business – as Dr Steyn – with actor Francis Matthews as his new sidekick Hans. Matthews is now very amusing about the whole process and how, even by then, Hammer had acquired a certain sort of name for itself. 'When colleagues asked you at the bar what you were currently in, you didn't feel inclined to tell them,' he said. 'If you were doing a Hammer, you tended to keep a little bit quiet about it.'

But this was contrasted with the tremendous sense of camaraderie on the set itself, and Matthews recalled spending the quieter moments of the day playing Battleships with Peter Cushing. 'People had this image of Hammer being all chopped-off hands and gore but it didn't feel like that,' he said. 'You brought all your skills to it as an actor though because the scripts were ... well, hardly brilliant.' And despite his protestations concerning the chopped-hands image, Matthews also remembered one of *Revenge's* ghastlier practicalities involving his character, Hans, having to carry out a form of multiple brain transplant to save Frankenstein, once again, from the grave.

> Well, for the Baron's brain and the monster's brain, we used exactly the same prop, a sheep's brain from the local butcher. And these scenes were shot over four days. But for some reason, someone forgot to put this brain in the fridge overnight. Come the fourth day, I uncovered it and the thing was alive with maggots. Everyone fled the studio. And someone had to go off to ring the butcher to see if by chance he had another sheep's brain in stock.

The *Observer*'s C.A. Lejeune was still having none of it. She wrote of *Revenge*: 'I want to gargle it off with a strong disinfectant, to scrub my memory with carbolic soap.' These days, Francis Matthews can't really square that response with the innocent enjoyment that he derived from his first Hammer experience. One other aspect of the film still makes him laugh. It concerned the line he utters when faced with the prospect of saving his mentor: 'Pray God I have the skill to do this.' 'We had the premiere at the Plaza in Haymarket,' said Matthews, 'and when I said that line, it brought the entire house down. More laughter than a Bob Hope film.'

As ever, the mismatch between the perturbed critics and the audiences was great. What those early critical voices missed was the genius of Hammer's relationship with its punters. Both sides were engaged in an act of silent and enjoyable conspiracy. One of the elements that made these films so irresistible was precisely the reaction that they provoked from the snootier end of the arts establishment.

Even from the start, the showmanship and sheer chutzpah of Hammer was very much in evidence. The original *The Curse of Frankenstein* opened at the London Pavilion in May 1957, and the foyer was done up to look like Frankenstein's laboratory, complete with Creature in tank.

In America, where the film was received with both enthusiasm and curiosity, the publicity stunts were even more inventive. In Baltimore, for instance, a lone young woman was invited by cinema management to watch the film all by herself in a 3,000 seat theatre, to see if she could withstand it.

Jimmy Sangster and others have tended to downplay the overtly gory aspect of these films, insisting that they could have been worse. Perhaps so, but what probably made this and subsequent Hammers so shocking was the question of context. In essence, what audiences were being presented with was something with the menacing amorality of a gangster film, but presented in Gainsborough period setting, and daubed over with blood. The studio might have felt that it was presenting some form of continuity with the old Universal films that so overshadowed it; but in actual fact, they created something that James Whale and Carl Laemmle would have recoiled from. Despite what director Terence Fisher was to say years later about his gothic horrors, what this film did was create a world in which good was seen not to triumph. For something offered up as colourful, scary, escapist entertainment, its view of human nature was extraordinarily bleak and severe. And it marked a real turning point in the story of British cinema.

Chapter Three

SEX, FANGS AND ROCK AND ROLL

 'The horror market,' declared an ebullient James Carreras in 1958 upon the opening of *Dracula*, 'is better than ever because of the whole new generation that has never been exposed to this type of film. The aim is to make the audience believe something that is too fantastic to believe.' He then went on to slightly spoil the effect by adding: 'I'm prepared to make Strauss waltzes tomorrow if they make money.'[1]

Such frankness and guileless vulgarity was very much the hallmark of Carreras throughout his career, but tends to mask the fact that he was extremely serious about the films that his company made. And this high seriousness arguably found its finest expression in *Dracula* (1958).

The reasoning behind the choice of film is not difficult to unravel: Carreras and Hinds had just stopped rubbing their eyes at the success of *Curse* not just in Britain but in the States and across Europe and even in Japan. Dracula had always been the next on their game-plan for disinterring the Universal crypt. The market was eager. And thanks to *Curse* they had their two principal actors standing in front of them. Cushing would naturally be the principled vampire hunter Van Helsing. And the imposing, strikingly handsome Christopher Lee would become the latest cinematic embodiment of the Count. A no-brainer in other words. They didn't even test any other actors for the role, it was Lee's right from the very start.[2]

Rather sweetly, a budget breakdown shows, however, that Carreras and Hinds had not allowed success to interfere with their canny instincts. The overall budget was £81,413. Out of this, screenwriter Jimmy Sangster was paid £1,000. The cast wages came to a total of £7,310. To date, it is estimated that the film has made over £500 million.

The film itself is an object lesson in taut adaptation and is arguably one of the finest things the studio ever produced. And Christopher Lee's still-definitive portrayal of the Count – turning blood-sucking into an overtly sexual activity – is the crucial point at which Hammer found that sex and death in equal proportions – and particularly barely repressed sexuality in a Victorian setting – was the real winning formula.

Anyone in the audience who had read Bram Stoker's novel would have found Hammer's abridgement dazzlingly fast. The film opens on a rather fine matte-painted prospect of Castle Dracula and its ramparts. The titles and credits are picked out in bright red. We track down to a crypt and to a stone coffin upon which we can see the legend: 'Dracula'. A second later and the name is obscured by lurid crimson droplets of blood.

Then we are whisked into the story. Jonathan Harker (Jonathan van Eyssen) arrives at the castle and informs us, by means of voice-over, that he is a librarian come to sort out the Count's collection. He enters the castle, alone, walks into a dining hall, reads a note left by his host – and is surprised by a woman in a low-cut white gown who claims that she is being held prisoner and begs for his help. But then she withdraws, frightened, and Harker is startled by a silhouette at the top of a staircase. The figure descends quickly, resolves itself into the figure of a handsome baritone aristocrat who introduces himself, in perfect English, as Dracula.

But Harker is no librarian; the woman in the white gown is no ordinary captive; and Dracula is no gentleman. All this is made apparent just minutes later in the Count's study. Harker is about to be bitten by the girl when a bestial Dracula – eyes reddened and blood dripping from his maw – materialises. This is all the proof that vampire-hunter Harker needs. The next day, he descends to the crypt, stakes the young woman (who turns into a gummy old woman) and fatally dithers as the sun sets over Dracula's tomb.

But who should this be at the village inn? None other than Harker's old friend Van Helsing, in a fetching astrakhan collar, who has decided to come and help him. Down in the castle crypt, Van Helsing finds that he is too late.

The action switches to Karlstadt (rather than Whitby in Yorkshire, as in the novel, for reasons that we shall hear about presently). Van Helsing is there to tell Mina Harker and Arthur and Lucy Holmwood the bad news about Jonathan. In the meantime, Dracula decides to come to Karlstadt and starts to make nocturnal moves on Mina. Van Helsing is forced to stake her. Then the Count starts moving in on Lucy. Van Helsing confronts him, pursues him back to Transylvania – just as Lucy's transformation to vampire is almost complete – and then traps the vampire in a vast beam of sunlight. Dracula crumbles to dust.

Two things stand out about the crispness of this version. Firstly, you can't immediately place what Sangster has left out, save Jonathan Harker's career shift from estate agent to librarian and the absence of fly-munching lunatic Renfield. Second is the presence that Christopher Lee carries in the film. One comes away with the impression that he was in almost every scene. In fact, he was in very few. And he had a grand total of thirteen lines throughout the entire thing.

'We were restricted to a certain extent by budget,' said Jimmy Sangster, 'and I had to tell the story in ninety minutes. God forbid if you should be longer than ninety minutes. If you've got to cut a book like *Dracula* down, you've got to make some pretty heavy cuts. I didn't bring him to England,' he added, 'because we couldn't afford a boat.'³

As with *Curse*, the screenplay for *Dracula* was sent to the censors for a read-through and approval, and once more got a chilly, nose-holding response, with reservations expressed about the tastefulness of depicting blood-sucking in Eastman colour.

'The battles we had with the British Board of Film Censors were ferocious,' said Sangster in his autobiography. 'They started long before shooting commenced. One of the BBFC's readers referred to the 'uncouth, uneducated, disgusting and vulgar style of Mr Jimmy Sangster'. In fact, Mr Jimmy Sangster wrote a lot of stuff into the first draft that he knew the censor would demand to be cut, in the hope that some of the slightly less 'horrific' scenes would be allowed in.⁴

And again, Carreras and Hinds pooh-poohed the BBFC's lily-livered sentiments and carried on much as before.

But there were improvements on *Curse*. The screenplay, for a start, was very much less baggy and delivered the frights at a far greater and more even pace than previously. And with Terence Fisher once more directing, there was also a greater assuredness in the production values, even if he overlooked some of the more blackly ironic jokes in Sangster's screenplay.

Carreras and Hinds had been uncertain how far they could stray from the established Universal vampire iconography of cobwebs, candelabras and great looming shadows. It was Fisher, with his distinctly catholic colour schemes of blues, reds and purples, who persuaded them that it was right to move away from these clichés.

On his side, he had the formidably good set designer Bernard Robinson, who was renowned for rustling up aesthetic wonders on leftovers. It was Robinson who was responsible for the striking ramparts of the castle, and for its curious interior, with banister-less stairs and rather delicate, feminine gothic screens. He was also responsible for the first example of what would become a Hammer leitmotif – the glass painting of distant peaks and evening sky.

In fact, it is worth taking a look at Powell and Pressburger's *Black Narcissus* (1947) with its breathtaking, painted Himalayan mountain landscapes and artfully lit gothic denouement. It is more than possible that this was an unconscious visual influence on both designer and director.

So much for the fancy stuff. But the real selling point of the film, as all the crew will have known very well, was the sex. It was there in the cinema posters – images of Dracula crouching over a woman's bed – and it was there in the screenplay from the off. Valerie Gaunt has the honour of being the first of Hammer's true vamps, with an overtly seductive manner, vertiginous neckline and the debut of those vast white eye-teeth, which are sunk sexily into the stiff neck of Jonathan van Eyssen.

Melissa Stribling, as Mina Harker, was the second vampire woman, and the shock factor from the audiences' point of view was not only the obvious sexual connection between the Count and his victims but then the subsequent scenes of staking – an implacable Peter Cushing as Van Helsing aiming the wooden point just beneath the gowned breast and then hammering it in. Even in 1958, this must have been regarded as an unsubtle metaphor.

Then there were the bedroom scenes – to be exact, the perceived erotic frisson of Christopher Lee appearing at the windows of the heroine's bedroom, and the heroine, mouth slightly open, the hint of a smile, lying there waiting for him. In terms of daring, this was a world away from Universal and all of its coy camera-panning-away-at-the-crucial-moment ways. For the young audiences – who by 1958 were starting to enjoy a slew of stimulating American cultural influences, from coffee bars to rock and roll – it must have seemed enormously refreshing to find a British film pushing the envelope that much further than anyone else in terms of relatively brazen sex.

The denouement also made a big impact at the time and still stands up very well today. Van Helsing is pursuing Dracula through his own castle as the sun begins to rise. For a moment, the Count turns the tables and it looks as though Van Helsing will be bitten. But at the last moment, the scientist feints, leaps up, makes a dramatic Douglas Fairbanks dash along a table, pulls the curtains down to let in the rays of the sun and, as Dracula helplessly hisses, picks up two golden candlesticks and makes the sign of the cross. Dracula is trapped and dissolves into dust, leaving just his signet ring lying in the folds of his cloak. The end.

And with this scene, Hammer was well and truly established as the master purveyor of gothic melodrama. The like of the special effects had not been seen before; and the sheer energy that both Lee and Cushing put into their confrontation gave horror – previously a rather stagy genre – a real breathing immediacy. This sense was also fostered by Fisher's lickety-split direction. Again, there was nothing flashy or fancy but the pace was intense. And of course it was the film that would forever mould and shape the working lives of both Cushing and Lee. But the mantle was to sit heavier on Lee's shoulders.

The film was a bigger success than *Curse*. The critics were still dismayed by what they considered the gratuitous blood and sadism; '*Dracula* is clearly aimed at adults ... I hate to think what kind of adults,' said the

Spectator magazine, archly. But in general, the shrillness of these critical complaints had lessened a little – in the manner of grown-ups sighing and realising that there was nothing they could do to stop their children playing a particularly raucous game.

By 1958, Prime Minister Harold Macmillan was presiding over what appeared to be a time of great prosperity and confidence for Britain. Goods such as cars, refrigerators and televisions were becoming more widely available thanks to hire purchase. Unemployment was low, which gave the unions a stronger bargaining hand. In other words, the young people – labourers, clerks, secretaries – who trooped along to see this colourful new world of sex and monsters were confident, their aspirations and expectations high. We might at a pinch say that Hammer's *Dracula* pre-dated Bond and The Beatles in terms of throwing open the possibilities of a more sexually permissive Britain.

The film also did tremendous business in the States and this of course was the development that Carreras and Hinds watched with hawk eyes. They cannot be blamed. Universal AIP was their backer, and it was said within days of *Dracula* opening that Hammer had saved the American company from looming bankruptcy.

Indeed, here we see the beginnings of James Carreras's real genius. Universal were distributing *Dracula* throughout the US, and there were a number of eye-catching stunts to promote the film, including handing audience members fake 'wills' lest they die of fright. Indeed, one cinema manager in Michigan spent the week before the film's opening dressed as Dracula and was arrested for a breach of the peace.[5] But Carreras was watching even more closely than that.

'I don't like the advertising I have seen put out by your New York office which is along the lines of the old Dracula pictures,' he wrote to Universal. 'A hideous face and bats flying all over the place. Our Dracula is handsome and sexy and not the old Bela Lugosi type. His victims are young attractive women. The campaign in London is on the horror sex lines and I would be grateful if you would re-examine.'[6]

Then, in an interview given several months after the film's release in the US (under the title *Horror of Dracula*, lest anyone confuse it with that earlier Lugosi version), Carreras was in exultant form as he explained Hammer's *modus operandi*. 'No exhibitor has yet lost money on one of our films,' he said.

> We have a small team, no elaborate offices, no vast corporate
> structure. When it's your own money you're spending, you look after
> it. And we are utterly and unashamedly commercial, just as

commercial as a company making pots of marmalade. We give the customers what they want, which is what any enterprise should do.

Suddenly the American exhibitors are forgetting all the old arguments about how Americans can't get an English accent and fighting to get our stuff for general release. Not for the flea pits or the arts cinemas but the regular circuits.[7]

There spoke a man who sounded as though he had had bitter experience of flea pits in the past. The ideas he set out there were to serve the company well for the next few years; and not so well after that.

And what of his great star, the screen's most charismatic and attractive Dracula? Since the project had been mooted, no one else was considered for the part but Christopher Lee, and this was the top-billing starring vehicle for which most actors would have been pleased. But Lee was an intelligent man (possibly a shade too intelligent for the trade he was in) and it was clear that he could instantly see what a trap the part of Dracula could become.

By this point the sequel to Frankenstein was already in hand, although Jimmy Sangster had rather brilliantly closed off one of the return routes. In the Universal films, it was by tradition the monster that was restored to life with every follow-up. Hammer, however, had lost that option by dropping their Creature into an acid bath. Also, it was extremely unlikely that Lee would agree to reprising that particular role. So the next possibility would be to bring back Baron Frankenstein himself. But the first film had left him facing the guillotine. How the hell was the Baron expected to get out of that?

The question was put to Carreras, who raised his eyebrows and said: 'We'll have to sew his head back on.'

Thankfully, Jimmy Sangster swerved his way past such extreme solutions in his screenplay for *The Revenge of Frankenstein* (1958). This was all very well for Peter Cushing; Frankenstein was an articulate and occasionally very amusing anti-hero and Cushing was cast so against type that it could only enhance his career. Dracula was quite a different prospect for Lee.

In the first place, it was clear that for the vampire to have real power, his dialogue had to be kept to a minimum. If the Count spoke too much, he would sound at best incongruous and at worst just silly. But on the other side of the argument, this limited Lee's options very heavily in terms of characterisation. How could he suggest that the vampire was anything but an unholy nocturnal animal? How could he suggest that there was anything else going on in there – vestiges of humanity, signs of loneliness?

And also, with the question of sequels, what more could be done with the Count? Hammer already knew full well that if they wanted the audiences back, they had to stick with the formula just as it was. And that meant more blood dripping from maws and more lying in coffins and opening eyes *very suddenly*. There would be not a hope in hell of seeing another level to the Count or indeed getting a glimpse into his soul.

The dilemma was delayed a little because the studio held off from making a sequel for a year or so; they had a couple of other monsters to disinter. Both again required the services of Cushing and Lee.

The first was a unique retread of *The Hound of the Baskervilles* (1959), the well-worn Arthur Conan Doyle/Holmes mystery. What made this fascinating was the spectacle of another genre – the detective thriller, albeit with hints of the supernatural – being done up as Hammer Horror, complete with James Bernard's swooping score, the mist-enshrouded studio realisation of Grimpen Mire and the thunderous prologue in which the Baskerville curse is explained as being caused by a vicious eighteenth-century hunting toff – Sir Hugo Baskerville – pursuing, molesting and murdering a servant girl.

Cushing was Holmes, Andre Morrell an admirably strait-laced Watson. And Lee – unusually – was the good guy, Sir Henry Baskerville, who first has to face a tarantula crawling on his shoulder and then, of course, the full horror of the phoney hound from hell. Once again, Fisher directed with gusto.

Then came *The Mummy* (1959). It had an impressive extended prologue, featuring Christopher Lee as the lovelorn Egyptian high priest who gets sentenced to eternal living death with his tongue cut out. There then followed thirty minutes of ennui, perked up when Lee's bandaged mummy, brought to England, rises from a swamp and goes off in search of the desecrators. In Lee's terms, this was another hideous make-up job. But the screenplay allowed more sympathy, and amazingly – despite the layers of putty – Lee was able to convey a startling degree of lovesickness when confronted with the reincarnation of his lost royal inamorata. Cushing was the monster's arch-rival, Banning, who was even flintier than Van Helsing, allowing room for Lee's mummy to grab some emotional identification. It was an excellent performance from Lee despite the indignity of having to perish in a studio swamp (possibly a left-over Grimpen Mire). The heroine, Yvonne Furneaux, who was carried into that swamp wearing regulation cocktail gown, was even less impressed by the scenario.

That same year, 1959, Edward Goring of the *Daily Mail* wrote: 'The biggest Anglo-American co-production deal in screen history was announced in New York last night. Hammer Film productions will make 25 films for Columbia. *The Curse of Frankenstein* and *Dracula* broke the jinx on British films and earned a fortune.'

So one could hardly blame Carreras and Hinds for deciding that 1960 should be marked with something that their marmalade-consuming public were clearly desperate for. And so it was that the initial ideas for *The Return of Dracula* were batted around.

But one enormous obstacle was placed in their way. Christopher Lee didn't want to return. He would not re-create the role of the Count. The actor was clearly concerned that the role would hang over him ever more, and at that stage he was clearly optimistic that this was a fate that he could escape. What made it all the more galling for the executives was that they had Cushing lined up to reprise Van Helsing in what would have surely been an electrifying confrontation.

So Carreras and Hinds had to think again and it wasn't long before they were blithely forgetting about Lee's absence and substituting him instead with one Baron Meinster (played by David Peel), a vampire who saucily – yet camply – conducts his campaign of terror around a continental girls' school. Also Hammer executives quite happily went about duping the dopier members of the public by calling the film *Brides of Dracula*. Of the Count, there wasn't even a mention.

It is little wonder some felt cheated, although once again Cushing gave an intense performance as Van Helsing, and the final showdown, where Van Helsing uses the vast blades of a windmill to cast a shadow in the shape of a cross upon young Meinster, was very exciting. On top of that, there was a quite brilliantly mad performance from Martita Hunt as Count Meinster's mother. If ever there was an Oscar to be awarded for deranged laughter, she would have to be a very hot contender.

But with no Lee, it wasn't quite the same. And for the next several years, Hammer had to cast its monster net a little wider in order to find new horrors to distract the public with.

At this stage, it's worth taking a very swift overview of Dracula's subsequent Hammer adventures – though we will also examine them further at a later stage as the studio's story develops – just to get these particular films into some kind of initial perspective.

At the end of 1965 – seven years after he first played the Count – Christopher Lee was finally tempted back into the scarlet-lined cape by James Carreras. Possibly the money Hammer was offering was a little more substantial this time around; possibly in the intervening years, Lee had seen that he had still yet to be cast as a hero by anyone. Also he was still being offered an awful lot of horrors. To say nothing of an eyebrow-raisingly incorrect series of Fu Manchu films in which he played the eponymous master-villain with heavily made-up eyes. So why not be the Count again?

But *Dracula – Prince of Darkness* (released in 1966) was not without its own problems, despite this joyful reunion of Lee, director Terence Fisher and Jimmy Sangster, once more pressed into gothic screenwriting service. For a start, it was now Peter Cushing's turn to go AWOL – too many other commitments, including a kindly portrayal of Doctor Who in two cinema spin-offs from the television series. And then there was the small matter of the script, which for some reason put Christopher Lee into a very bad mood.

The plot was reasonably simple: four respectable Victorian English travellers find themselves lost in Transylvania. In no time, they are at Castle Dracula. The late Count's sinister manservant Klove tricks one of the men into the crypt, stabs him and pours the blood into his old master's coffin. Dracula is revived and vampirises one of the women, and at this point Van Helsing substitute Father Sandor (Andrew Keir) steps in. After some further toing and froing, including one unnerving scene in which Dracula cuts his own chest and almost induces the other woman traveller to drink his blood – the vampire is once more chased back to his castle and doesn't even make it through the door. As Dracula crosses his frozen moat, Father Sandor shoots and shatters the ice; the vampire perishes in the running water beneath.

Lee's chief problem with the script was the fact that he thought all of the dialogue given to Dracula was rubbish. And it was on this basis that he refused to deliver any of it. Not one line. This did not appear to phase director Fisher; and Sangster, the canny old craftsman, was supremely unbothered. He had already removed his name from the film anyway. Instead, the Count did a lot of standing, glaring, squinting, hissing, snarling and pointing. And in some curious way, it's quite effective. One can see that the idea of the Count is somehow easier to believe if he is not opening his mouth. One might also argue that he becomes something slightly more archetypal, a representation of a certain sort of evil.

Possibly it was all once more down to questions of dignity – it would be nice to know now what sort of lines Lee was refusing to say, and Sangster has said that he cannot remember – but as it is, the film still works perfectly well, a very nice slice of vintage Hammer Horror with all the trappings so beloved by its now vast regular audience. After this, though, the problems multiplied.

It was obvious that Lee was reluctant to keep playing the Count but none the less, he did so. Was it simply because other work was scarce? Not in the least. As an example, Hammer kept him sweet by giving him the lead in *Rasputin the Mad Monk* (1966), which turned out to be one of Lee's all-time favourite vehicles. Filmed immediately after *Dracula – Prince of Darkness* on exactly the same sets and with a very similar cast, including Barbara Shelley and Francis Matthews, this lurid drama chronicled the sexy exploits of Russia's 'greatest love machine', as the pop group Boney M once put it. The production was a handsome one, and it was a splendid role for

Lee as the hypnotic monk seduced and declaimed his way into Tsarist high society, removing Barbara Shelley's aristocratic frock, throwing acid into the eyes of Dinsdale Landen and finally finding himself in a rip-roaring fight to the death with Francis Matthews among other noblemen.

But no matter how much pleasure Lee took in this historical/melodramatic change of pace – no coffins or crucifixes here – the fact remained that Rasputin was hardly the shining good guy in the piece. Lee, in essence, was still pre-sold to the audience as the villain.

There were huge numbers of roles for Christopher Lee in other horror films, including those produced by rival studio Amicus (of which more in Chapter Five). But he was well and truly identified with Count Dracula, and with the portrayal of the power, fascination and attraction of evil. He had simply done the job far too well.

And for a certain amount of time, he was obviously enjoying himself as well. Interviewed in 1964 by Francis Wyndham, on the set of *The Gorgon* (a vastly entertaining effort which we will focus on more clearly in good time), Lee was effusive about the Hammer philosophy while being comically reactionary about other domestic film products of the time.

'I try to emphasise the loneliness of evil,' said Lee. 'Frankenstein's monster and the mummy didn't ask to be brought to life. Dracula couldn't help being like he was. I hate the word "horror". I prefer to call them "adult fairy tales".'

Then Lee got into his stride. 'I don't mind telling you that I resent the present trend in British movies,' he went on (and again, bear in mind that this was 1964).

> If there's a pile-up, it's their own fault. They should make films
> people want to see. Mind you, I haven't actually seen *Saturday Night
> and Sunday Morning* or *A Taste of Honey* but from what I hear
> about these so-called realistic films, the men are either thugs or
> queers and the women look like whores. If I want to know about the
> boy and girl next door, I can knock on the door. If I want to be sick, I
> can go to a hospital.[8]

One might have forgiven the interviewer for invoking the words 'pot', 'kettle' and 'black' at that moment but the line Lee was drawing was interesting and indeed kept Hammer separate and aloof from other British film companies for some years. In some ways, even by the mid-1960s, it was a jealous and inward-looking operation.

For their part, Hammer executives also started to show a little reluctance to keep on hauling the old Count out of his coffin. Remember, frugal and cheap though the studio was, nobody there liked the idea of making fun of what they did – and it was clear already that no one quite knew what else to do with Dracula. None the less, come 1968, the increasingly proficient press and publicity office started the drum-roll for *Dracula Has Risen from the Grave.*

In fact, it was a bit of a close call for the studio, for Hammer executives had secured American backing from Warners on the assumption that Lee would happily pop the fangs back in once more. This was not quite the case. And when the actor discovered that such a guarantee had been given, he reacted angrily. Executives had to enter into 'a great deal of slightly hysterical and acrimonious discussions' with Lee.[9] They paid off.

And anyone can say what they like now but this isn't a bad film at all. In fact, it is rather sprightly, good natured, and is carried off with some verve by director (later Oscar-winning cinematographer) Freddie Francis. Dracula has some presence, the juvenile leads are unusually engaging, and stylistically, the innovative use of colour filters in any scene involving the vampire is very pleasingly done.

But one can see the first cracks. As the nationwide advertising campaign had it (together with an image of Lee's hand reaching around a coffin lid), 'You can't keep a good man down.' The larkiness of the slogan immediately robbed the vampire of some power. The dialogue poor old Lee was to receive robbed him of a little more.

This time round, it is an alcoholic priest who accidentally revives the Count by cutting his head open on an ice block in which the Count is frozen. Within seconds, Dracula is back at the door of his castle but the way is blocked by a giant gold cross that has been fixed to the door by a peevish monsignor. 'Who has done this thing?' thunders Lee, and that is practically Dracula's only line throughout the film. The vampire then settles on a course of revenge on the cross-fixing monsignor and his family, which involves taking up subterranean residence in the cellars of the local inn, as mentioned before. Here, Veronica Carlson and Barbara Ewing (as barmaid Zena) are the women alternately falling for and being pursued by the Count, and very spirited and perky their performances are too. There is even a more likeable turn than usual from our old friend Michael Ripper of innkeeper fame. But the film is not very frightening.

The problem was clear. You kill Dracula off, you bring him back, but the next time you bring him back there are diminishing returns in terms of thrills because you know what he is going to do. At least this time round Christopher Lee was still bringing relish to what he did. All of that was to fall away somewhat in the years to come.

The film made a huge amount of money, by far the most successful sequel that the company had made. And so the die was pretty much cast. The next entry in the series followed barely a year later. Its genesis was even more agonised than the last.

Hammer's original plan was to do a story about three thrill-seeking Victorian gentleman – respectable by day, depraved by night – who in their quest for the ultimate thrill end up accidentally summoning Dracula. Among the three thrill seekers was Peter Sallis (now, sweetly, of *Wallace and Gromit* fame and just prior to his first appearance in the BBC's *Last Of The Summer Wine*); and the young degenerate aristocrat who carried out the black magic was Ralph Bates, who was being groomed as a young Hammer star.

But catastrophe once more loomed: Christopher Lee was not up for it. Later, he said:

> I felt I had discharged any obligations I had to the company. By this time, I had discovered just how successful Hammer films were in the States and how well-known I was. I told my agent to tell Hammer that if they really didn't have any money, then they could pay me a percentage of the American distributors' gross.[10]

It is almost possible, even after all these years, to see the vintage brandy going the wrong way down James Carreras' gullet, and the old man, face crimson, shouting out his response. That response, in essence, was: forget it.

And with the sort of pique that one might consider surprising (Carreras and Lee were, after all, rather good friends), the Hammer supremo put plan 'B' into operation. They would have themselves a new vampire. A younger, sexier vampire in the form of Ralph Bates. His sinister aristocrat Lord Courtney could take the Dracula role – presumably at a fraction of the cost of the original.

But at this, Warner Brothers/Seven Arts started to complain. They wanted Christopher Lee. Why couldn't they have him? So once more there followed a round of acrimonious, slightly hysterical discussions, this time conducted by the popular and emollient female producer Aida Young. Lee was talked down from the gothic turret tops and agreed to take part. But with notable ill-grace, it must be said. As shooting started, he informed his fan club: 'The tasteful title is *Taste the Blood of Dracula*. As usual, words fail me, as indeed they will also do in the film.'[11]

Like *Grave*, the film had a larky advertising campaign, this time a send-up of an old milk ad: 'Drinka Pinta Blood a Day'.

But again, there is actually much in this that is good. The three Victorians – also among them John Carson and Geoffrey Keen – are quite pungently revolting; the juvenile leads (including Martin Jarvis, Linda Hayden and Anthony Higgins, then under the name 'Anthony Corlan', who was to find art-house fame in *The Draughtsman's Contract*) are lively; there is rather nice atmospheric use of Highgate Cemetery at the film's climax and the new Hammer director, a young Hungarian called Peter Sasdy, gives it some shape and form. Not to mention a tremendous and romantic James Bernard score.

But it is no way Christopher Lee's fault that the least effective thing about the film is Dracula himself.

He has not many more than three lines of dialogue, and those delivered immediately after the dispatch of a victim: 'The first!', 'The second!' and 'The third!' The vampire's motivation is utterly inexplicable. Young Lord Courtney (Bates) has performed a ceremony whereby the vampire is summoned back to life from a powdery form in a desanctified church in Highgate. Sickened by what they have seen, the three older thrill-seekers set upon Bates and beat him to death. Then they flee. Dracula, upon reviving, makes a note of this and vows vengeance on the three men, despite never actually having met this Lord Courtney or indeed being especially aware that these men had murdered him.

Still, vengeance he must have, so Dracula goes about it in the traditional way, i.e. targeting the pretty youngsters and making them kill their fathers.

Playing one of those youngsters was a bouffant Martin Jarvis who recalls what a presence Christopher Lee was off-set as well. 'Of course, this was all in period costume and there had been some problem so on the days he wasn't filming, the costume fitters let me wear Dracula's shirt,' says Jarvis.

> But you could tell when Christopher Lee was coming in because these male costume fitters were all much more intense than usual. 'No, Mr Jarvis, you can't wear his shirt today.' And even though Christopher Lee wasn't in for long, he did lurk perfectly. He didn't have a lot of patience with us giggling youngsters. But he had the demeanour, the height and – incredibly important – the voice. He was a great Dracula.

Jarvis's character Jeremy incidentally gets fanged by Isla Blair and then ends up destroying his father John Carson in a chilly, undead fashion. The scene was remounted for international audiences, this time featuring Jarvis with his beloved fangs in.

Back to the story. Eventually, Dracula is stopped in his tracks by Anthony Higgins who somehow re-sanctifies that disused Highgate church. To the accompaniment of choral music and vertiginous camera angles, the vampire, reduced to throwing organ pipes at our unimpressed juveniles, finally flops down on to the altar and dissolves. Throughout all of this, it is very clear that Lee's heart was not in it. How could it have been? The thing made no sense.

None the less, the cash registers were once more kept busy and yet another entry was regarded as an inevitability. The American backers had not finished with Dracula yet and barely was he cold in that sepulchre than he was being cajoled back to life once more for what appeared to be a form of prequel, *The Scars of Dracula* (1970). This was the nadir of the series, and Lee could only have been returning to the Hammer Studios out of loyalty to Carreras.

Although this entry, directed by Roy Ward Baker, placed the vampire back in his familiar Transylvanian milieu, things were looking very sparse (possibly due to the sad death, the year before, of Hammer's designer par excellence, Bernard Robinson).

The castle was smaller, the inn even more brightly lit than usual, the local priest more camply crazed, the vampire's manservant (as played by Patrick Troughton) more gurning and salivating than ever before. The juveniles, Dennis Waterman and Jenny Hanley, looked straightforwardly bewildered and little wonder. This was an entirely purposeless story in which Dracula bites a few people, is beastly to his manservant, tries to bite the young people seeking revenge for the previous bitings, and goes over his own ramparts in flames. It is a staggering waste of eighty-five minutes; one of the very few occasions in Hammer where the viewer ends up feeling utterly cheated. History, thankfully, has bestowed upon us Dracula's live-in lady friend as played by Anouska Hempel, whom we will focus on a little more fully elsewhere.

And by this stage, Christopher Lee had become totally unforgiving. 'The Scars of Dracula was truly feeble,' he wrote.

> It was a story with Dracula popped in. Even the Hammer make-up
> was, for once, tepid. It's one thing to look like death warmed up,
> quite another to look unhealthy. I was a pantomime figure.
> Everything was over the top, especially the giant bat whose
> electronically motored wings flapped with slow deliberation as though
> it were doing morning exercises.[12]

By now, in terms of Dracula, everyone must have thought that that was surely that. It was not as though Hammer was running short of other ideas. In fact, as we shall see later, the early 1970s brought a surprising new rush of inventiveness to the studio. But there was also one last twist for the old Count up the sleeves of the executives. Quite an entertaining twist, as it turns out, but one that appeared to drive Christopher Lee round the bend with exasperation.

The idea, conceived in 1971, was originally entitled *Dracula Today* – making him sound a little like a current affairs programme. And the twist was this: remove the Count from nineteenth-century Transylvania and instead have him pop up in swinging Chelsea.

The notion was not, in itself, completely risible; by this stage, Hammer could see that the days of period costume horror were numbered, and there were both dramatic and (though it sounds unlikely now) sexy possibilities in having the Count move among the swingers.

The script went into production and was retitled *Dracula AD 1972*. Among the young ones this time were Stephanie Beacham and Christopher

Neame. Also, for the first time since the original in 1958, Christopher Lee was reunited with Peter Cushing as Van Helsing – well, the grandson of the original, who features in the film's prologue, a terrific coach-and-horse chase which ends up with Dracula impaled on a wheel spoke.

For some reason, his remains end up beneath a disused church in Chelsea, 1972, and this, now, is where the film's inadvertent charm really lies: the *hilarious* depiction of groovy young people (and that 'young' is qualified) deciding to freak out with a black-magic ritual that, naturally, ends up invoking the Count. From the pad of bad-boy Johnny Alucard (do you see what they did there?) to the purple-lit nightclub, with *very* soft music, in which the groovesters congregate, here is a brilliant pastiche of what older people imagined fashionable London looked like. In other words, it is a masterpiece of kitsch. Even venerable Peter Cushing, as Lorrimer Van Helsing, has the grace to look a little amused by the whole thing. One man is not laughing: Christopher Lee. Once again largely shorn of dialogue, and once more squinting and baring teeth like mad, the look behind his eyes gives it all away. This is hideously beneath his dignity. How did it all come to this?

Lee claimed to have not minded this film quite as much as the one that was to follow. '*AD 1972* had certain things in its favour,' he wrote.[13] Which prompts one to think: 'Yeah – name two.'

'I was, at the beginning, aghast at the plan to bring the story into modern times,' Lee continued, 'but a compromise was effected whereby at least Dracula's gothic homestead and the church were retained.'[14]

The film as it turned out was a moderate success, sufficiently so for the studio to try the same gambit again a year later in *The Satanic Rites of Dracula*. That proved to be the beginning of the end for Hammer, as we shall see in more gory detail at a later stage. It also marked the moment that Christopher Lee reached his breaking point with the studio.

It was the early 1970s and there was not an excessive amount of film work around for anyone, even for an actor as good and fundamentally recognisable as Lee. But his feelings about these later Draculas can be summed up easily: distress and anger.

Lee went off to play the Bond villain Scaramanga in *The Man with the Golden Gun* (1974) – he was excellent, one of the series' most memorable bad guys, but the film itself was a very shabby, tired effort. Lee also managed some strenuous swordplay as the dastardly Comte de Rochefort in Richard Lester's *The Three Musketeers* (1973) and got to be in a spaghetti western. In script terms, Lee did extremely well in the now much-loved cult classic *The Wicker Man* (1973). In fact, he considers it his favourite performance and the film is counted as one of the best this country ever produced. This was emphatically not the case at the time: *The Wicker Man* was regarded as a honking turkey and forgotten two weeks after release. The mid-1970s were not a good time to be a British film-maker. After this, Lee went on to do all sorts of other roles – from parts in Disney efforts, such as *Escape from Witch Mountain* (1978), to a well-received comedy appearance on the American TV showcase *Saturday Night Live* – but was to find for a few years that he could never quite shake the old vampire off. And you can see why. Lee's Dracula, even now, is one of the most iconic monsters of modern times, instantly recognisable all over the globe.

So what was it with the original in 1958 that so captivated audiences and kept them flocking back until 1973?

We might disregard the sentiments of one of the original 1958 audience members; a young chap was filmed by the BBC in a cinema foyer as the first Hammer *Dracula* opened and as the corporation solemnly reported this new horror phenomenon. Without a moment's thought, the young chap told the camera: 'I just love to see the blood spurt.' When Michael Carreras saw that clip, his immediate response was: 'Oh Christ – what have we done?'[15]

But it can't have been just the gore element in that 1958 Dracula, because in fact, the amount of blood is an optical illusion. Most of the time, it just isn't there. Terence Fisher simply tricked us all into believing that it was.

More likely it is the sense of doomy romanticism that hangs over the thing, not necessarily in the kerplunking dialogue or in the toe-curlingly awful performance from Michael Gough as Arthur Holmwood, but in the design, in the music, and in the look of the Count himself. Bela Lugosi's Dracula always opted for full white-tie evening dress, including some form of honour on a ribbon. Public-school educated Lee, who had a large say in his character's costume design, thought it slightly preposterous that a centuries-old nobleman living in the middle of Transylvania would do himself up like a social-climbing Rotary Club member.

So instead Lee looked much more sombre: Black suit, black cloak, all very simple, no adornment or fuss. A much more presentable figure to loom in the frame of a young lady's French windows.

One might also commend Lee's unforced upper-class demeanour, the hauteur and detachment of the vampire, all of which helped to make him a perversely alluring figure. And say what you like about the fangs, they were clearly a step up from most contemporaneous British dentistry.

A crucial element in Hammer's success that no one – save the studio executives – picked up on was this: the films were popular with women. As a genre, horror was – and still is – traditionally the preserve of young men. Sometimes there will be cross-over in the event of the horror film being used as a date movie. But Hammer executives knew that in order to really succeed, they had to draw the women in of their own accord.

And that explains much of Christopher Lee's Dracula: he is the embodiment of the handsome, seductive foreigner, an exotic object of desire. And he in turn has a most intriguing effect on the women he conquers. Very often they begin as repressed figures; when bitten, it is as though Dracula has released all of their inner sensuality. A striking case is that portrayed by Barbara Shelley in *Dracula – Prince of Darkness* (1966), prim English wife one moment and sexy white-gowned vamp the next. The romanticism of the Dracula cycle extended beyond the look of the productions. And this, it might be added, was perfectly deliberate on the part of the studio from their first Dracula onwards.

Director Terence Fisher explained: 'Dracula preyed on the sexual frustrations of his women victims,' he told one interviewer.

> The [Holmwood] marriage was one in which she was not sexually satisfied and that was her weakness as far as Dracula's approach to her was concerned. When she arrived back after having been away all night, she said it all in one close-up at the door ... I remember Melissa Stribling who played Mina saying, 'Terry, how should I play the scene?' So I told her. 'Listen, you should imagine you have had one whale of a sexual night, *the* one of your own sexual experience. Give me that in your face!'[16]

It is interesting to see how Christopher Lee's iconic silhouette insinuated its way into other corners of pop culture. Capes and morning dress could be found in Carnaby Street, on Adam Adamant, finally on Jon Pertwee's Doctor Who. Funnily enough, by the time we get to *Dracula AD 1972*, the Count actually looks rather fashionable, and not that much out of place next to the crushed-velvet fools who surround him. And even here, in Lee's middle years, the Count is, from the point of view of the female characters, far and away the sexiest man in view. The image is, even now, overwhelmingly familiar: the widow's peak, the burning eyes. Hammer had created a pop art monster.

These days, now that he is better known to a whole new young generation as Saruman, the wizard-turned-to-the-bad in the first of the *Lord of the Rings* trilogy, it is understandable that Christopher Lee wants as little mention of the 'D' word in his life as possible.

Just recently he recorded an album of operatic solos – Lee has always been a keen singer but none the less this is still rather impressive for a man in his mid-eighties – and held special signing events in order to promote it. Fans were invited along but one polite, if rather strained, request was made beforehand: Lee did not want to sign any memorabilia to do with the Transylvanian count.

You might immediately think: 'Oh come on, get over it!' But actually, put yourself in Lee's shoes: you have a film career spanning six decades –

countless productions, countless roles, countless different themes and characters. It just so happens that seven of those hundreds of films concern a vampiric nobleman. And indeed, you regard the later examples of these films to be especially poor. So yes, you might dearly wish that everyone would simply shut up about Dracula.

Actually, even at the time, especially in the early 1970s, to their credit, it was clear that Hammer executives saw the growing indignity of the role, and Christopher Lee's growing unhappiness with the part: the truth of the matter was that they had no wish for it to be so.

For all the talk of selling marmalade, this was a studio that did, however absurdly, pride itself on its family atmosphere. Indeed, this is one of the key elements that led both actors and technicians to return again and again to that country house at Bray.

This feeling of being one little bustling cottage industry began in the late 1950s and was to find its full flowering as the studio grew in confidence, in the early 1960s.

Vampire lady Carol Marsh in a sarcophagus with a cup of tea and a sponge finger (1958)

Francis Matthews
and Peter Cushing
in Frankenstein's
laboratory (1958)

Christopher Lee, in
Curse of Frankenstein
make-up, takes lunch
alone in the Hammer
canteen (1957)

Jonathan Van Eyssen surveys the studio ramparts of Castle Dracula (1958)

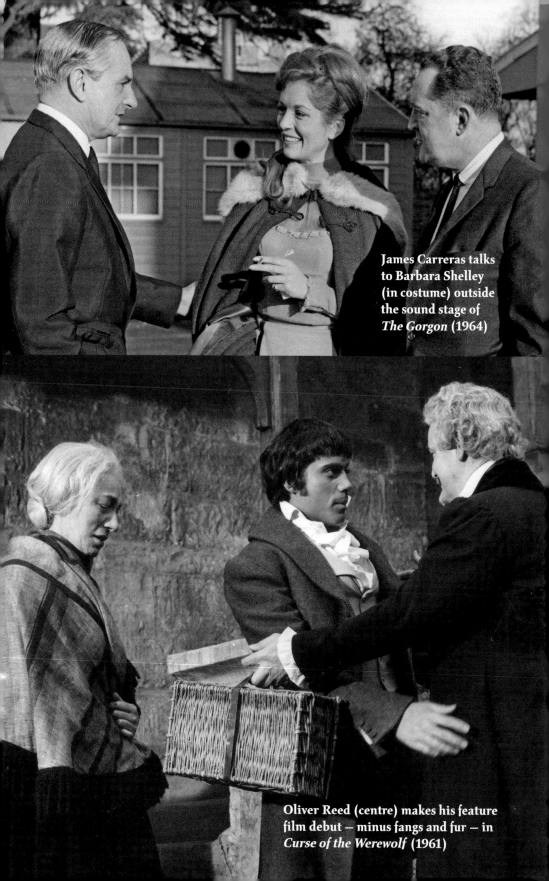

James Carreras talks to Barbara Shelley (in costume) outside the sound stage of *The Gorgon* (1964)

Oliver Reed (centre) makes his feature film debut — minus fangs and fur — in *Curse of the Werewolf* (1961)

The Reptile enjoys a cigarette break (1966)

Jacqueline Pearce poses on the front steps of Bray's House of Horror (1966)

Christopher Lee looking glum on a coffin, flanked by the lovelies of *Dracula AD 1972* (1972)

Terence Fisher (centre) celebrating with the cast of *Frankenstein Created Woman* (1967)

Peter Cushing and Christopher Lee off-camera enjoying a joke (1964)

'Please remember it isn't me'. Peter Cushing and Veronica Carlson close their eyes and think of England for *Frankenstein Must Be Destroyed* (1969)

A romanticised
Hammer graveyard,
with a wholly
unconvincing grave
being opened in
The Gorgon (1964)

wallowing in secret, hidden sleaze grips like iron and leaves one feeling squirmingly uncomfortable, as well as straightforwardly frightened. Imagine then how even the censors must have felt back in 1960.

Certainly, the critics rose up in a way not seen since *The Curse of Frankenstein*, but this time with even greater vehemence and venom. There was utter disbelief that a director such as Powell could have concocted something so vile and depraved. Incredulity that he could have persuaded people such as Moira Shearer to have a part in it. Huffing outrage at his depiction of a society mired in sordid sex. There was no comforting sense of distance here, not even the sense that the psychopathic Boehm was completely alien to the society in which he moved. In effect, the film famously brought Michael Powell's career to a halt and it was years before he was rediscovered and exalted by the likes of Scorsese.

So even by this stage, Hammer, though causing similar outbreaks of repulsion in the censor's office, was more of a mischievous bad boy than a disturbed delinquent.

By the turn of the 1950s/60s, Hammer was still turning out the odd noirish monochrome thriller such as *Hell is a City* (1960) – these really were the specialised favourite of screenwriter Jimmy Sangster – but James Carreras wanted these increasingly sidelined in favour of the horrors. 1959 brought *The Man Who Could Cheat Death*, starring Anton Diffring and Hazel Court, a reworking of an old ghoulish tale called *The Man in Half Moon Street* about a man who can stay alive indefinitely *only* if he kills someone to replace some kind of gland every now and then. It does not repay viewing now, being in essence a staggeringly dull film.

The studio also tried out a form of historical horror, in the shape of *The Stranglers of Bombay* (1960) which involved India in 1827, Thuggees, square-jawed British soldiers, scenes of elaborate torture and other elements that audiences weren't necessarily used to seeing in period costume. This curiosity got some enthusiastic reviews and made some money. So the studio tried the formula again in 1961 with another burst of unintentional racism: *The Terror of the Tongs*. This time it was a nineteenth-century Hong Kong criminal cult that was going around dishing out the atrocities, including 'bone scraping'.

The key thing at this stage was that – whether Hammer had saved Universal Studios or not – the British now came to an agreement with the Americans whereby Hammer could pillage any monster it liked from the Universal crypt in order to keep the lucrative horror revival going.[2] And there was more there than simply Frankenstein and Dracula.

For its next project, Hammer even tried a little investment outside the walls of Down Place. This is something that very rarely happened and, when it did, tended to end in tears. This time, it hired the screenwriter of *Expresso Bongo* (i.e. a clever and proven touch with daft young audiences) to deliver a script for *The Two Faces of Doctor Jekyll*. Wolf Mankowitz, a very bright writer, duly gave it some oomph, sexing up what was already, to be honest, a reasonably sexed-up story, and made it all a little more high-brow than usual, with clever lines about dualism and the nature of identity.

Jekyll/Hyde was to be played by Paul Massie and, as well as the traditional steaming potions in glass beakers, the film included a sleazy nightclub which Mr Hyde would frequent. And the twist this time was that Mr Hyde would be a handsome devil, whereas Dr Jekyll would be a bearded nerd. And the more the potion took a hold on the man, it wouldn't be Hyde who kept re-asserting himself, but Jekyll. The aim was to highlight the attractiveness of evil. Just to reassure audiences that frightfulness really would occur, Christopher Lee was cast as Jekyll's friend. Lee, it seemed, was a trifle put out not to have been given the Jekyll/Hyde role.[3]

It was all very colourful and rather stylishly done but it wasn't a dazzling success (although Mankowitz's whopping £5,000 fee was recouped in Europe where, as ever, the film was sold in rather sexier terms than in Britain).

And here, for the first time, is where the spotlight falls properly upon Michael Carreras, eldest son of James and eventually the heir to a troubled family enterprise. This popular man began working alongside his father after the war, learning every angle of the film craft: 'I had the advantage of going through all the different departments of [Hammer predecessor] Exclusive Films,' he explained. 'Logging, buying, accounts. I ended up in the publicity department which was responsible for sending out the stills and posters.'[4] Marketing was a terrifically important component of the Carreras strategy – indeed James had a knack for it that was almost ahead of his time in its snappy, larky post-modernism.

So come *The Two Faces of Dr Jekyll*, Michael Carreras found himself in the position of producer. Christopher Lee may have been grumpy that he was never offered that lead role but in fact this was down to young Carreras: unlike the great majority of the cinema-going public, he felt tired of always seeing Lee and Cushing's faces in these parts and turned Lee down when the actor approached him about it.[5]

And yes, Carreras wanted the film to be a cut above in intellectual terms, hence the signing of Mankowitz who was regarded as one of the brightest young things of that age. Jimmy Sangster later said of Carreras: 'Michael always tried to make better pictures. He would always try to get better writers, better actors, better budgets.'[6]

Already, by that stage, there was a sense abroad that the son did not have quite the same level of vulgar enthusiasm as the father. That he did not have quite the same taste for gothic horrors as James. In fact, as the years went on, this lack of enthusiasm for the genre was to become more and more glaringly apparent.

But none the less, Michael Carreras and *Dr Jekyll* were very unlucky with the Board of Censors and its Chairman, John Trevelyan, and the result was fatal for the film. This was in no way the fault of young Carreras. But *Jekyll* was coming out in the wake not just of *Peeping Tom* and *Psycho* but a couple of utterly gratuitous Nat Cohen thrillers – the sadistic *Circus of Horrors* (1960) and the equally exploitative *Horrors of the Black Museum* (1960). Interestingly, these last two films, involving thugs, sulphuric acid, disfigurement and other such diversions, were an early result of other independent studios, even more penny-scraping, attempting to pick up the gauntlet that Hammer had thrown down. How strange it now seems that, by 1960, Hammer seemed immensely sophisticated and even refined in comparison with these brutish efforts.

Nevertheless, Trevelyan was in an especially sensitive mood and as a result, *The Two Faces of Dr Jekyll* was cut heavily – it was felt that with the nightclub scenes, there was simply too much sex, and the violence levels were deemed unacceptable – and as a result the film was rendered, in parts, largely inexplicable. Both Carreras and his screenwriter (who got paid more than double the usual Hammer going rate) were philosophical about it all. Said Carreras: 'Within the company, it set me back a lot. Everybody said you shouldn't have done it.' Mankowitz was very loyal: '

Michael had one great characteristic, and it was that if he put the talent together, he never messed with it. He never tried to control it or manipulate it – he just directed it, very gently. And he could have done that very well if it hadn't been for the 'old man' up there [James Carreras], and the remorseless mills of Hammer.[7]

Those mills clearly seemed a little too remorseless for young Carreras, and in 1961 he left the company to found Capricorn Films. Not, of course, that this was the end of his association with the company. Very far from it. He was soon to return as a freelance director, then a little later in an executive role – first to preside over its most spectacular financial success, and then to oversee its slow, desperate fight against decline.

By 1961, it was clear to the production office what the public was after and that was more Dracula. In fact, there had been another putative vampire script – *Dracula the Damned* – which, in the absence of Christopher Lee, was metamorphosed into the fraudulently titled *The Brides of Dracula*.

And it was here that the Hammer 'family' (excluding Michael) was really consolidated. At the top, the increasingly genial and publicity courting James Carreras; in the background, the more reserved, thoughtful, publicity-shy Anthony Hinds who was soon to start doubling-up as screenwriter 'John Elder' when it was felt that the skimpy Hammer budget did not necessarily have to run to pricy freelance writers. By this stage, the elderly William Hinds (still known to some as old Will Hammer) had died and had left his entire share of the company to eldest son Anthony. It made Anthony what some described as 'a man of independent means'.

Incidentally, that jewellery business that old William Hinds had been involved with in the 1920s, before he threw himself into film production, might ring a bell today. It was continued by another branch of the Hinds clan, and, to this day, F. Hinds is an extremely familiar name on high streets across the nation (in the manner of H. Samuel), over 100 branches still involved in the same business of wedding rings and carriage clocks.

Then there was director Terence Fisher, still as stalwart a figure as the British film industry ever produced; a man who had worked at Gaumont and Gainsborough, making stolid, oatmealy productions, and who had somehow progressed into these cheap but technically razor-sharp productions with the dual bonuses of colour and embonpoint.

No one had – or has – a word to say against a man whose birth certificate might well have been amended to 'Dear Old Terence Fisher'. Actor Francis Matthews, having co-starred in *The Revenge of Frankenstein* then co-starred in the eventual Dracula follow-up, *Dracula – Prince of Darkness*, remembers a quiet figure much given to dissolving into laughter. 'The thing is that Terence Fisher is now regarded as a sort of *Cahiers du Cinema* genre genius,' he said.

The French in particular worshipped his Hammer films. But in fact I found that he was one of the least hands-on directors I'd ever worked with. He smoked little cheroots and, in terms of the filming, had the habit of liking absolutely everything. You would never go back and change anything if you felt your performance wasn't quite right – he was always pleased. You see, the thing is, he was brilliant on the technical side but as was common then, when it came to the acting, it was just left to you really.

There was once scene on *Darkness*, which my wife saw afterwards and told me never ever to act like that again. I think my screen wife had just been kidnapped, my screen brother slaughtered and Barbara Shelley turned into a bloodsucking demon. And I said, with hand clenched to mouth, 'I've heard of vampires but never seen one.'
I mean, really. But Terry used to laugh and get on with it.

Alongside Fisher was production designer Bernard Robinson who, as we have already seen, was an expert in conjuring fantastic worlds from tatty old odds and ends, and who worked closely with Fisher on making sure that his colour schemes worked. Robinson once said of himself that he was 'the Marks and Spencer of his profession, giving value for money'. His widow Margaret recalled how this would work in principle on such films as *The Mummy*. This entry actually had an Egyptology adviser. 'The adviser went mad,' she recalled.

> He insisted the ushabti, the little vases, would have to go back
> because their noses were wrong – they were Hittite, not Egyptian.
> Well Bernard naturally wasn't going to send them back because who
> was going to notice, in a funeral procession with a sacred cow and a
> leopard and a lot of nubile dancing girls?[8]

Crucial to all of these early films were cinematographers Jack Asher, who was a perfectionist and who lent those early Hammer productions a gloss that made them look five times more lavish than they really were, Arthur Grant, who could lift even the drabbest location shoot and give it real depth and atmosphere and Michael Reed, a colour photography expert who would go on to much bigger films afterwards. Even now, part of the reason for the visual attractiveness of the films is the camerawork, Asher's in particular. Take a look at the climax of *Dracula – Prince of Darkness*, where the Count is trapped on splintering ice on what – let us not forget – is actually the back of an old house in Berkshire. First, the wintry pale blue of the sky and the ice are contrasted with the pink of a (suggested) setting sun; next, the ice, extraordinarily, looks rather convincing; then, there is the progressive darkening of the shading as the scene proceeds to its chilly climax, the predominate blues in the picture steadily deepening. In other words, the camera team took what was little more than a scribbled-out bit of nonsense and made it visually unforgettable. Even now it remains one of the studio's finest – and oddest – sequences.

When it comes to a sense of depth and resonance not wholly warranted by utterly absurd scripts, there was another utterly indispensable, never-seen member of the Hammer family: the composer James Bernard. Classically educated at the Royal College of Music and a protégé of Sir Benjamin Britten, he had, as a young man, provided the studio with his first score for *Quatermass II*; it is a remarkable piece of music, many times more nerve-jangling than the film itself. And Bernard was flexible; although he gave Dracula a three-note theme that would last throughout that series of films, with each new Frankenstein, Mummy or Zombie, he always provided a fresh, completely new score, which was properly orchestrated and conducted. This was a level of care not always taken by other small independent studios. But

Carreras and Hinds understood this element to be absolutely crucial; no matter what other corners were cut, the music had to be strong; there were occasions when it could lift the unremarkable and give a punch where none had existed previously. Bernard's high, neurotic violins and violent percussion are instantly recognisable and unmistakable even now. And he took to the form instantly. To this day, he still stands – perhaps a slightly dubious distinction this, but unique, at any rate – as the finest composer of horror film music there has been.

Like many of his generation, Bernard was a modernist, drawn to atonality; but he also knew that while this worked for the monsters, a strong contrast, and relief for the audience, could be provided with plangent romantic themes. There was a flavour of the Methodist hymn about a lot of Bernard's themes. Listen to the music of, say, *Taste the Blood of Dracula* (1970) in isolation to the film and one could actually imagine that it was a domestic drama set deep in the Welsh valleys.

There was power there too, though: the score for *Frankenstein Must be Destroyed* (1969) not only underlines but actually amplifies the extraordinary pathos of that story of lunacy and brain transplants. It is percussive and the violins are neurotic, but there is a real heart as well and it is this element that so often lifted the Hammers above their rather more cynical competitors. Bernard, rather like Peter Cushing and Christopher Lee, was indispensably Hammer.

And talking of Cushing and Lee, the Hammer family was also made up of a recognisable near-repertory company of actors, who would recall being bussed from West London out to Bray first thing in the morning. Among the women were Barbara Shelley and Yvonne Monlaur. In those early days, Miles Malleson and George Woodbridge would be on hand to be undertakers and policemen. Thorley Walters began his long association with the studio, specialising in burgomasters, nincompoop police chiefs and alcoholic doctors. There was, of course, Michael Ripper, an example to all inn landlords everywhere, who plied his trade from deepest Carpathia to nineteenth-century Cornwall.

It is a curious aspect of horror movies – the old Universal efforts did the same too with stalwarts such as Lionel Atwill – that they seem to work better with familiar faces in the familiar stereotypical roles. Possibly the reasoning was that Hammer felt that one way to leaven its otherwise wholly bleak view of the world – both this one and the one beyond – was to give the audience light relief with these faces. When Michael Ripper or Thorley Walters are in shot, one feels a certain reassurance that nothing too untoward can happen. The other reason was that with very tight shoots, the studio had to be certain that the actors were reliable and would get it right on the first take: seasoned old professionals like Ripper and Walters were more than reliable; the studio always knew that they would get cracking performances from them.

But in terms of scripts, untowardness there still was, and back in the early 1960s Hammer was still engaged in wrestling matches with the censors. One notable clash was over their remake of the Wolf Man cycle, this one called *The Curse of the Werewolf* (1961). The back story of this particular hairy article is that his mother, a peasant girl, was raped by a demonic vagrant. The actor Richard Wordsworth, who portrayed this ghastly vagrant, recalled with laughter what director Terence Fisher required him to do to demonstrate horrid lust – and what the censors then had to say about it. Wordsworth was told to keep a little egg white in his mouth and then dribble it out. 'But keep it tasteful,' Fisher told him (and that comment alone makes for such a boggling image that one feels it should be accorded a DVD extra all of its own).[9]

Understandably, film censor John Trevelyan was revolted by that, and the subsequent attack on the girl. Hammer was told: you can either have the dribbling or you can have the vagrant 'having relations' (as they put it) with the girl. But you can't have both. Fisher and Carreras felt that the dribble and the relations were inseparable, but it was the dribbling that had to go, otherwise, in narrative terms, the boy who grows up to be werewolf would never have been born.[10]

Here it is time for one of the luminaries of the Hammer family to step forward and take his posthumous bow: Oliver Reed. *The Curse of the Werewolf* marked the twenty-two-year-old actor's screen debut. And this tragic tale of the lycanthrope whose condition was not of his own making was sufficiently moving as well as frightening for the young Reed to instantly be awarded the accolade of his own fan club.

Reed's association with Hammer was to grow, including a collaboration with Joseph Losey (of all people). But one other thing about *Curse* is worth noting at this point and it is Hammer's brilliance at making do with what it had got. The novel on which *Curse* was based, by Guy Endor, was originally set in Paris. So why was the film's narrative relocated to Spain? The reason, quite simply, is that Hammer had previously intended to make a horror drama based around the activities of the Inquisition. When various Catholics advised Carreras and Hinds that such a film would be regarded as tasteless in the extreme, they unusually backed down but then found themselves with some brilliant Spanish sets built by Bernard Robinson.[11] So how best to use them?

In one way, the idea makes us laugh affectionately, this professional film studio using sets as children might use a dressing-up box. But on the other hand, we now must also applaud the ceaseless inventiveness involved in such a system. A couple of years later would see similar resourcefulness deployed to use sets for two films back to back (which is how Castle Dracula also came to double as the Tsar's palace in *Rasputin the Mad Monk* [1966]).

And it was into this strange celluloid cottage industry that Oliver Reed moved, becoming an integral part of the Hammer family in the early 1960s. Executives were impressed with his presence in *Curse* and set out to deploy him in a wide range of their other films. He took the lead role in the bleak Joseph Losey science-fiction drama *The Damned* (1962); this was a highly unusual and experimental Hammer feature concerned with a hidden community of deliberately irradiated schoolchildren, intended to be the survivors in the case of nuclear Armageddon. Losey, not long harried from the US in the wake of the McCarthy witch-hunts, was given (for Hammer) an astonishing amount of artistic leeway. More than this, he was also allowed to ramp the costs up (notably by staging an expensive helicopter chase). Oliver Reed was to prove the anchor for an otherwise exceptionally doomy effort.

Incidentally, when it came to experimentation, James Carreras was having none of it. 'It's not our cup of tea at all,' he said later. 'Losey is a very eminent director and he has a great following among the critics and the film, I'm sure, was a good film. But unfortunately, you know, we can only judge it on results. Did it get its money back? And the answer is no, it didn't.'[12] As neat a summary of the Hammer philosophy as was ever given.

Young Oliver Reed was also enlisted for two of Hammer's popular early 1960s offshoots. At that stage the studio was attempting to branch out into swashbuckling family adventure in the form of pirate films and they were also making a bid for the Hitchcockian end of the market with psychological thrillers.

So young Oliver was first drafted on to *The Devil Ship Pirates*, a spirited enough yarn (although how Carreras in heaven must be sighing over the semi-supernatural nonsense of today's *Pirates of the Caribbean* and clicking his fingers with frustration at a missed opportunity). Hammer also dipped a toe into Romney Marsh with the smugglers of the *Dr Syn* novels, but ran into copyright difficulties and so Dr Syn metamorphosed into *Captain Clegg*. Both directions were a very nice try. One might say that the pirate and smuggler pictures were Hammer Horrors for children, in the sense that they combined high adventure with a taste of the macabre. This was nicely illustrated by an ingenious smugglers' ploy. Those travelling at night across Romney Marsh live in terror of the so-called 'Marsh Phantoms'. And indeed, duly, these apparitions materialise – luminous skeletal figures riding black horses. Or to be more precise, eighteenth-century smugglers in cunning phosphorescent disguise.

Peter Cushing voiced the view that his own role in this drama as the reverend-cum-smuggler was among his favourites, and he always sought a way to make further episodes of these sagas.

Where Oliver Reed came into his own were Hammer's black-and-white suspense thrillers. These had begun in 1961 with Jimmy Sangster's *A Taste of*

Fear, which established the template for this particular style of film. First, it had a lip-smackingly helpless heroine in a wheelchair (played by Susan Strasberg). Second, it featured no other character who could be completely trusted. Third, there seemed to be some plot to drive the heroine out of her mind. Fourth, this involved her glimpsing corpses of relatives who may or may not have actually been corpses, for we never got to find out until the concluding reel. Fifth, in the case of *Taste* was the jumbo, juicy red herring thrown in mainly for the American market in the shape of Christopher Lee.

Many of the same sort were to follow including *Maniac* (1963), *Nightmare* (1964), *Hysteria* (1965), *Fanatic* (1965), *Crescendo* (1970) and, almost as an afterthought, *Fear in the Night* (1972); the chief leitmotif of these films is that the heroines, be they Stefanie Powers or Judy Geeson, are going off their pretty little heads. But Oliver Reed's chief contribution to this mini genre was *Paranoiac* (1964) which involved long-lost siblings who may or may not have been murdered, a sinister old dark house and someone scary in a pumpkin mask. Because of his dark, brooding looks, Reed, rather like Lee, made an excellent red herring. And Hammer gave Reed a jump-start in his career that anyone would have been proud of. He was to return years later narrating a nostalgic television series about the company.

One other monochrome thriller went on to find a life beyond that of most straightforward Hammer Horrors, and that was 1965's *The Nanny*, starring Jill Bennett and, unforgettably, a scenery-guzzling Bette Davis as the title figure. Davis had of course made herself an icon of gothic camp three years previously in *Whatever Happened To Baby Jane?*. Here she delivered a pop-eyed performance as a homicidal child-carer. Thanks to unnerving cutaways involving dead bodies in baths, the film swiftly got a reputation as one of the studio's most unsettling, and it did tremendously well at the box office. It also pioneered, in its slanty camera angles and arch dialogue, a very particular sort of British psychological thriller, where dead-eyed psychos tell housewives that they mustn't worry, and where dead girls in bras fall out of wardrobes. In other words, the film's appeal now largely rests on the game performance given by Bette Davis.

In terms of family atmosphere at the studio, it was not only a question of artists and crew; at the end of that country house driveway down near Maidenhead, close to the rippling Thames, Hammer was also to prove a home and a family to its backroom staff – from the accounts men to the press secretaries to the PAs. About 130 people were employed at the studios at this time.[13] In 1964, the quietly spoken Anthony Hinds withdrew from his day-to-day producing duties and made way for the even more gentlemanly company general manager Anthony Nelson Keys. Nelson Keys (known among the bright sparks as 'Bunch of') was fondly noted for his inability to stand confrontation – he hated it. For instance, Hammer's technicians, the electricians and so forth, were as bolshie as all their counterparts elsewhere in the film industry, but Nelson Keys never quite knew what to do when their demands became loud and pushy. It is said that he set up studio floor microphones so he could hear initial rumbles of discontent among the staff; they cottoned on to this and started staging fake outbreaks of socialist agitation. The next thing they would hear would be the sound of Nelson Keys' car door slamming, and of him driving away.[14]

It was around this time, in the early 1960s, that James Carreras, never one to shy away from press attention, started jocularly referring to himself as 'The Colonel'. This was a fairly widespread social tic in the years immediately after the war – the tendency to jokingly use one's old rank as a nickname. The war might have ended in 1945 but for those who fought, it had been the single, defining formative experience of their lives, and it would not have been either seemly or appropriate to simply file it away and forget it so soon afterwards.

But whatever Carreras's loud idiosyncrasies – and even those who weren't fans couldn't deny his natural aura of showmanship – it is undeniable that people loved working for Hammer and stayed with the studio for years. Down Place at Bray was a super-motorised cottage industry. The films may have been funded mostly by the Americans, via an influential figure called Eliot Hyman of Seven Arts, but the working practices were undeniably British and the scriptwriting, directing and acting almost absurdly so.

Jimmy Sangster recalled the Carreras style fondly. 'Jim Carreras, known as The Colonel ... was an extraordinary man. He was the ultimate salesman.' There was just one set-back, a minor, trifling thing: 'He knew very little about the physical business of movie-making. Not fully understanding the technicalities, he'd get upset at the number of people on the company payroll standing around, apparently doing nothing.'[15]

And so the gothic horrors went on. After *Werewolf* came a re-working of *The Phantom of the Opera* (1962) with Herbert Lom. The prelude to production saw the Hammer team get unusually excited; for one day, quite out of the blue, they had received a surprise visitor at the studio's London office in Wardour Street: Cary Grant.

Grant, it seemed, had popped in because he wanted to let Hammer know that he was keen to appear in one of their horrors.

Hammer naturally wasted no time in circulating this story. And then it seems Cary Grant's enthusiasm dissipated almost as soon as it had arrived.[16] Aside from getting the studio worked up about the almost infinitesimal chance of Cary Grant playing the organ-thumping Phantom, *The*

Phantom of the Opera presented the studio with another slightly unusual problem. Even though Gaston Leroux's novel, plus the Lon Chaney and Claude Rains film versions, had been high on melodramatic thrills, they were a little short of what might strictly be termed horror. The story – mad deformed composer lives in catacombs of opera house and kidnaps the ingénue he taught to sing – was short on coffin-lid opportunities.

They tried: a grisly extra murder or two here and there, extra grotesque make-up for Lom. But it was no use. And so – one might say ignominiously – the film was submitted for *self*-censorship by the studio, any seriously horrid bits were cut, and it was issued as part of a child-friendly 'A' certificate double-bill with the smuggling adventure *Captain Clegg*. This is the only occasion when it might be said that Hammer toned itself down.

It was clearly time for the studio to go back to their old dependables. In 1963, Terence Fisher proved unable (or possibly unwilling, for there was a suggestion that he was in a huff after the fate of *Opera*) to helm *Evil of Frankenstein*, that saga's second sequel. The directing duties were handed to cinematographer Freddie Francis, who was many years later to win the Oscar for his camerawork on *The Elephant Man* (1980). No Oscars on this occasion, however. Peter Cushing returned as the Baron in a frankly curious story involving local bureaucrats, a drunken corrupt hypnotist, the old monster found frozen in a block of ice and the return of the monster's 'square-headed' Karloff look as the copyright holders of this image, Universal, were now bankrolling the film.

It was a spirited effort but it was never entirely clear what the film was actually about, or how Frankenstein's involvement this time around was any more especially evil than on other occasions. Added to this was the absence of composer James Bernard. Stand-in composer Don Banks gave it plenty of pacey melodramatic oomph but none of the strange, nervy soul that one automatically links with Hammer. According to the make-up artist Roy Ashton, whose thankless job it was to make wrestler Kiwi Kingston look as soulful and bathetic as Karloff and Lee before him, the whole thing was a bit of a mess, with executives from all over the studio trying to put their tuppence worth in. 'To tell you the truth,' he told Hearn and Barnes, 'they did not know what they wanted.'[17] And the result was that Kingston ended up looking (and acting) like a drunken body-builder plastered in foundation. Tellingly, the film made a great deal more money in America than it did in Britain.

It was also time for a bit more fang action, though once again without the involvement of Christopher Lee *or* Peter Cushing. *The Kiss of the Vampire* (1964) this time features Noel Willman as the chief bloodsucker and Clifford Evans as his nemesis. In all other respects though, the winning formula was there in the shape of wooden Edward de Souza as the respectable young protagonist, who at one point has to face mortal biting peril bare-chested; a cult of white-gowned vampire ladies; a painted castle on a hill and a score from James Bernard that in its extensive use of more melodious piano gave it all a pleasingly retro feel of old melodrama.

Incidentally, while Bernard was in the middle of composing that score, he was simultaneously working on a musical based on John Vanbrugh's *The Relapse* called *Virtue in Danger*. Actress and singer Patricia Routledge, who starred in this production, recently joked: 'I was always a little nervous of his Hammer connection. Every time James came back from that studio, I took a little step back.' Nevertheless, Bernard certainly demonstrated range.

The one glaring setback of *The Kiss of the Vampire* was the climax: on paper, having the vampire cult destroyed with an army of blood-sucking bats must have seemed a tremendous wheeze. On screen, the outbreak of flapping rubber bats, all too clearly attached to wires, now forces the viewer to look away not with horror, but with horrified embarrassment. And no, there is no way that attaching such a rubber bat to a young actress's neck makes the effect any more realistic. Pleasingly, the offending bats were bought at Woolworth's. But audiences were slightly more forgiving in 1964, and the film not only brought in a decent profit but also some rather good and affectionate reviews. Everyone was now used to Hammer's style and – perhaps in contrast to the rougher new English cinema being wrought from gritty northern towns – the studio's films were actually greeted as something of a colourful relief.

And *The Kiss of the Vampire*, perhaps more than any other production set in concrete was to become known as 'the Hammer look', including, integrally, the location work – a crisply autumnal Black Park doubling as Transylvania, together with the now turn-of-the-century Victoriana and a brightly lit sinister castle. All the paraphernalia was secured in place. Increasingly from this point onwards, Hammer realised that no matter what the nature of the horror was, the audience must have as many of these guiding leitmotifs as possible. Certainly James Carreras was very clear on this score. If that was what the audience wanted, then they should have it.

It was clear that Hammer's core audience had become consolidated by this point too: still young, still working class and now eager to consume films in double-bills, for that way one really got one's money's worth. The pirates and the Captain Cleggs – and even several Robin of Sherwood blockbusters that they produced – were Hammer's attempt to become known as a studio for all the family, and perfectly decent these films were too, largely saved up for the half-terms and the school holidays. But by that time to the majority of cinema-goers, the word 'Hammer' could only really signal one thing.

Nor is it possible to ignore the vast cultural shifts that were now at last becoming apparent, from the *Lady Chatterley* trial to the advent of the Bond films to the explosion of popular television.

In truth, Hammer had demonstrated in 1957 that audiences were not quite as easily shocked, or as prudish, as the censors apparently believed. But the early 1960s saw the censors besieged from all sides. The advent of the Bond movies in 1962 with *Dr No* took the idea of what was acceptable family viewing to its (rather stylish) limits, while monochrome films such as *A Taste of Honey* and *This Sporting Life* gave cinema-goers a rough sexual frankness that could not have been imagined a generation before.

New Wave cinema, in Britain, projected a world filled with soot, smog, damp pavements, dank kitchens, whippets, coarse pubs, gin and knitting needles, Richard Harris, Tom Courtney and northern accents. After the coy, deodorised decorum of Rank films, this was the rough-talking backlash (though naturally always directed by impeccably public-school educated figures such as Lindsay Anderson).

And their influence has stretched far. Those of us born later than the early 1960s find ourselves unconsciously using these films as a visual cue whenever contemplating Britain during this period. It can't be helped. Cinema shapes the landscape of our collective memories.

This was the time when The Beatles were scoring their first chart hits, and it was clear that the tectonic cultural shift under way in Britain was not attributable to creeping Americanisation, although in terms of music and film the transatlantic influence still held sway. It was more that an attitude that had clearly been brewing up in Britain since the end of the war finally came to the boil.

A very great deal has been written about that grim extended period of austerity in the late 1940s – an exhausting war effort followed by the grey grind of rationing, well into the 1950s – and how it was thrown off by the newly affluent younger generation who had been brought up in it. Cultural historians tend to alight upon the 'satire boom' of the early 1960s as a means of illustrating the apparently restless and iconoclastic mood of the time.

Spearheaded by the launch of *Private Eye* magazine and Peter Cook's Establishment club in Bohemian Soho, this was a movement that swiftly spread to a much wider national audience with the BBC's *That Was The Week That Was*. Young Oxbridge graduates such as William Rushton impersonated Harold Macmillan on stage and mocked received notions of class and authority.

Allied to this was a surge in the worlds of art and fashion, the keynotes of which at this stage again were rebellion and heightened sexuality; a pushing against notions of acceptability and respectability.

The Profumo scandal of 1963 was to prove the point at which all these disparate threads would be tied together: sex, the establishment and a notion of deference that was no longer recognised. Mandy Rice Davies's pert comment of 'He would say that, wouldn't he?' seemed to hold a mirror up to an unprecedentedly confident younger generation that was eager, after the hardship and horrors that the previous generation had had to endure, to inherit the world.

And Prime Minister Harold Macmillan had been right in 1957 when he proclaimed that we had 'never had it so good', no matter how shaky the economic foundation of this prosperity turned out to be. The British may have been losing their empire but the general mood of optimism (always easy in times of full employment), together with the exuberance of flourishing pop culture, created a period in which the ephemeral was being consumed in greater quantities than ever before.

In America, the popularity of television had been threatening cinema screens for a decade – hence the invention of such fight-back strategies as Cinemascope and 3-D. In Britain, although the more popular second channel, ITV, had started in 1955, television as a popular medium was still very much in its primitive early days – fine for intimate dramas such as soap operas but unsatisfactory for other genres. Such series as *The Avengers* (which began in 1961) and *Danger Man* (1960) were nods to Ian Fleming's Bond novels but studio-bound fuzzy black-and-white videotaped television could never hope to offer something on the scale of widescreen cinema.

This, for a time, was also a unique selling point for Hammer, on both sides of the Atlantic. Yes, television had hurt cinema in the sense that it had made staying in a much more attractive proposition; but television could never make the sort of chillers Hammer was engaged in. Also it was still the received wisdom that a horror movie could only really be scary in the darkness of a cinema, where the directors really understood about the art of throwing shadow and light. And so the audiences would queue up of a Friday night for their shocker of a double-bill, boyfriends and girlfriends, lads out for a laugh, innumerable youths under the requisite sixteen years of age then demanded by an 'X' certificate trying to bluff their way past the box office. Astonishingly, it was only really by 1964, as Hammer was starting to hit its stride, that competitors began to wake up to the market that they had ceded so easily to these upstarts from Bray.

Indeed, the Hammer style became so familiar to that generation that it was rewarded with its own send-up: *Carry On Screaming* (released in 1966), which featured young Victorian women being kidnapped from Hocombe Woods (the sweetest pun imaginable, unless I have misheard, and the word was actually 'Fircombe'); they are turned into waxworks by Kenneth Williams, the vampish Fenella Fielding, and a pair of Frankenstein monsters who were actually rather more effective than Kiwi Kingston could ever have been. To have made it to Carry On homage was the clearest sign that Hammer was nestled affectionately in the bosom of the pop culture establishment.

And yet it is also noticeable in this and later periods of Hammer development that James Carreras and his son Michael would allow no trace of knowing, arch humour in the films. To be fair, directors such as Terence Fisher wouldn't have known a joke if one punched them in the throat, and even Christopher Lee was described by one other actor as a man with an occasional lack of sense of humour. But for other cast and crew, the urge to nudge the films towards self-referential send-up must have been extremely strong – it only took three Bond movies before that particular formula was becoming camped up – and it says something for the tight control that a small private studio can exert that the discipline was maintained, even as the horrors steadily became more formularised.

Other stalwart audience members around this point were to be found in France, Germany and Italy, where the films were achieving wild popularity. Part of the reason was that they were seen as the repressed English finally letting themselves go to reveal that they were actually wildly sensuous creatures. As such, the films were given a much sexier sell (for instance, *Dracula has Risen from the Grave* (1968) was retitled as *Dracula and the Women* for the French, as one might expect). Another factor helped enormously throughout France, Italy and Spain too: Catholicism. A classic Hammer Dracula, filled as it is with golden crucifixes and proactive priests, also eventually depicts the vanquishing of the fiend by those who have God on their side. True, Dracula's nemesis was usually an unbeliever, but he was reliant upon the power of the cross to vanquish his foe. In other words, for a churchgoer, Count Dracula offered a rather satisfactory Saturday night out at the pictures.

And there was one extra element here that British audiences would have known nothing about: for these overseas audiences, slightly different versions of crucial scenes were shot in a slightly different way. A slightly bloodier way, that is. Whereas for native cinema-goers, stakings were represented by a cutaway shadow on the wall, or the vampire held below frame as the actual point went in, the continentals were deemed to favour a more blood-spurting full-on shot that left nothing to the imagination. This was also the case for the Japanese. Naturally it was all done for minimal cost, with minimal disruption to the main production.

If only Macmillan and his Labour successor Harold Wilson had looked to Hammer for inspiration in terms of basic economics. No matter how much money was pouring into the coffers (and it must have been an absolutely blush-making amount by the early 1960s – the world of film accounting being what it is, though it is difficult to ascertain just how much), James Carreras was still keeping a steely grip on those budgets. It might serve as a small comment on the company's regard for cash-flow that by this time, it had been joined by a junior accountant by the name of Roy Skeggs. Perhaps unusually for the film business, he rose through the ranks and ended up, when it all came crashing down some years later, as the man entrusted with the legacy of Hammer films.

When one surveys today's small-budget British films – the Loaches, the Leighs, the tyro directors making grindingly gritty urban dramas – one hears little but complaint about limited resources. It was a complaint that was never heard at Bray. Well, rarely.

Certainly, by 1964, 'know thy limits' was enshrined as a production motto. From the word 'go', a Hammer schedule would tend to run as follows: first, either the notion for the film or indeed simply a title, which could be used to start the American backers salivating. Followed swiftly by mocked-up poster art. As mentioned before, Hammer marketing was all. If the title was good and the poster sufficiently eye-catching, then the troublesome business of actually making the film could begin.

One drifts into a daydream where one imagines Ken Loach or Michael Winterbottom commissioning an artist to paint a poster for an as-yet imaginary film in order to lure in American backers. You can't help but wonder if ... but no, that way madness lies. That was the way films worked then. It couldn't surely be the case that such an approach could work now?

And in any case, it didn't always work. There is still in existence a 1970s Hammer pre-production poster featuring (and this borders on the night-marish) Peter Cushing in Nazi uniform holding a whip with the title 'Shadow of the Eagle'.[18] Thank the merciful heavens that no such disaster ever made it to the screen.

Then, once the script was written and the casting was in place, what would follow was an extremely brisk filming schedule. James Carreras himself was proud of this production line: 'After the first idea for a film is born,' he told a newspaper interviewer back in 1963, 'it's on the [studio] floor within six months. Shooting takes six to eight weeks and about three months after that, it's out in the cinemas.' And he wanted to make it clear that that was by no means the end of the studio's work.

> We start getting our money back after the London release and it comes back very quickly when you have a success. If we can get them into the London Pavilion, then fine – otherwise we don't bother with the West End. We believe in following our product right the way through. Our [cinema] manager incentive schemes offer prizes to managers who present our films with imagination, so the managers look forward to Hammer programmes. There's always some sort of angle you can exploit.[19]

The other side of that, however, was that any new director or even executive producer coming in with fancy ideas would more or less have to forget them immediately, for nothing would be allowed to slow this production line up. One example came later on in the mid-1970s when Brian Clemens (presiding genius behind the cult TV series *The Avengers*) helmed the inventive *Captain Kronos – Vampire Hunter*. He wanted to refresh the old vampire myths and this would be achieved through special effects – such as, for example, vampires having the ability to slow time down when they are moving in on a victim or having flowers wilt as the monsters walk past. But this added a layer of complexity to a breakneck schedule and Michael Carreras, by that stage completely in charge, vetoed the suggestion, leading to a measure of friction between the two veterans.

Back in 1964, young Michael had himself come back to the fold in freelance capacity and had joined Hammer's team of directors. He found himself in charge of another great gothic dependable: *The Curse of the Mummy's Tomb*. One might say that one cannot go far wrong when that title is your starting point, but in fact, from the beginning, the film was riven with difficulties. The first one was that, for some reason, it had been decided to set the film in the present day, with the revived Mummy having to face tanks and fighter planes in the desert. Quiet coughs from the accounts department soon became a loud series of harrumphs in higher offices and the script was revised, taking the saga back to its familiar Victorian-People-Opening-A-Tomb-That-They-Oughtn't-And-Obviously-In-A-Studio. Slightly too late for the poster campaign, sadly, which showed a vastly out-of-scale Mummy looming over a modern world.

Michael Carreras was the ultimate exemplar of the studio keeping it in the family but his professional relationship with his father seems at best to have been a little rocky. As an executive producer and a director he was clearly given a lot of elbow-room in the Hammer set-up. But there were incidents when father and son would not see eye to eye and the results could be heard all over the studio floor.

One such occasion was in 1968, on the set of Hammer's strange Sargasso Sea science-fiction saga *The Lost Continent*. In this, a group of travellers lose their way on this rather obviously studio-bound ocean and make land only to find weird monsters and a peculiar civilisation that terrorises its citizens with what look like rubber balloons. The only possible explanation for the entire enterprise was that it was the late 1960s and Hammer were interested in the idea of branching out into science fiction.

But the costs of the film began to rise inexorably and Pa Carreras, clearly not pleased by what he was seeing, one day came down to the studio floor and had a blazing stand-up row with his son about the whole thing. And then called a halt to production.[20]

A short time later, production resumed but Carreras the older had demonstrated who was in charge. In the way that one sees families bickering in front of strangers when they are at home, without embarrassment, so we see Sir James and Michael openly fighting in front of their 'family' – cast, crew and technicians. It seems so difficult somehow to imagine that happening on any film set now. Incidentally, Sir James was proved completely right; *The Lost Continent* was abysmal, although the unused title song has a zonked-out period charm. It was followed by another ill-advised weirdo Hammer science-fiction effort called *Moon Zero Two* starring Warren Mitchell in a camp futuristic costume. In Michael's favour, however, two of his other non-horror projects for the studio were in fact to haul in its biggest profits ...

All this was to come later, and was to form the background to Hammer's ultimate descent, and its fight for survival.

Turn the reels back to 1964, though, and we see the period when the studio was reaching its height, creatively and financially. Interestingly, as Hearn and Barnes have noted, *The Evil of Frankenstein* was the one entry where the studio attempted to emulate the look of the old Hollywood horrors and it is the film that got the most tepid response in England.[21]

It was a time in which domestic cinema audiences were at once seemingly undemanding and also starting to dwindle rather badly. The epics were there: *Lawrence of Arabia* (1962), *Cleopatra* (1963). The Bond films had become an annual event, with 1964's *Goldfinger* being an extraordinary phenomenon. But in terms of slightly more modest home-grown films, things were just starting to look a trifle thinner than before. As mentioned previously, Rank was in trouble, Ealing had ceased production in 1959, British Lion was almost played out and there was a beginning of an exodus of directors – such as Charles Crichton and Sidney Hayers – to television filmed series such as *The Saint* and *The Avengers*.

But at the cheaper end of the film market, holding back the tide against suburban Odeons being transformed into bingo halls, were such tiny concerns as Anglo-Amalgamated. In fact, it was this company that first saw the potential in the idea of a series of Carry On films. Interestingly, there was a big piece in a 1964 issue of the then trendy *Sunday Times* colour magazine that focused in on the production of both the Carry Ons and the Hammers, already seeing them as spiritually related.

In one way, the pairing was obvious and charming: here were two studios that, through dint of canny economy, kept churning out monstrously vulgar films for working-class people, but did so with humour and panache.

But James Carreras can't have been too delighted to have been squashed in with Sid James and Peter Rogers, for there was a very fine distinction between the films: when once asked what fresh Carry On comedy he was working on, Peter Rogers replied glibly: 'Same film, different title.'

The Hammers were different though, especially as they moved into the mid 1960s. For all their lack of money, the production values were consistently and remarkably high. Despite the modus operandi – title and poster artwork first, screenplay later – producer Anthony Hinds and all his associates worked hard to ensure that although the films shared a certain look and feel, they were also original and non-repetitious. It was terrifically important to them that the audience, no matter how daft, should not feel let down in any way. So there was not a breath of cynicism in the studio. There was craftsmanship, over sets and make-up, lively engaged directing and screenplays that sought to take audiences on to reasonably fresh ground each time. They really did think they were making good films.

Of course, some weren't good. Some were atrocious. This is why you will rarely see Hammer's version of *Phantom of the Opera* on television. Other films, though, have in the subsequent years caused the art-house critics to swoon. *Brides of Dracula* is one such effort, now praised for its taut narrative and its inventive lighting. One writer has described it as 'Hammer's flawed masterpiece'. Steady.

But one thing Carreras and the Carry On gang did have in common is that they were regarded as being below the salt by other grander figures within the film industry. Carreras, especially, had become regarded by some as 'persona non grata' at the start of the decade as the money from the films started to slosh in. He was regarded by many as being a loud braggart. In those straitened days, as Rank ground to a painful halt, much of this sneeriness might now be attributed to burning jealousy.

There was also perhaps a certain level of irritation too. James Carreras was very much involved with the charitable Variety Club, and it was noted by many that he spent a huge amount of his time at this side of things, rather than on the films his company made. As the 1960s progressed, this would go further, giving one the impression that all Carreras really wanted was to be embraced by what he regarded as high society.

For the moment, at that point in 1964, Anthony Hinds could see that the films needed another fresh look. And as part of the quest to prevent the audiences getting jaded with fangs and gowns, Hammer were now to begin the search for brand-new monsters that would sustain them through the next few years, but monsters that would always be presented to audiences in the very English context that they seemed to enjoy best.

Chapter Five

COMPETITIVE STREAKS

 It might be the case that a sense of assuredness is not a good thing in a horror film. That if a production is too sleek, the imagery too familiar, then that production will lose power. All the films in this genre cited as causing a seismic reaction among critics and audiences have tended towards the rough and ragged and raw – from *The Curse of Frankenstein* to *Night of the Living Dead* to *The Texas Chainsaw Massacre* to the recent gross-out spew-fest *Hostel*. There are times when the function of a horror film is to push the boundaries, grab audiences by their necks and drag them – very unwillingly, heels squeaking – to places where they have never been before. This is unlike the more considered, reflective sub-genre of ghost films, in which the emphasis is strongly on suggestion and a sense of *unheimlich* (from Jack Clayton's deeply unsettling *Turn of the Screw* adaptation *The Innocents* [1961] to *The Sixth Sense* [1999]); the horror film is there to arouse differently atavistic emotions, a wild heart-beating terror.

That is, unless the horror film in question is the work of a widely recognised production team which is thought of with affection. It happened with Universal in the 1930s and 40s after the initial sensation of its versions of Dracula and Frankenstein made way for the familiarity of the many sequels. And so too with Hammer. In 1964 – seven years after the studio had been accused of both sadism and vulgarity (and which, in the eyes of the censors, was worse?) – the Hammer films were now a fondly regarded staple of the British cinema circuit. They were always colourful and arresting and by this stage never pushed things too far in terms of inspiring nausea. Actually, they had pulled back a little on the gratuitous gore front. In other words, for the young men who lapped this sort of thing up, they were – crucially – films to which it was all right to take your girlfriend. And we have seen that the studio was keenly aware of its female audience and the need not to drive it away. Christopher Lee, that most unlikely of sex symbols, was always a help in this regard: give the old Count a bit of guttering candlelight, a heroine lying back on some nicely plumped pillows and a few swirling autumn leaves rustling through those bedroom windows and it was clear that he fulfilled a certain sort of 1960s naff continental erotic fantasy. (Remember, ladies, this was a nation that just one decade later considered simian missing-link Robin Askwith to be a sex symbol.) On top of this, there was something about the very essence of gothic that appealed to both women and men: perhaps the moody trappings and the evocation of a distant contrived world made the broaching of certain taboos surrounding sex and death acceptable.

Producer Anthony Hinds, regarded by all who worked for him as the philosopher of the Hammer outfit, was unquestionably behind the various gradations of tone throughout the films and there are two projects in this period that highlight not only Hammer's quest to broaden out its range of subject matter but also its desire to give even a tale of monsters a little more emotional resonance than they had done before.

And so 1964 brought an entry entitled *The Gorgon*. This, most unusually for Hammer, arose from an unsolicited screenplay from someone called William Devine. Hinds saw it, liked the idea, realised that the script needed some polishing in order to make it work for the big screen and handed it to writer/director John Gilling. When Gilling was done with it, Hinds did not like some of the excesses that the rewritten story went to and, as 'John Elder', set about re-inserting some of the lost material from the original. Gilling grabbed hold of it again, however, and there was further see-sawing. Then – after some ill-will from Gilling – the thing was deemed ready to put before the cameras.[1]

As always, with one canny eye fixed firmly on the budget, this is how it went: on a hill outside the middle European village of Vandorf lies Castle Borski, the matte-painted establishing shot of which rings several *very* loud bells. And, local legend has it, this deserted old ruin has, in the last century, come to be haunted by a nameless evil. Every seven years, it is said, this spirit walks abroad and those who chance upon it die a slow, hideous death – by turning to stone. Can you guess what it is yet?

Yes, it is the one surviving Gorgon sister Megaera who has, for obscure reasons to do with tight budgeting, shifted her activities from ancient Greece to nineteenth-century Transylvania. And all right, on paper, the idea doesn't sound all that promising, even when you assemble a cast featuring Christopher Lee, Peter Cushing and Barbara Shelley. Or even when you throw in director Terence Fisher, back after his *Phantom of the Opera* huff and having been directing Sherlock Holmes adventures for rivals.

But actually, it does work – that is, if you have a taste for the eerie and the unsettling as opposed to slam-bang horror. Those who are foolish enough to venture up to the castle – and those include Richard Pascoe – are greeted with a creepy solo alto note on the soundtrack prior to the green-gowned monster making her pounce. And there are some fine scenes with actors in grey mottled make-up, well, turning to stone. The sets are good, the acting strong, and there is also a genuine sense of not quite knowing how this monster can be disposed of.

The only slight setback is the hideous Gorgon itself, as portrayed by an actress called Prudence Hyman (and how, we wonder, did Prudence's agent sell her *that* particular role? 'It's a super part, darling, it's Hammer, you get to be the monster, ah no, *not* really hours in the make-up chair, more of just a wig fitting ...'). Oh, she emerges from the dark shadows of that house to turn men to stone with a single glance with real aplomb. Fisher's camera goes in lovingly for those moments of fright. She even has Christopher Lee style red contact lenses. But there is a problem to do with what we might call suspension of disbelief.

The Gorgon in legend does of course have, instead of hair, a head of writhing, hissing snakes. And Hammer's special effects division promised that such snakes would be delivered.[2] They would sit atop Prudence Hyman's head writhing like anything. But they didn't. In fact, the green toy snakes they used were as rigid as broom handles and wholly inert. The over-all effect, in those fleeting scenes when Megaera comes looming out of the darkness, is that of a furious boarding house landlady interrupted in the course of setting her hair.

But this footling criticism is not entering into the spirit of the thing, and in any case, we only see this creature fully disclosed once or twice, and only then sparingly. By day, this monster has possessed Barbara Shelley and this time round both Christopher Lee and Peter Cushing are red herrings: unusually, Lee is the good guy, Cushing the almost-bad guy, and both are baffled by the outbreak of stone deaths.

The point is that there is greater pathos – we are allowed to feel genuine sympathy for Barbara Shelley's character Carla. It is made rather obvious from an early stage that she has been taken over and thus we know that none of this can end happily.

Also there is something quite satisfactory about this use of a monster from ancient legend, an aesthetically pleasing change of pace, that fits in well with Hammer's established milieu. Of course it must be set in middle Europe – it wouldn't be a Hammer film otherwise – and there must be night-time scenes in woods – ditto. But the eerie doominess of the high singing, and the nature of the novel death that the protagonists face is unfamiliar enough to make one snap to attention and appreciate the inventiveness that's going on.

And although there is one *absurdly* unnecessary autopsy scene, involving
a very minor dead character, Peter Cushing pursing his lips holding a scalpel
and a *very* half-hearted brain in a jar (anything, it seems, to get an 'X' certificate), the blood count in this Hammer effort is actually non-existent. And the
autopsy scene wins the prize for the studio's most absurd line when
Cushing sighs at the brain and says: 'God's most wonderful work – and yet
it is the most revolting thing to see.'

When this film is eventually re-released on to DVD, it is difficult to
imagine that it will muster more than a 'PG'. In other words, through the
good offices of Anthony Hinds, it looked as though Hammer had both
mellowed and – just very slightly, given that this was still abject nonsense
for Friday night escapism seekers – actually grown up a little.

And also, it looked as though Terence Fisher himself had softened somewhat. The look and feel of the film are of a lush romanticism, from the deep
misty blue of the painted backdrop skies to the warm amber of Bruno's
artistic studio to a foggy studio graveyard that would have found favour
with Rossetti. All served up for tuppence – even the 'grave' that Richard
Pascoe digs down into is barely a foot deep. And Fisher is clearly very much
in love with Barbara Shelley – the camera simply cannot keep its lens off
her. But in a tasteful way.

In other words, it now looked as though the studio's primary aim was no
longer to shock, outrage and titillate, but to actually give a little more
thoughtfulness and aesthetic resonance to these crimson melodramas.
Certainly, hands-off though he may have been, James Carreras noted this
shift of tone. And it was very much *not* to his taste.

Although *The Gorgon* wasn't the cause, this in fact was the last Hammer
for which Anthony Hinds would be a hands-on producer. From that point
onwards, he was going to be the slick back-room operator, writing scripts,
fixing problems, overseeing the general flavour and direction of the films.
Critic Denis Meikle says of him: 'Hinds was always a very private individual, with interests far removed from the world of films ... he was the power
behind the throne and *his* was the creative philosophy that Hammer had
enshrined: that is, to make films economically and effectively, only the best
people were good enough.'[3]

Astonishingly, it was a good seven years into Hammer's undisputed mastery
over what was called the 'exploitation' market – the cinema circuits were
packed with the company's double-bills – before a domestic competitor really
launched any kind of serious, concerted challenge. The late 1950s and early
60s had seen many monochrome cheapies such as John Gilling's *The Flesh*

and the Fiends (1959), concerning Burke and Hare, and Nat Cohen's *Night of the Eagle* (1961), which featured voodoo spells, crisp photography and one of the most hysterically overwrought casts and screenplays ever gathered together for a film. And that includes Robert Wise's *The Haunting* (1963). But then another producer, Milton Subotsky – who seven years previously had accepted a payment from Hammer for its non-use of his Frankenstein script – now gave the matter of horror some fresh thought.

He was in partnership with producer Max J. Rosenberg and their company was called Amicus. Its influence is now fondly cited by modern comedians such as the stars of *The League of Gentlemen*. Perhaps Subotsky and Rosenberg both realised that it was futile to engage Hammer on the same middle European gothic territory. Perhaps they felt that such territory was now starting to look faded and worn at any rate. But for their debut horror feature, they determined on: a) a contemporary setting and b) using the format of the old American EC horror comics that had caused such moral indignation in the 1950s and that was also used to great effect by Ealing in its ghost film *Dead of Night* (1945): that is, instead of one narrative, the film would consist of five separate tales, held together by a single linking narrative. The link in this case was Peter Cushing (was there a film in the 1960s in which he did not appear?) playing a creepy tarot card reader called Dr Shreck. And the film was to be called *Dr Terror's House of Horrors*.

It is a title that makes James Carreras seem Bergmanesque in terms of restraint and subtlety. The film also featured a rather extraordinary cast. The vague narrative link is that Dr Shreck and five other people are sharing a compartment in a train that breaks down. And as they wait in that eerie darkness, the passengers get their tarot cards read one by one. And each, it seems, is facing an ordeal of terror. Among those facing such a fate are Roy Castle, Christopher Lee and, rather amazingly, the DJ Alan 'Fluff' Freeman. So we have, among other things, a tale of Soho jazz and voodoo, something about vampires, a disembodied hand, and something else involving a science-fictional creeping plant with murderous tendencies that lays siege to a suburban house.

Apart from the absurd script and bizarre performances, the film contrived to look cheaper than it actually was: extra-bright studio lighting exposed the wallpaper masquerading as brickwork. None the less, the film had a cheery, cheeky energy even if it was not remotely frightening, and it has a sort of cult following today. It was the first sign that Hammer had any kind of a proper, organised rival. Also the film went down well with contemporary audiences. After years of Hammer taking itself terribly seriously, it must have seemed quite jolly to have a horror film that poked fun at its own deficiencies, and also refreshing to have such a film set in the modern world – a complete change of scenery, no matter how tatty.

Subotsky and Rosenberg next decided to go for the science-fiction angle and leapt in to snap up the rights to the BBC's *Doctor Who*, which had begun in 1963 and which had become something of a phenomenon with the arrival of the Daleks. In 1965 and 1966, they managed to get two films based on the series into cinemas, and for these they upped the budget a little, using then-revolutionary plastic sets. These films too were a financial success – you couldn't go far wrong with a Dalek, even then – though only really in Britain.

Because *Dr Terror's House of Horrors* had been so well-received, it was only natural that Subotsky and Rosenberg should want to dish up more of the same. So 1967 brought a new compendium entitled *Torture Garden* featuring imported *Batman* star Burgess Meredith as a sinister fairground owner who tells five people of frightening events ... well, you get the picture. One of the stories, involving a resurrected Edgar Allen Poe, still delivers a minor jolt today. Then in 1969 there was *The House that Dripped Blood* – all five stories taking place in the eponymous house, handily for the budget – which featured one quite unsettling episode involving a small girl and voodoo, and one startlingly post-modern one, involving Ingrid Pitt and Jon Pertwee on the set of a Hammer-esque vampire film.

The friendly rivalry with Hammer went on for several more of these films, possibly the most notable and financially successful of which was *Tales from the Crypt* (1972), which featured, rather astonishingly, Sir Ralph Richardson as the crypt keeper. Clearly, horror films had attained a certain chic in the smarter acting circles. Unlike Hammers, the Amicus productions never let their tongues leave their cheeks. Also unlike Hammers, Amicus didn't do such storming business abroad. But in 1964, when they kicked off, they might have been tapping into a feeling that the genre needed a little more than painted castles on painted hills. Interestingly, at this stage, James Carreras didn't see it that way. His view was that if the public liked something, then they must be given more.

In 1966, Hammer road-tested another new monster and in traditional fashion, came up with the title and the poster art before going to all the expense of commissioning a script. The poster this time bore the image of two snake people – that is, a man and a woman in Victorian dress, but bearing the fanged heads of snakes. Title? *Curse of the Reptiles*.[4] It was certainly an arresting image – even if, with a squint, the figures rather resemble Arthur Mullard and Hylda Baker – and the film that arose from it was similarly striking.

The Reptile was the end title, directed by John Gilling back-to-back on the same sets as *The Plague of the Zombies*. Down in darkest nineteenth-century

Cornwall (another refreshing change of pace, this) Ray Barratt's brother has died suddenly in mysterious circumstances, so he and wife Jennifer Daniel go down to take possession of the house they have inherited and to investigate. Living nearby in the big house is unfriendly Dr Franklyn (Noel Willman) and his beautiful but withdrawn daughter Anna (Jacqueline Pearce), together with a Malayan manservant. The big house is *very* overheated and every time there is a local death, the lights are left burning.

Local eccentric Mad Peter (an excellent role for John Laurie) predicts death and suffering and, lo, is bitten by a mysterious monster; he starts foaming and his face turns black. Others have died in the same horrible fashion and it swiftly becomes apparent that owing to an ancient curse accidentally invoked by Noel Willman, Jacqueline Pearce is doomed every so often to turn into a snake woman. The denouement involves a blazing house fire, a sulphur pit and the reptile woman perishing, after a window is smashed, in a slightly bathetic cold draft.

But the point is this: what the film lacked in white gowns and heaving embonpoint it more than made up for not only in the shape of a novel and rather disconcerting monster but also in a suffocatingly claustrophobic drama involving, essentially, abusive family relationships. The oppressive heat of the Franklyn residence is symbolic of the unhealthy bond between father and daughter. And Jacqueline Pearce's performance as the daughter whose terrible fate is the fault of her father is rather moving (as well as weirdly sensual, especially in the scene where Anna the Snake Woman gets quite overheated while giving a sitar recital).

Also unusually for Hammer, the lighting is very low-key – instead of confronting us with bright gouts of gore, for the first time we have menace lurking in shadow against a colour palette of dark reds and greens. Like *The Gorgon*, there would be little in this now to trouble the censors – although the blackened faces and foaming of the victims are strikingly horrid – but the piece is inventive and gently unnerving in its unfamiliarity. Naturally the whole thing still had to be in period dress and – hooray! – Michael Ripper was there as the Cornish inn landlord, this time explaining carefully to the hero precisely why it was that the locals did not care for strangers.

These days, Jacqueline Pearce is wry about this particular starring role. 'I had to be a reptile, darling,' she recently told *The Times*. 'Dreadful make-up – very claustrophobic – which had to be glued on, fangs, long fingernails which had curled up with heat by the end of the day.'[5]

These cosmetic discomforts were one thing; but in terms of overall tone, the restraining hand of Anthony Hinds could on this occasion be detected in steering Hammer towards – shall we say – a slightly more respectable, less thuggish style of horror film.

The Reptile also got good, appreciative reviews and now enjoys status as a sort of cult rarity – never on the telly, tricky to come by on video and DVD. As a one-off, it was a very good go.

It was also in part a response to the only serious competition from America, which had been posed by schlock director Roger Corman and his star in residence Vincent Price. Back in 1960, Corman – up until that point best known for teen drive-in exploitation flicks, often turned around in as little as three days – had hit upon the idea of adapting Edgar Allen Poe stories. At first glance, these might appear to be fundamentally unfilmable, so weird and poetic and abstract were they. Corman found a way.

He kicked off with *The Fall of the House of Usher* and, in the name of costs and (he claimed) atmosphere, kept it entirely within the studio. Possibly just as well because the 'singularly dreary tract of country' in which stood 'the melancholy House of Usher' would have been a bother to conjure up under the Californian sun. There is a very wooden hero, a suitably stilted Madeleine who ends up being accidentally buried alive, and a memorably nervy, white-wigged Vincent Price to whom, as Roderick Usher, every loud noise is agony and whose senses are tuned so far as to take him to the brink of insanity.

Given that it was made for about ten dollars, the film did extremely well, prompting the follow-up *Pit and the Pendulum* (1961), *The Premature Burial* (1962), *The Raven* (1963) and the self-conscious artiness of *The Masque of the Red Death* (1964). This last film, together with *The Tomb of Ligeia* (1964) saw Corman do more than simply pay tribute to his Hammer competitors: he came to England and camped out on Hammer's doorstep.

As well as having a young Nicholas Roeg behind the camera for *Masque* (and a striking job he does too), Corman rounded up English talent familiar and new – Hazel Court, Patrick Magee and, making her debut, the very young Jane Asher. There was a level of ingenuity involved in getting a ninety-minute film out of a five-page short story – here, a little bit of devil worship provided some ballast. And it was a visual treat – from Prince Prospero's different-coloured chambers to the finale of the Red Death itself. And boy, was it a Hammer rip-off. Vincent Price as the prince gave it villainous welly, his guards setting fire to peasant villages, his revels weird and sadistic and involving dwarves.

For his next film, *The Tomb of Ligeia*, Corman went further. 'We went into the English countryside,' he said. 'We shot a fox hunt, a wedding at a very pretty English church, a sixteenth-century monastery in ruins ... it was the first and only time the sun shone in any of those films.'[6] In other words, this rather effective tale of possession and sinister black cats was an American film-maker's most direct acknowledgement that horror had to be done the Hammer way.

The Europeans were at it too, although they felt they could be a little less restrained. Thus, Italy's Mario Bava stepped up with *Mark of the Vampire* (1965) to put Barbara Steele through her paces as a reincarnated neck biter. Then there were multi-national efforts such as *Castle of the Living Dead* (1964), which featured not only a Euro-pudding cast but also our very own Christopher Lee who had decided to go and live in Switzerland. The upshot is that Hammer itself had become incredibly pervasive and strangely international in its cultural impact. It was as though horror couldn't be conceived of in any other way.

Back in 1960, Derek Hill in *Sight and Sound* magazine had this to say about the genre: 'Every horror film cycle has coincided with economic depression or war. Now we have the biggest, ugliest threat of all, and a bigger, uglier horror boom than ever before.'[7]

Could he have been right, even five or six years later? Was the continued enthusiasm for Technicolor screen monsters a symptom of Cold War anxiety? A sign of nuclear neurosis? On the face of it, films such as *The Gorgon* and *The Reptile* are so far removed as to be almost fairy tales. We might scrabble a bit at the surface and find themes of invasion/perils of colonisation, but you'd be hard pressed to argue that the production team had intended any such thing. As for economic depression – the argument clearly has been inspired by the 1929 variety, and the apparent Universal monster boom that came in its wake. But if anything, what these Hammer films tell us is that precisely the reverse was happening, at least in terms of people's expectations. It is not that they are frothy, unlike the tenor of much of pop culture at that time. But they are light and cheerfully disposable – they contain nothing designed to trouble the audience beyond the confines of the cinema foyer.

There was another force at work though, a rival cultural one, that was causing those cinema foyers to see thinner and thinner crowds. According to film historian Robert Murphy, in Britain 'between 1957 and 1963, the number of cinemas halved and admissions fell from 915 million a year to 357 million.'[8] Thanks to the growing proficiency of television production, and the near blanket-coverage of sets nationwide, the cinemas were one by one succumbing to hideous transformation into bingo halls.

Rank, as we have seen, was suffering badly, and had to merge with American company Xerox; British Lion was operational but holed; Anglo-Amalgamated yielded the Carry On series to Rank in 1966 and stumbled. At the very bottom of the market, the notorious Harry Alan Towers carried on producing Fu Manchu films and Amicus continued with its cheap and cheerful horrors. So how was it then that Hammer boss James Carreras continued to look so cheerful and ebullient?

There was a telling piece in the colour supplement of *The Sunday Times* in 1964, which took the readers behind the scenes of *The Gorgon* before it was released. The guide for this tour was not just with any old hack, but the novelist Kingsley Amis. Of course, Amis was a great fan of James Bond so it isn't too much of a leap to see his enthusiasm for Hammer too. But as he describes the sprayed-on cobwebs of Castle Borski and the make-up preparations that Prudence Hyman had to go through, we can suddenly see this piece through the eyes of Carreras and suddenly we understand why this old man was laughing.

He had the perfect audience triangulation. Here was a leader of what we would now call the chattering classes and the nation's trendiest newspaper going out of their way to celebrate his films while at the same time the escapism-seeking young working classes continued to patronise them.

What Carreras appeared to crave most of all was industry respectability, and we can see that even if it was Anthony Hinds who influenced the tone of each individual production, it was Carreras who ultimately whipped up the Hammer world, with his pre-selling posters and ever more exclamatory film titles. It mattered to him enormously that Hammer was seen not as a ghoulish, morbid concern, but something that was fun, amusing and ultimately throwaway.

Actually, *The Gorgon* and *The Reptile* are unusually unrepresentative of the society that made them – these two films could in some sense have been made at any time. Which is part of their immense charm now. The acting and the style of set design might instantly betray when they were made but the stories themselves have an almost defiantly timeless quality. There is the issue of gothic romance too, a term that just a few years previously, Hammer would have snorted at. But the fact is that these two films are now among Hammer's most aesthetically pleasing. *The Gorgon*, as directed by Terence Fisher, is a symphony of early romantic imagery, from distant painted mountains to a shot of autumnal leaves on moonlit water. The production is shot through not so much with the sensibility of Mrs Radcliffe as with the German romantic imagination – a backdrop to an ultimately tragic story of loves that are doomed. No one gets a happy ending. Hero Richard Pascoe, having fallen in love with Barbara Shelley, fails to realise that she is in fact possessed and after he does battle with the Gorgon (using a mirror reflection) and decapitates it, he in fact turns out to have decapitated Barbara. But he cannot gurgle in horror for too long, for Barbara has in fact turned him to stone. It is left to Christopher Lee to utter the wonderfully comfortless final line: 'Paul, she is free now.' Cheers mate. That helps.

Similarly, *The Reptile* is not destined to end with the cast laughing together and embracing. But as we ponder the tragic end of Anna the Snake Woman, let us turn to inn landlord Michael Ripper, who in fact was an actor of great range, depth and experience. He was happy to return to Hammer again and again for one simple reason: the people who made the films appeared to care about what they were doing.

'In any business, there are artists and there are craftsmen,' he said in an interview with Denis Meikle. 'There were more artists at Hammer than in any other film production company I worked for.'[9]

Let's also hear from the late Anthony Hinds, who was in no doubt of the importance of his position in this company of artists. 'I set the tone for the gothic Hammers, Jimmy Sangster and I. There was nobody else involved. Nobody else had anything to do with it.'[10]

Certainly that may have been the case up until 1966. But James Carreras, now facing the prospect of Universal dropping by the wayside, and fixing up a new US distribution deal with Warners/Seven Arts, clearly felt that while dreamy-spooky gothic had its place, what the company needed more than anything was an infusion of fresh horrors. One of the casualties of this line of thought was Jimmy Sangster's sub-genre of bendy, twisty, lets-drive-the-heroine-mad psycho thrillers. And it was time to up the temperature of the gothic horrors. The results were oddly to take the studio right the way back to the working-class sentiments of a century beforehand.

Chapter Six

CLASS WAR

 As a nightmare sequence, it still has some potency; two Victorian men standing in a crumbling churchyard, the mist and the very air green-tinged. Then it begins; the earth by the headstones moves, is scrabbled away. Fingers start to protrude through the soil. The dead are rising from their graves. The two men look on as zombies with whited-out eyes and rotting grave clothes pull themselves up from the mud and grope around. Then the ulti-mate horror: the newly buried dead wife of one of the men emerges from her recent grave, eyes unseeing but the body lurching grotesquely towards her husband. He cries out and the other man picks up a shovel, stands behind the zombie woman, raises the implement – and then decapitates the corpse with it. As her head tumbles to the soil, eyes still wide and unseeing, her husband screams with horror – and then launches upwards in his bed, as his friends run into his bedroom to comfort him.

For a long time, this scene from *The Plague of the Zombies* (1966) was the clip most often used in any television programme that happened to be dis-cussing the Hammer phenomenon. It is often said that it inspired American director George A. Romero when he came to make his seminal zombie hor-ror *Night of the Living Dead* two years later. It was also referenced in the 1970s US vampire saga *Count Yorga*, and it is fair to say that as an image of the macabre it is still very much with us today.

All of which is a fine tribute to the film's director John Gilling, and his way with a miniature budget. But actually, it is a scene that is extremely unrepre-sentative of Hammer and indeed of *The Plague of the Zombies*. Hammer, as a rule, has no time for the ethereal half-world of bad dreams. Instead, the studio seeks to convey the impossible through a sort of brutal confrontationalism. In fact what *Plague* represents is a studio keenly aware of the class make-up of its core audiences. For at the heart of the film is not so much gothic horror as the equally pulse-quickening theme of upper-class vileness.

A swift précis. Down in nineteenth-century Cornwall (this film was made back-to-back with *The Reptile* (1966) so the sets and indeed the setting were exactly the same) there are dark doings going on. A subterranean voodoo ceremony is connected to a welling wound on the wrist of Alice (Jacqueline Pearce). She is the (very poorly) wife of village Doctor Thompson (Brooke Williams) who writes to his old mentor Professor Forbes (Andre Morell) for help. It seems that it is not just the doctor's wife who is suffering – a mystery malady has caused many fatalities in this small Cornish village and the locals are none too impressed with the quality of the medical advice on offer. Professor Forbes and his daughter Sylvia (Diana Clare) travel down and swiftly fall foul of the local squire John Carson. It is not long – after frightening encounters with vicious fox hunters, a screeching zombie at the head of a tin mine, and the death of Alice – before black magic is found to be at the core of the village's ills. The squire, it turns out, had been over to Haiti and on his return decided to import some of the supernatural power-wielding tricks that he had learned there. But he is no match for wily Andre Morrell and thus we reach a fiery climax at a voodoo ceremony in the old tunnels of the tin mine.

Again, in the space of eighty-four minutes, John Gilling manages to pack quite a lot in – none of the characters really have a chance to draw breath. But what is set out almost from the start is the theme of class and the abuse of unearned privilege. As the professor and his daughter are driven across a heath towards the village, Sylvia witnesses a fox hunt, and sees the fox escape. The coach is flagged down by the hunters – all threatening boors – and Sylvia lies to them about the direction the fox took. Upon arrival at the village, the pair immediately witness a funeral procession – one that is horrifyingly broken up by the red-coated hunters, clattering into the village, upsetting the coffin and swearing vengeance on the professor's daughter for misleading them. In the midst of this horrible chaos, the coffin is shoved from the pall-bearers' grasp; it falls from a bridge into the churchyard and the box cracks open, revealing the hideous corpse within.

Thus the scene is set: arrogant aristocrats versus oppressed villagers who can do nothing but silently rage when even sacrilegious acts such as this are committed. Worse is to come for Sylvia. Out in the woods at night, following her hypnotised friend Alice, she finds herself pursued by the red-coated young men on horseback; cornered, they take her to the squire's house – and only the squire's sudden entrance at the last minute saves her from a fate worse than death.

The part of the squire is one of actor John Carson's finest hours, as many acknowledge. By turns haughty, charming and sinister, he is one of the most believable villains to have been presented in these films. His back story (one that saves Hammer the trouble and expense of filming a voodoo story in the Caribbean, as tradition might demand) involves an off-screen trip to Haiti from which he has returned with some top tips on labour relations. In particular, he has found a most economical way to work the tin mines.

The squire is also the local magistrate and coroner and, as such, pretty much appears to hold the power of life and death over the village. So domineering is he that none of the red-coated bucks who by day make up his hunting contingent and by night his black-magic gang dare to set themselves against him. But the squire is also a silver-tongued brute, as Sylvia is to find when he pays a house visit and contrives to leave with a tiny phial of her blood. But over and above all this excellent villainy there is a hint of something more, a very loud echo of familiarity.

Bear in mind that in 1966, two years into his administration, Harold Wilson consolidated what had been a rather fragile hold on government, seeking to increase his parliamentary majority of three in a fresh general election. He did so triumphantly, and Labour's majority increased to 100. This was the era of Wilson's famous 'white heat of technological revolution' through which Britain's future would be forged. A clever image but one that in 1966 was still rather a long way from the country's grimy industrial reality. This was a country in which heavy industry was still the absolute bedrock of the economy, from mining to steel smelting to shipbuilding. And for all of the prevalence of youth in pop culture – if the breathless colour magazines were to be believed, London was now swinging, and every dolly bird sported white plastic boots as they visited Granny Takes a Trip in the King's Road – the reality of life for the majority was still rather closer to the black-and-white films of the early 1960s. Meritocracy may have held a certain sort of sway in the entertainment business, but everywhere else the bonds of the old school tie were as tightly knotted as ever. In factories the work whistles still signalled the start of the shift, management still took lunch in the panelled boardroom while the machinists knocked off at five and headed off for a pint in the Marquis of Granby. This was a nation still very much polarised.

And naturally, Hammer, producing a certain sort of film, was the sort of studio that was interested in the sort of friction that old school notions produced.

Actually, class conflict had been one of the central leitmotifs of Hammer films from the very start. We look back to their 1959 version of *The Hound of the Baskervilles* where, as you will recall, the curse is originally triggered by a red-coated toff molesting and killing a servant girl and where the villain Cecile (different from Conan Doyle's) reveals that the whole plot had been cooked up as a means of class revenge.

We think too of those Dracula and Frankenstein films; Count Dracula especially is the well-spoken embodiment of feudal power, and those who live in the shadow of his castle take it for granted that they will be subject to his blood sacrifices. Baron Frankenstein too is an unrepentant toff to the tips of his fingers, as we see most strongly in his first film: his treatment of 'staff', in the shape of Paul Krempe, and his horrifying behaviour towards the servant girl Justine – first making her pregnant and then coldly throwing her to the Creature – put him into the very highest ranks of upper-class villainy.

And this is where the echoes of familiarity could be heard in *The Plague of the Zombies*; the lineage of Carson's squire goes back to well beyond Frankenstein and Dracula: recall David Farrar's lip-licking crop-wielding performance as Squire Jack Reddin in Powell and Pressburger's richly Technicolored melodrama *Gone to Earth* (1950). He himself was modelled upon the clear template of the nouveau faux-squire Alec D'Urberville in Hardy's *Tess of the D'Urbervilles* (1897). Early British cinema gave us another villainous squire in the person of Tod Slaughter in *Crimes at the Old House* (1932). As long as there has been English literature and film, the story of corrupt and effete nobility set against the honest toilers has been absolutely central and Hammer – perhaps unconsciously – revived the theme.

There are also echoes here – and these simply must have been unconscious – of *Jane Eyre*. The loose parallel is that of an Englishman who ventures to the Caribbean and returns home with a dark secret that he must hide. But squire John Carson has none of Rochester's stormy romanticism. He is instead the very image of the cold, calculating aristocrat, a man who relishes wielding dark power over his tiny dominion. And his grand house is the hub of the evil. However, *Plague* can hardly be seen as a progressive anti-racist tract. The few black actors here are little more than extras, called upon to beat drums in a frenzied fashion. But given the fast disintegration of empire throughout the late 1950s and the 60s, *Plague* is interestingly anti-colonialist; the villagers' lives would not have been blighted were it not for the squire's journey and the greed which led him to bring back those voodoo powers.

The Plague of the Zombies is Hammer's clearest expression of distaste for the landed gentry but there were numerous other outbreaks: from the villagers' revolutionary overthrow of the depraved aristocrat Count Mitterhouse in *Vampire Circus* (1972) to the quite surprisingly moving tragedy of young lovers Christina and Hans in *Frankenstein Created Woman* (1967), upon which we will focus fully in Chapter Eight since it forms one of Hammer's most intriguing entries and was the favourite of Martin Scorsese. For the moment, suffice it to say that in *Woman*, barmaid Christina – who has a scarred face, a gammy leg but a faithful lover in the shape of Hans – is tormented by three vicious young toffs. Indeed, the nature of this torment is so extraordinarily malicious that Hans (who happens to be Frankenstein's assistant) is driven to attack them. They then contrive to have him framed for a murder that *they* commit and – like his father before him – doomed Hans is sent to the guillotine and Christina takes her own life. Of course the three young toffs show not even the faintest flicker of guilt or remorse; as lower-class folk, Hans and Christine do not register as full human beings. Even now, this simple parable of class-based beastliness gets the blood boiling in a rather surprising way. This must have been the effect among the original audiences, although this strong emotional response might have been tempered with puzzlement about where exactly the monster had got to in this Frankenstein film.

Outside of London's West End, the cinema chains – the ABCs and Odeons, which even by 1966 were struggling and were starting to be transformed into bingo halls – were catering to audiences very largely made up of young working men and women. Their screens would be obscured with cigarette smoke and their programmes ran continuously, so that one could walk in halfway through a film, and then leave once one had got to that point in the next showing. In 1966, the spy genre dominated all and the Bond tide was still high – the previous year's *Thunderball* had been the most commercially successful entry yet in that series; in a counterpoint to the glamour of Bond, Michael Caine had started playing Harry Palmer in Len Deighton's down-beat espionage saga. Less satisfactorily, episodes of America's *The Man From UNCLE* were stitched together to form full-length films, while the lower end of the British studio system produced such painful micro-budget knock-offs as *Where the Bullets Fly* starring Tom Adams.

On the whole, espionage was expensive escapism, largely impossible on a bijou British budget. In another genre entirely, working-class audiences were flooding in for the latest entries in the increasingly ubiquitous Carry On series. 1966 was a vintage year, bringing them ... *Doctor*, ... *Cowboy* and ... *Screaming*. Carry On producer Peter Rogers must have been horribly tormented by the success that Hammer and James Carreras enjoyed in America because it was during this period that Rogers started trying harder to angle his comedies towards transatlantic markets. These days, one entirely fails to see how a cowboy comedy starring Sid James, Kenneth Williams, Jim Dale and Joan Sims, and very obviously filmed in the grounds of Pinewood Studios, could have caused American cinema-goers to do any-thing other than purse their lips and sit and experience feelings of irritation and bewilderment. Actually, that was the effect on many of the British view-ers too. The point, though, is that in cultural terms, the Carry On series, in its direct appeal to working-class audiences, was perhaps the closest parallel to the Hammer films at that time.

Like the Hammers, the Carry Ons relied on a repertory company of stock actors who would play roughly the same sorts of roles in successive films, from Sid James's yak-yakking lech to Kenneth Williams's extravagantly nostrilled queen. Like the Hammers, the behind-the-scenes production staff remained largely the same throughout the twenty-odd years over which the films were produced. Like the Hammers, the Carry Ons were served with some truly wonderful music, this time by James Bernard's Royal College of Music contemporary Eric Rogers. And of course, like the Hammers, they were cheap (famously going to the lengths of filming *Carry On Camping* in winter and painting mud green to give the impression of green grass).

Unlike the Hammers, though, many of those who worked on the Carry Ons viewed them with – at best – disdain. Kenneth Williams was openly rude about the lowness of the humour and even the producer Peter Rogers would have been struck dumb had he been asked to expand upon their artistic merits. The Hammer staff were quite different. There might have been a telling pause if they were asked to sum up the studio's aesthetic values – but they were certain they were making worthwhile films that would never leave an audience feeling cheated, or indeed shabby. No one protested louder about the essential innocence and good-heartedness of the Hammer films than James Carreras. He told the *Evening News*:

> It's fascinating to watch the audience in a horror film. For 25% of the time, they're rocking with laughter. 30% of the time they're fairly quiet. For the rest of the time, there's silence. But they leave the cinemas smiling and laughing because they don't reckon they're going to run into a werewolf up a quiet country lane. It's pure escapism.[1]

You can, in some ways, understand that Carreras was professionally and socially in a tricky position. Here was a man who had a good war, excelled at sport in his youth, had always been the most ebullient of salesmen and the most assiduous of charitable workers. What he wanted was no great secret: he wanted complete respectability, and a proper place in what he perceived to be the establishment. Unlike other producers of what might be termed 'exploitation' films of that period, he cared what his peers thought about him. He cared very much.

So Carreras spent as much time involved with charitable business for the Variety Club as he did overseeing the output of the studio that his father and William Hinds had built up. He was acutely aware, in the late 1950s, as the profits of the horror business piled up, that he had become persona non grata in the slightly more elevated areas of the industry. By the mid-1960s, through his tireless Variety Club activities, he had sought to rectify that. Critic Denis Meikle wrote of him:

> Amazing he certainly was, as well as amiable, affable, and always available for lunch. Jimmy had become a commodity in himself – sought out, sought after and prized – as friend, consort or colleague. He was larger than life. He had a chameleon ability to be all things to all men. He was, in short, almost too good to be true.[2]

And yet, as he eagerly exchanged pleasantries with notables such as Prince Philip at big charitable occasions, Carreras never lost sight of the audience who were making that side of his life possible. Nor, despite his hands-off approach, did he lose any enthusiasm. Not at that point anyway.

When we consider the question of Hammer's habit of making the upper-class people the villains, we must also remember that this was done not only with the domestic audience: it was also aimed squarely at the American market, and the European market too. For reasons that students of cinema still debate and speculate about today, evil with a smart English accent hits the button with American audiences. In fact, it always did, ever since the very first days of the 'talkies' in the 1930s. Bela Lugosi's phonetic Hungarian aside, many of the stars of those original Hollywood Frankensteins and Draculas – Colin Clive, Boris Karloff, Ernest Thesiger, Lionel Atwill, Claude Rains, Basil Rathbone, Sir Cedric Hardwicke – were British and jolly well sounded it too. So perhaps it was to be expected that Cushing and Lee, with their perfectly modulated tones, would go down a storm in the States. So too, of course, did the notion of a degenerate aristocracy. The very notion had an atavistic emotional appeal.

By the mid-1960s Hammer also had the advantage that the whole idea of Britishness had become fashionable and desirable as foreigners latched on to the idea of a swinging nation. This is why everyone in Hammer films enunciates so clearly – even those like Duncan Lamont who are always called upon to play the village drunks. The monsters are clipped, the heroes have a relaxed middle-class drawl, and the village policemen, no matter how countrified, are never unintelligible.

In 1966, Hammer received another jokey homage, but this time from the European art-house end of the market: Roman Polanski was at the helm of a semi-serious spoof called *The Fearless Vampire Killers*. It was semi-serious because, despite the farcical nature of the screenplay, Polanski, by his own admission, had very strong views about Hammer aesthetics, and how they could be improved upon. In short, while acknowledging the essential resonance of the films, Polanski had little time for 'day for night' shoots in Black Park. Nor for some of the painted landscapes. He wanted to take these elements but give them greater depth.

The story itself is very slight: Professor Abronsius (Jack MacGowan) and his apprentice Alfred (Polanski himself) are the vampire killers of the title and their target is Count Von Krolok, played by Ferdy Mayne. First they have some nocturnal adventures at the village inn (Alfie Bass in attendance as the Jewish landlord who, when vampirised, is not remotely bothered by crucifixes). Then they go to Von Krolok's castle, to save a pretty lady (Sharon Tate) from being the victim at the vampires' annual ball.

The most marked visual differences between this and Hammer were that the locations featured a very real, snowbound Europe, and the set design, on what appeared to be a much grander budget than the usual Hammers, gave the vampire's castle, and indeed the village inn, much more texture. This was an eerily empty world in a perpetual blue twilight – an intentional one, as opposed to Hammer's economical camera filters. And yes, it is all rather beautiful to look at.

Where it also differed from Hammer, however, was not merely in the feeble jokes (not helped by a deadeningly unfunny turn from Jack MacGowan) but also the lethally boring longeurs, as Polanski's camera lingered over beautifully framed and lit shots for what seemed like whole minutes at a time. On top of this, the scenes that Polanski clearly did intend to be genuinely horrific – Von Krolok's kidnap of Sharon Tate, and the climactic vampire ball itself, are ker-plonking, over-stretched and rather too obviously pleased with themselves.

Even bearing all this in mind, though, Polanski paid full tribute to Hammer by sticking with the essentials of their carefully constructed universe: a sinister, decayed aristocracy feeding on the poor people in the villages below the huge castle. And happily, despite the diversion of the director's artistic sensibility, the film also proved that this particular corner of the film market was best left to Hammer: even if Hammer always played it straight, they managed to be ten times pacier and more entertaining. Moreover, any hint of a class element in the villainy always sounded that much better in Received Pronunciation.

The Plague of the Zombies can now be seen to represent one of the high-points of the Hammer oeuvre, a film that was low on gore and high on intrigue, filled with striking imagery and, of course, the blood-thumping sensation that a feeling of injustice could bring on. Of course, this was no Marxist text, and nor was any other Hammer: in *Plague*, it takes the solidly bourgeois doctors Andre Morell and Brooke Williams to get to the core of the mystery; sympathetic though the villagers are (and hats off at this point to Michael Ripper who on this occasion is the remarkably clear-sighted local bobby), it is made quite clear by Hinds that without the help of the benign middle classes, nothing could be done about their situation. One senses something quite similar about old Van Helsing, being high-handed and gently patronising with inn regulars, waving garlic flowers at them. In *Frankenstein Created Woman* (1967), Christina and Hans are unquestionably the heroes but their destiny – for good or as it turns out, ill – is irrefutably in the hands of Baron Frankenstein.

In the aftermath of the fashion for kitchen-sink drama – and through a flurry of the knockabout 'spoof' swinging comedies – all revolving Post Office Towers and Rita Tushingham – Hammer held a solid course when it came to questions of class (though not of sex – see Chapter Eight for further details). Later this would make the studio look staid, but in fact, in the mid-1960s, it is remarkable how closely Hammer's offerings match the yearnings of the studio's boss. In cutting back on the gore – and indeed on the fissly-fussly nightwear – the films were struggling their way towards complete respectability. These were no longer shockers to be savoured by bloodthirsty Teddy boys. These were well-crafted, nicely acted thrillers. We look at the amusingly bombastic, effortlessly patrician Andre Morell in *The Plague of the Zombies* and, with a little imagination, we see the embodiment of that middle-class authoritarian man of action who can move easily between the classes, talk to them all on equal levels, while providing the motor for change and stability in their lives. The sort of man 'Colonel' James Carreras fancied himself to be, in other words.

Of course, Carreras's emphatic way with poster art and titles – and the poster for *The Plague of the Zombies*, with its luridly coloured lurching monster is no different – always ensured that the truly refined wouldn't go near his films clutching a barge-pole with rubber gloves on. Their other big offering from 1966, *Dracula – Prince of Darkness* – the film that Carreras managed to lure Christopher Lee back from Switzerland for – was also not going to be in line for the Royal Command Performance.

In fact, here Hammer seemed to be trying to push the envelope of acceptability again, if only in terms of what was suggested as opposed to anything shown on screen. For instance, even now, Klove's sacrificial murder of Charles (Charles Tingwell) – stabbing him, then hanging him upside down and slitting him further to let his blood run over Dracula's ashes – leaves many viewers with the distinct impression that they have just seen a man's stomach being ripped open. They have seen no such thing. Terence Fisher merely suggested that that was the case. The audience did the rest. There was also the controversial scene involving the staking of a vampiric Barbara Shelley by a group of monks, which in subsequent film studies has been likened to a scene of gang rape. This is mainly because film historians have just been looking at the one still, of Shelley held down on a table while the monk advances with the stake. While the scene is most certainly unpleasant to watch, it is not quite as gratuitous as all that. None the less, it was the sort of thing that Hammer had finally become best known for. Indeed, it was around this point that Warners christened Down Place 'The House of Hammer'.[3]

This would probably not have pleased Carreras's son Michael, who was still only semi-detached from the Hammer family fold and was eager to do something to put the studio's reputation on a more respectable footing. It clearly made him uncomfortable that the studio was becoming best known solely for exploitation horror.[4] But even as young Michael was allowed to go off and produce two films that could have changed the course of the company's future – putting the emphasis on family adventure, glamour and exotic foreign locations – Sir James, answering to his American distributors, was unrepentantly committed to more vampires and yet more Frankenstein monsters. These, he believed, were the real bankers. But, for the moment, we will stick with Michael and his efforts to diversify the Hammer repertoire.

Chapter Seven

EPIC AMBITION

 By the mid-1960s, any reference to the 'British film industry' meant, slightly more precisely, an industry working with British talent but funded almost entirely – about ninety per cent in fact – by American studios. The screens now were awash with bright colour but this must have been an exhausting time to be either a critic or indeed a member of the audience. What might loosely be termed British cinema was entering into a phase of manic self-indulgence. For this we might be tempted to blame films such as Richard Lester's first Beatle epic *A Hard Day's Night* (1964) with its jump-cutting, speeded up sequences, meaningless montage and molecule thin narrative. After the tide of that initial New Wave had receded, the bubble machine of escapism – possibly the most mindless produced by any generation before or since – started blowing, and the films grew frothier and frothier.

We don't need a great list to make this point, simply an acknowledgement of the key texts: the 1963 version of *Tom Jones* starring Albert Finney, with all its post-modernist winks to camera and the new emphasis on 'bawdy' fun; *What's New Pussycat* (1965) with Peter O'Toole as a magazine editor who wants to have as much sex as possible and Peter Sellers as an astoundingly unfunny Viennese psychiatrist with a wig and an accent. Then there were two huge spy spoofs which, whenever they are shown now, tend to produce frowning gasps of disbelief in younger viewers: *Modesty Blaise* (1966), with Monica Vitti and Terence Stamp, and the sprawling Bond-a-thon comedy *Casino Royale* (1967), with David Niven, Orson Welles and Ursula Andress, amongst others. Both are noted for moments of strained surrealism, and an even more desperate sense that 'anything can happen, and probably will'. There are lavishly painted sets, plastic special effects, girls in minimal glittery costumes, the obligatory speeded-up sequences and impenetrable all-star custard-pie fights. Narrative is abandoned in favour of the stars winking and mugging their way through a thicket of puns and clonking sexual innuendo. No one could have imagined this to be sophisticated, even at the time. Yet these films – oh, and aforementioned efforts with Rita Tushingham in a revolving Post Office Tower with bubble machines *and* custard-pie fights – came to dominate domestic cinema for a brief period.

In retrospect, it is fairly clear that this frenetic frivolity was in itself a reaction to the grittiness of the late 1950s and early 60s productions – *Saturday Night, Sunday Morning, This Sporting Life* and indeed anything else starring Rachel Roberts. Even Bryan Forbes's *Whistle Down the Wind* (1964) was relocated from the Home Counties to the north. But after the second Beatles film, *Help!* (1965), which featured more zany doings, and this time in colour, British cinema started getting unbearably knowing and self-conscious.

Also, what no film-maker at the time could have seen – and this goes as much for David Lean and Lewis Gilbert as it does for James Carreras and his cheery crew – is that, in financial terms, this was the last high-water mark for the British film industry. The big Hollywood studios had busy production offices in those Home Counties studios, from Pinewood to Elstree, and investment in British productions was heavy. 'It was unquestionably a very good time to be in film,' recalled Bryan Forbes. 'Finding investment for production wasn't difficult.'

But the influence of Carnaby Street and the pop industry seeped through all corners of the entertainment business.

And the result, very often, was patience-trying childish self-indulgence. Even an allegedly socially aware production such as *To Sir with Love* (1967), involving Sidney Poitier as a black teacher at a sink school in London's East End, features as its resolution the school hall transformed into a colourful discotheque, with a bunch of wallies on stage on the guitars, and Lulu belting out the title song.

For the sake of misplaced nostalgia, there are some who might tug at my sleeve and point to an effort like Antonioni's *Blow-Up* (1966) as being a better example of that period. Shall we say not? Everything that is most self-referential and boring in this period finds its apogee in this echoingly empty and quite magisterially tedious murder mystery. Whose is the body in Maryon Wilson Park? But who on God's good earth cares? For here we are with more para-sexual activity (photography as opposed to spying) and more scenes of nightclubs and parties and allegedly trendy people leading their lives in a London hipper than anyone in the audience could ever hope to see. David Hemmings is the only person who can muster interest in the enigma. And as a bonus for an already ashen-faced audience, the whole thing finishes with a surreal tennis match, once again in that grim south London park.

Many imagine that the British film industry died in the 1970s. Actually, in some ways, one could hear the first death rattles at this point. And, ironically, the rising prosperity that did so much to fund these films also, on the other side of the screen, enabled cinema audiences to find alternative ways to spend their leisure time, either at pubs or dinky little trattorias. In the 1940s, most people would have gone to the cinema once a week. By the mid-1960s, those numbers were starting to fall dramatically.

But if there were ever any doubts in the mind of Michael Carreras about the future of the industry that he had followed his father into, he never let them cloud over the clear enthusiasm and optimism that he brought to his work. Nor, as a relatively young producer, did he allow himself to be influenced by the more experimental directors of his generation. Like his father, he had an idea of cinema as being a form of pure entertainment.

And I would contend now that if any sensible person had the choice between watching *Blow-Up* or Hammer's adaptation of H. Rider Haggard's *She* (1965) that person would go for *She* any time.

It is a silly film, to be sure, and a cheap one too, despite the location filming in Israel. It is unintentionally camp in places. But by heavens, Hammer's attempt at H. Rider Haggard's epic is sincere. And the sincerity pays off enormously today. Unlike a great many of its contemporaries, it stands rather proud, having the prime virtue of being supremely watchable.

And now it is time for Michael Carreras to take his first real, proper bow, for *She* was his work, in production terms at least, the film for which he was invited back to Hammer. He saw the epic possibilities of Haggard's well-worn pot-boiler and felt that this was a way for Hammer to break away from gothic horror, but to do so with its established stars, and with one very major star who would have all the punters flooding in: the original Bond girl, Ursula Andress.

Here, then, is the thing in a nutshell: John Richardson, Peter Cushing and Bernard Cribbins (an actor who is the true hallmark of value in a 1960s film) are in Palestine in 1918. The Great War is over. Richardson is lured to a mysterious house where he meets the beautiful Ayesha (Ursula Andress), or She, who is convinced that he is the reincarnation of her long-lost lover Killikrates, but in order that they may be reunited, he must undergo various desert-based ordeals. This Richardson does, with doughty Cushing and Cribbins helping out. They reach the Lost City of Kuma; She demonstrates her great cruelty by throwing slaves into a sulphur pit; Christopher Lee booms as her high priest; Ayesha steps into the blue flame of eternal youth but bathes too long in it and shrivels to dust before Richardson's horrified gaze.

In terms of production values, it wasn't quite Cecil B. De Mille, despite Carreras telling journalists that 'there's no doubt the future lies with bigger productions.'[1] But it was all convincing enough though. Andress made a suitably foxy and cunning Ayesha – the poster's shout line simply ran: 'The World's Most Beautiful Woman!' – Cushing and Lee gave substance to thinly written parts, and Cribbins brought an unexpected dignity as the batman who is expected to do his duty by his posher masters.

And it was refreshing to see Hammer out on location in Israel – for those bits that weren't obviously contrived in the studio, that is. And the studios weren't all that bad, considering there was still not a great deal of money. Ayesha's central chamber, dominated by the sinister and rather effective lava pit, was a fine piece of work, and the gold ornamentation looks convincing enough. The camp golden headdresses sported by Andress and Lee are minor distractions, as is the abundance of casual racism (so what sort of Africans *were* Andress and John Richardson exactly? And as for the others – do they just spend all day performing suggestive ritual dances?). What is nice to see now is the way that Peter Cushing and Christopher Lee look somehow so much more relaxed and happy with what they are doing. Ursula Andress couldn't act even if someone had pointed a revolver up her pet cat's backside but she gets across the main point about Ayesha, that she is both stunningly attractive and utterly lethal. The fact that she only starred because her director husband John Derek had a deal with Seven Arts allowing him to make films elsewhere in return for her appearance is neither here nor there.[2]

Oh, and another word in praise of composer James Bernard, who infuses the slightly shakier set-pieces, mainly involving people in costume processing across the scenery, with a genuine exotic grandeur.

The film did extremely well: certainly enough to warrant an immediate sequel – and indeed another sort of family adventure film altogether. And we can imagine how Michael Carreras must have cheered at this development. Many who knew him have said that he was never entirely comfortable with the genre of gothic horror. *She* was a perfectly decent 'A' certificate film, one which would wear well across the years, could be endlessly reissued, and subsequently endlessly reshown on television without losing any of its very slightly gimcrack charm.

The sequel, *The Vengeance of She* (1968), was an unfortunately patience-trying thing, devoid of Andress and starring another blonde stunner – twenty-one-year-old Czech newcomer Olinka Nelova – who at that stage had even less aptitude for acting than Andress. It is a meandering story, set in the modern day on the French Riviera, where an apparently reincarnated Ayesha is being sought high and low by an equally reincarnated and badly combed-over Richardson. It seems more an excuse for Michael Carreras to enjoy some glamorous location shooting than anything else.

But he had another, much more profitable, wheeze in 1966, one which would haul in Hammer's greatest profit and launch one of its most engagingly silly sub-genres. Carreras recalled seeing a 1940 effort from the Hal Roach Studios called *One Million BC*, set at the very dawn of time itself.[3] The unique selling point was that the loin-clothed cast, among them Victor Mature and Lon Chaney Jr, were merged via special effects with shots of lizards blown up to dinosaur size. In 1966, Michael Carreras (along with everyone else who had ever seen a film on a bank holiday) was aware of the spectacular stop-motion work of Ray Harryhausen, especially in *Jason and the Argonauts* (1962), and he proposed a remake of this dinosaur epic to Harryhausen.

The filming was to take place in the Canary Islands. The scenario would have rival tribes of early humans face not only fearsome dinosaurs, but also pterodactyls and even a vast giant tarantula. But at the very core of the thing, the one element that would have audiences piling in the world over, and which would provide the basis for one of the most iconic poster images of all time, was the casting of the main cave girl. It was time for Raquel Welch's day in the sunshine.

The poster remains familiar now – Welch in chamois leather, posed one hip slightly forward, blonde hair waving, prehistoric décolletage plunging, as behind her a tyrannosaurus and a stegosaurus slug it out. At the time she said she had only taken the role in the mistaken belief that 'nobody will remember this thing. I can shove it under the carpet.'[4] If only she had known!

Actually, iconography aside, the film itself is seen less often these days. In truth, there is not really a great deal to it other than Welch and co-star John Richardson looking fetching under the Mediterranean sun, and the hypnotically watchable, subliminally jerky dinosaurs themselves. True, Welch does get kidnapped by a pterodactyl and for a few moments, the modestly-placed chamois bikini is under threat, even if, in long-shot, it is clear that the actress has been replaced by a doll. She also gets to hide behind a rock when dinosaurs engage in life or death battles. And that's about it. But it was the most enormous hit.

For the most part, it was obvious that the audiences had been lured in by the poster image of Welch and the promise – unfulfilled – that her prehistoric adventures would cause her costume to fall off as the film went on. But Michael Carreras managed to serve up his cake and eat it – like *She*, this was a Hammer film that the entire family could enjoy, an exotic epic that would be ideal for school holidays. And again, it could be reissued endlessly as a half-term treat and shown on television in BBC1's prime 'Saturday Night at the Movies' slot. Oh, and it also did tremendously well in America. After the 1960 debacle of *The Two Faces of Dr Jekyll*, one might say that young Carreras had been completely rehabilitated. But still he remained a freelance, heading up his own operation at Capricorn Films.[5]

With *One Million Years BC* fast setting the studio's record for monster profitability, Carreras was drawn to exploring further films that would point the studio away from gothic horror. One was the science-fiction curiosity of *The Lost Continent* (1968), based on a little-known Dennis Wheatley story, which, as already mentioned in Chapter Four, drew father James Carreras into a rare visit on to the studio floor to halt production, so baffled was he by the weirdness. Funnily enough, this Sargasso Sea tale of mutant monsters and lost travellers has gained some critical reputation across the years, possibly because of its sheer undaunted quirkiness. It was not mere self-indulgence on the part of the younger Carreras, but rather an attempt, from the Freudian, glowing-eyed sucking monsters living in the rocks to the striking red weed that entraps the travellers, to do something completely new. But once you have unleashed your giant mutant scorpion – a prop on a trolley being yanked around the studio as unseen hands made the legs skitter up and down – then you do not leave yourselves many dramatic avenues to explore.

Then, again as mentioned, there was an attempt at a space western, called *Moon Zero Two* (1969), rather bravely following Stanley Kubrick's *2001 – A Space Odyssey*. Even for Michael Carreras, it was a rather curious new direction – apart from anything else, science fiction other than Kubrick's was not a profitable genre at that time. Even the excellent *Quatermass and the Pit* (1967) had only performed middlingly in Britain, and fared even worse in the States, where it had been puzzlingly re-entitled *Five Million Years to Earth*. Possibly, like so many others, Michael Carreras was inspired by that year's real life moon landings, and took a gamble that a great public taste for space rockets would re-emerge. It didn't after this production. Perhaps the posters hadn't helped. '*See* the first space gun battle on the moon!' they yelped. '*See* the fabulous Go-Jos dancing on the moon!'[6] The Go-Jos were the mini-skirted in-house dancers for *Top of the Pops*. The public may have caught a little whiff of desperation. Once again, though, *Moon Zero Two* has now become an object of curiosity, owing to its unselfconscious way-outness and prospect of Bernard Bresslaw in silver space clothes. Not to mention a rather charmingly dated theme song that sounds like an intergalactic version of 'Up, Up and Away'.

It was time, come 1969, for Carreras the younger to do the obvious and bring on more cave girls which he did in *Creatures the World Forgot* (1971) and *When Dinosaurs Ruled the Earth* (1970), a film that was winningly retitled by Peter Cook as *When Diana Dors Ruled the Earth* – and who wouldn't have paid good money to see that?

Better money, certainly, than you would pay to see the real things. Incidentally, the screenwriter of *When Dinosaurs ...* was none other than J.G. Ballard, who has said of this work: 'I'm very proud that my first screen credit was for what is, without doubt, the worst film ever made.'[7]

These are now Hammer's most obscure efforts – never seen on television, not available on DVD, certainly never shown in the art-house retrospectives, and never fondly chewed over by the fans. They deserve their fate, for they are at best bizarre and at worst insanely and naffly perverse. Try one of the productions from this period, *Slave Girls* (1968), where woodentop Michael Latimer treks through the jungle and happens across two tribes of women – the powerful brunettes, led by Martine Beswick, who have enslaved the winsome blondes, led by Julie Ege. Cue a series of chamois leathered girl-on-girl fights against painfully obvious studio backdrops. (This one has actually made it to DVD, but under the title of *Prehistoric Women*.)

In *Creatures the World Forgot* it is half-naked men who are doing the fighting – in caveman thongs. If the homoeroticism was unconscious – and more than possibly at the time it was – then it makes the film doubly hilarious. Mix in with these elements some jerkier-than-normal and slightly out of focus dinosaurs and you see how Carreras's idea of a family epic could sometimes go amazingly awry.

As a pleasing footnote, the whole cavewoman sub-genre was rather wonderfully sent up in *Carry On Up the Jungle* (1971) in which Sid James's party of Victorian Amazon explorers are captured by the bikinied Tonker Tribe led by Valerie Leon. The voluptuous tribe (with its ritual chant 'Tonker, tonker, stick it up your honker') needs Sid James, Charles Hawtrey and Frankie Howerd for breeding purposes. In some extraordinary way, this notion was more palatable than the grunting dialogue-free fights being served up by Hammer in the name of heavily disguised soft porn.

But then of course these later Carreras productions were made at a point – the early 1970s – when there was no further American investment and Hammer was left for the first time to make its own financial arrangements. The circumstances, as we shall see later, would have been enough to turn anyone's artistic judgement to putty.

As for the earlier Mediterranean efforts, we must at least take our hats off to Carreras for having tried these things out. For in a sense, he was right about the longevity of gothic horror as a genre. It couldn't be sustained for ever, simply because tastes and fashions always move on. But back in the late 1960s, he found himself in profound philosophical disagreement with his father.

Some years later, in the mid-1970s, when Michael Carreras was being interviewed by John Brosnan, he had to reluctantly admit the pull of the horrors and indeed the craft that went into them. Michael said:

> As a film fan, which I am very much, I don't go to see horror films as my first choice. I naturally see our own a number of times and then I go and see the opposition or, to be more honest, I get the better examples of other peoples' horror films in and screen them during the day as part of my working routine ... it's not as if we sit here concentrating on horror films the whole time ... but they're probably the most enjoyable things to work on because you can let your imagination run riot.

He went on to add:

> I think that one of the reasons our horror films became leaders in the market was that they were always beautifully photographed, the sets were always extremely believable. They've never been shoddy productions.[8]

Well, give or take a tribe of slave girls or two at any rate.

Come 1966, Warner Bros/Seven Arts were pretty much calling the shots with Hammer, and they happened to concur with James Carreras's view that the studio should be experimenting with new ideas and formats less, and focusing on simply providing more Peter Cushing and especially Christopher Lee. The Baron and the Count were perceived to be at the very centre of Hammer's output, the public could never have enough of them, and there simply should be more of them, as opposed to one-off zombies, reptiles and gorgons.

That year, Christopher Lee had, as we have seen, been lured back for *Dracula – Prince of Darkness* and the film did extremely well, despite the Count not saying a word throughout. It was time now to get Baron Frankenstein back into his laboratory. As ever, Carreras had his poster in mind – this time featuring Frankenstein, and a beautiful woman. The film was conceived almost as a spoof. The finished result, however, was to prove one of Hammer's most haunting, complex and strange works. It was obviously not recognised as such at the time – cheap cinema rarely earned any accolades at all other than the odd snide review in the national newspapers. But as time has gone on, it became clear – to Martin Scorsese amongst others – that *Frankenstein Created Woman* is perhaps the ultimate Hammer film, and one with an unusual richness, depth, and sense of poetry. It is also a film which now gives us a snapshot of Hammer's relationship with women generally, both on and off the screen, and how the studio acknowledged the burgeoning women's movement.

Chapter Eight

FANGS ARE A FEMINIST ISSUE

'Frankenstein has created the ultimate in evil' screamed the posters. Let us be quite clear from the start: Frankenstein on this occasion had done nothing of the sort.

Like many of the later efforts from Hammer, the idea had originally sprung from a jokey notion. Having seen a reissue of Roger Vadim's *And God Created Woman* (1958) starring Brigitte Bardot, screenwriter Anthony Hinds larkily suggested that Hammer's riposte should be 'And Frankenstein Created Woman'. He even ventured that the studio should try to engage Bardot for the film.[1]

But as we have seen before, Hammer, on the whole, did not do jokes; so *Frankenstein Created Woman* was pitched to Warners executives, the grins faded and the story took on the most extraordinary life of its own.

And as a narrative, it is unusually involved. In a prologue, we see young Hans unwillingly witness the execution of his father. Years later, now grown up, he is in the employ of Baron Frankenstein, who has been conducting experiments on himself, involving deep freezers and the isolating of the soul. Hans (Robert Morris) is in love with Christina (Susan Denberg), the innkeeper's daughter. She has serious facial scars and a malformed leg which torment her; Hans doesn't care because he is in love. In a complicated series of events, Hans falls foul of three young toffs (take a bow, *Heartbeat's* Derek Fowlds) who have been viciously tormenting Christina. Later, these toffs drunkenly kill Christina's father; Hans's coat was left at the scene and it is Hans who is framed and convicted for the murder, mainly on the basis that *his* father was a murderer and the predilection must have been passed on. And so it is that Christina witnesses her lover's execution – then throws herself into the river and drowns.

Frankenstein, meanwhile, procures Hans's headless body and is contriving to hold his soul in stasis in a force field. Then Christina's body is brought to him and now the Baron (for reasons that only he can guess at) sees the chance to transplant the soul of this dead man into his dead lover's body ...

From the start, what makes this Frankenstein unusual is the characterisation of the Baron himself who, on this outing, is an almost kindly, fatherly figure. He has – for him, anyway – a warm relationship with both Hans and Dr Hertz (Thorley Walters). At Hans's trial, he is called upon as a character witness (and there's a very nice touch from Cushing as, in the witness stand, he flicks through the Bible with an expression of bored superciliousness). And after the Baron brings Christina/Hans back to life, he is brisk yet ultimately much more caring than we have ever seen him before.

And that's because, for all the talk of souls, and the spooky scenes of Christina/Hans exacting bloody revenge on the three young toffs, this is Hammer with a new note of romanticism and tragic pathos. In previous films, the young love interest parts were at best thinly drawn. Here, they are very much in the foreground, and by golly, we are made to feel for them. There is an uncommonly tender scene as Hans and Christina lie in bed together; she cripplingly conscious of her face, and making him blow the lamp out before they make love.

In *The Plague of the Zombies*, we saw how the narrative was given an extra kick with class friction; here, class antagonism is the motor of the thing. The three young toffs are utterly irredeemable: their venomous taunts to Christina, their high-handed threats to revoke the landlords' licence, their general all-round top-hatted arrogance are the things that cause Hans and Christina's world to be destroyed. The appeal to the core of Hammer's domestic audience could not be more direct. And it works. The horror and the poignancy of the blameless young couple's death resonates strongly. And when the resurrected Christina sets about avenging these deaths – killing the toffs one by one with meat cleavers, kitchen knives, etc., we can't help feeling, at a very deep gut level, that these loathsome men had it coming.

Frankenstein here becomes, as critic David Pirie writes, 'the enchanter'. In other words, rather than being the malign prime mover in the narrative, it is the Baron who introduces the possibility of a metaphysical resolution, allowing the lovers to be avenged at last by supernatural means. In the frame of the narrative, it gives him an unusual degree of moral neutrality.

And rather than the expected paraphernalia of severed hands and organs in jars, the Baron's experiments this time have a sense of genuine curiosity, as opposed to horror, about them. For a start: capture the soul? What on earth can the man mean? We are very much with the drink-addled but kindly Dr Hertz on this one. And while it still seems exceptionally ghoulish to have acquired Hans's headless executed body, we can see that, for once, the Baron intends, in his own particular way, to do good.

By the end, after the dual Christina/Hans has dispatched Derek Fowlds, his/her soul is in quite understandable confusion and torment. She runs to a cliff. Frankenstein tries to stop her and explain to Christina that her actions were not her own. But she knows that – and jumps into a waterfall anyway, her body this time never to be recovered. And for once, none of it is Frankenstein's fault. Indeed, in happier circumstances, his bizarre experiment might have worked.

What are we to make of the mellowing approach here? Can this be the same director who gave us the comfortless and nihilistic *The Curse of Frankenstein* just ten years previously? Anthony Hinds suggested around this point that it was time they got more 'compassion'[2] into the films generally and it is obvious that Terence Fisher was in wholehearted agreement.

To be sure, there is a far greater assuredness on his part now; the striking shot of the sky above the guillotine in the opening credits, the curious lighting of which is somehow reminiscent of the work of Caspar David Friedrich; greater fluency of camerawork in the fight scenes; and those deep pools of sinister colour and shadow deployed when Christina/Hans is setting about her revenge on the three toffs.

This time, Baron Frankenstein is not a fugitive, merely a figure regarded with a little suspicion by the small society that he lives amongst; and indeed the loveable soak Dr Hertz and young Hans confer added acceptability on him. And loopy though his experiments seem, the burden of badness has been lifted from him.

Some twenty years after the film was made, American director Martin Scorsese singled it out for special attention at an NFT retrospective of the Hammers in 1987. In particular, he explained why it was his favourite Hammer of all: 'It's because they actually isolate the soul, a bright blue shining translucent ball,' he said. 'The implied metaphysics are close to something sublime.'[3]

There were other critical fans. Thus David Pirie in *The Heritage of Horror* (1973) tried to explain the core of the film's appeal:

> The film rapidly develops into an extravagant fairy tale full of decadent romantic imagery, with Fisher using the spurious scientific contrivance of soul transplants to take the recurrent nineteenth-century image of the Fatal Woman to its logical conclusion, ... The 'beauty of the Medusa' theme is fully indulged here when, for example, Christina's lover Hans touches her scar admiringly while the camera lingers ... the scene is set for the miraculous series of sexual events which are to occur: in a succession of incidents, for which

three young men are responsible, both Christina and Hans are killed and Frankenstein, unashamedly in the role of an enchanter on the side of justice, employs his energy machine to merge the two of them into Christina's rejuvenated and healed body ... like Keats's *Lamia*, she is the illusory incarnation of female beauty.[4]

That may perhaps have been slightly over the heads of the core Hammer audience but there is no denying the intense and heavy romanticism of the film; from the curious and attractive attic laboratory set (where Frankenstein appears to be using a combination of alchemy and nuclear physics) to the symmetry of those bleak heathland scenes; from the pathos of Christina's understanding of her dual nature to the highly moving score by James Bernard – one of his best – we have here a film that would surely have been scoffed at for soppiness by Jimmy Sangster just a decade previously. And it is remarkably not of its time. In a year dominated by pop silliness, spoofs and high camp, *Woman* is an eyebrow-raisingly serious and sincere effort. Even the climax – Christina stabs villainous young Derek Fowlds and flees through the woods to kill herself, Frankenstein helpless to stop his creation – is unusually moving for a Hammer effort. At last we see the true colours of Terence Fisher; having inaugurated the studio's success with two notably brutalist efforts, it is as if his inner softy has broken out and triumphed. This was the only time that we would ever see the otherwise deranged Victor Frankenstein playing it light in a court scene when he is testifying for the good character of his assistant. And we are remarkably short on Guignol, save for a not-wholly convincing human head in a lady's hatbox (this gruesome prop, incidentally, was larkily thrown at the Bray canteen dinner lady Mrs Thompson one lunchtime – she caught it with a scream);[5] the head is the disconcerting means by which the reincarnated Christina keeps in touch with her inner Hans.

Of course, Fisher and Hinds by this stage could do almost anything they wanted – they were the elder statesmen of Hammer films. It is interesting to see though that – apart from Fisher's *The Devil Rides Out*, which he directed the following year – this was the last time that any such production would be tolerated by James Carreras. He – and indeed Warners – were after something a little more full-blooded. As in the late 1950s, Carreras wanted to push the envelope.

What *Frankenstein Created Woman* also represents is Hammer's first tentative toe in the water of the burgeoning feminist movement. To be frank, Susan Denberg's Christina is hardly Mrs Emma Peel. But this was the first time that Hammer had made a woman the centre of the narrative, no matter how much the character was simply manipulated by and reacting to the male figures around her. This was only partly in order to hold out the offer of sauce to the male audience; it was also a clear appeal to the sizeable female audience, an attempt, however patchy, to give women a horror that they could identify with a little more closely.

I use the term 'patchy' because in the first half of the film, as a girl saving up to have operations to remove her disfigurements, Christina has a faint fairy-tale quality, closer to Cinderella than anything else, and with not much more depth. Only when we see her with her lover Hans do we get a sense of a deeper character. But when Frankenstein is done resurrecting her – and with Han's soul inhabiting her body – Christina becomes one of Hammer's most intriguing creations, one that both Hinds and Fisher could clearly not quite work out themselves.

New, rebuilt, non-scarred, non-lame Christina at first appears to be vaguely amnesiac and bewildered to be back in this new physical form. Frankenstein and Hertz go through a montage of weeks of teaching her to walk again, reacquainting her with the world. But there is an unreadable quality there, a sense that the old Christina has been replaced with someone more watchful. And then of course come the scenes of her revenge. Whether pooled in darkness or bathed in a crimson light, this new, unrecognisable Christina sets about luring the toffs one by one with seductive allurements we would never have seen her old self using. At the moment when each of the men is under her sexual power, we suddenly hear Hans's voice exhorting her to 'kill!' as Christina strikes with cleaver or dagger. What both Hinds and Fisher can't quite determine is to what extent the woman is possessed by the man, and to what extent the man is driving the woman's body. Indeed, they also seem to be stumbling over the same-sex implications of the seduction scenes. But rather than hobbling the film, this ambiguity gives it a further bizarre resonance as a story that operates more with the logic of a folk tale than a science-fiction horror film.

And while, clearly, there is nothing remotely feminist about this 'text', as they say, the film did mark an important step forward for Hammer; in that they realised that a film could gain a lot by having a woman as the key pivotal character. Indeed, as the 1960s gave way to the 1970s, Hammer did it increasingly frequently.

At this point, it is worth a very swift side-step to take a glance at the studio's various later attempts to embrace the burgeoning spirit of new womanhood. The films briefly mentioned here will be discussed again later on but for the moment, I just want to address one myth surrounding the later Hammers of the 1970s: that they were gratuitously exploitative of women. Yes, as the years went on, there were flashes of nudity. This wasn't just Hammer – there were similar flashes everywhere. But at Hammer this was balanced by a very much fresher approach to writing and performing female roles. Indeed, Hammer women started to take centre stage in a way that they did at no other studio.

The most famous and fondly remembered example is the Ingrid Pitt vehicle *Countess Dracula* (1971); rather than blood-sucking, as the cheat title implies, the countess Elizabeth Bathory bathes in the blood of virgin women and by doing so miraculously regains her youth. But it all goes horribly wrong on her wedding day as groom Sandor Eles is confronted with a suddenly transformed wrinkly old crone. Pitt also effortlessly held the screen as Sheridan Le Fanu's Carmilla in *The Vampire Lovers* (1970), giving a lesbian twist to the whole genre of biting and sucking. We had a hilariously arch Martine Beswick playing Ralph Bates's feminine side in the absurdly enjoyable *Dr Jekyll and Sister Hyde* (1971) and also dominating the screen in the aforementioned *Slave Girls* (1968). Hammer heroines progressed too – in *The Satanic Rites of Dracula* (1973), Joanna Lumley, as Lorrimer Van Helsing's daughter, gives an amused, and amusing, performance.

On the production side of the films, there were also a few steps in the direction of equality. In 1966, a young assistant director called Aida Young was promoted to the rank of producer – then an extremely rare achievement for a woman in British film. She was to recall:

> I was the only woman doing my kind of job anywhere in the feature industry. I was the first third assistant director, the first second ... If you were a woman, you had to do continuity, or you were a secretary, or you were wardrobe, make-up and hair – that was it.[6]

Young was the first at Bray to break out of all of that, doing much of the hard graft as associate producer on both *She* and *One Million Years BC*. She then went on to the horrors, kicking off with *Dracula Has Risen from the Grave* (after which she managed to get into a scrap with composer James Bernard, having complained about his 'atonal' themes – at first, Bernard got huffy but then, for the subsequent *Taste the Blood of Dracula*, relented and made the music more melodic). Aida Young was unintentionally pushed slightly into the background in the early 1970s after having produced the visually impressive *Hands of the Ripper* (1971); at this point, Hammer was becoming overrun with freelance producers wanting to try out fresh ideas. As a result, she left the company and joined EMI instead.[7]

One other woman producer, Josephine Douglas, a friend of James Carreras, emerged from the world of television – she had previously produced the BBC pop show *6.5 Special* – and was assigned, perhaps rather thanklessly, to *Dracula AD 1972*. Having said that, she made the most of it, excitedly telling one on-set journalist that 'Dracula is thirsty – but I'm not happy with his face. It's not green enough.'[8] In an overwhelmingly male industry – and of course, every industry then was overwhelmingly male – the fact that Young and Douglas got through those walls of prejudice at all was extremely impressive. They are also a further sign of how sensitive Hammer was to its female audience. Up to a point at least.

There was a publicity shot taken in 1970 for *The Vampire Lovers*. It featured five of the film's actresses, including Ingrid Pitt, Kate O'Mara and Madeleine Smith, posing in the regulation Hammer flimsy nightwear, but all standing on top of an oaken coffin, with some garish lighting in the background. Today, it looks so cheesy and outrageously sexist that one might take it for a joke. Indeed, it's the sort of image that could very well be used now in a sort of post-ironic joke by any one of a number of ad agencies. What on earth can these actresses be thinking as they stand there posing with their arms outstretched? What photographer thought that multicoloured backdrop was a smart move? Exactly how undignified is it to pose in a nightie anyway? These days, Kate O' Mara still finds herself looking back on it with bemusement. 'It wasn't just shots with the arms outstretched,' she said. 'There was another shot of all of us having to pose around the now upright coffin with Ingrid Pitt standing in it, grinning. Actually, the whole thing was rather unplanned.

'As is usual with filming, we were on one day taken off to do the publicity stills around the back of the set,' O'Mara continued. 'And this being Hammer the photographer could only find this one prop, the coffin, so that was that, with the coffin, and us, all at different angles. But the hair! The nighties!'

O'Mara ruefully acknowledges that as a symbol of where women stood in the Hammer universe, it was far from ideal. But she is also clear that Hammer was a long way from being the worst offender.

In 1970 – a year in which beauty pageants still topped the television ratings, in which even Shakespearean actresses would send photographs of themselves in bikinis to casting directors, and in which the main narrative role of any woman in any popular drama (other than *The Avengers*) was to either scream or to be the love interest – you can see a certain level of self-mockery going on in that publicity shot. It's not quite the same as camping it up – hugely camp though the image is. Nor is it quite the same as being a straightforward lure for male audiences. The image is somehow a little too knowing and amused for that. Rather, what the picture seems to be saying is: a Hammer film will guarantee you beautiful women and acres of cleavage but it will also amuse and entertain you – in other words, it is not solely there to titillate the fiddling plastic-mac platoon. In a cruder way, it's also saying: in this film, women are the predators. A quick glance too at the expressions in the eyes of all the actresses will reveal that they too are finding this all rather enjoyable.

One actress specifically brought in to inject an element of what was known as 'Hammer Glamour' was the then twenty-three-year-old Veronica Carlson, cast as the female lead in *Dracula Has Risen from the Grave* (1968). She found herself on the receiving end of a huge amount of press attention. This of course was the era of the Bond girl, when it became an annual ritual to show off Sean Connery's latest lead actress to the world's photographers. Hammer happily picked up the habit. The US trailer of the film trumpeted Veronica Carlson as 'Hammer's newest star discovery!' In any case, she has affectionate memories of James Carreras and Christopher Lee going out of their way to make her feel welcome and giving her the (correct) impression that she had joined a happy band. It seems extremely unfair to suggest that she might have been selected less for her acting skills than for the awesome dimensions of her bust. But in fact Miss Carlson came to embody the classic Hammer girl in that Dracula entry, and two subsequent Frankensteins.

She was the young heroine whom Peter Cushing was forced to ravish in *Frankenstein Must be Destroyed* (1969); this scene was the result of a distasteful script intervention by the American backers Warners, who halfway through production decided that they wanted the film to have 'more sex'. This wish was conveyed to the actors and director Terence Fisher on the studio floor by James Carreras himself. All concerned were rather shocked and dismayed. And Carlson's account of all the awkwardness before the scene was shot throws a quite wonderful light on the workings of the studio's lead actors.

> Dear Peter, at his most gallant, took me to dinner. His original dream was that we go to dinner in costume, his favourite being my purple velvet dress and tri-corn hat. However, the urgency of dealing with the impending (rape) scene upstaged that romantic notion. We discussed all the possibilities endlessly, especially how to execute the ghastly deed within the bounds of good taste. It was impossible, in the end, Peter said – and I can still hear him today – 'Please remember, please remember it isn't me, Veronica, it isn't me,' and he hugged me tight.
>
> Just prior to shooting the scene, Roger Moore (with whom I had filmed an episode of *The Saint* three years before) heard of my distress and came to comfort me. The scene called for me to have my nightgown partly ripped off, even though there was a 'no nudity' clause in my contract. Ultimately it was director Terry Fisher who called 'Enough enough, I've had enough' before walking off the set.[9]

In her Dracula film, Miss Carlson was the actress who pioneered the technique of being chased by a horse-drawn hearse through a pine forest while wearing a nightie in what is supposed to be the middle of the night. Her character is the niece of a monsignor being wooed by Barry Andrews and she is the film's 'good girl', placed in dramatic opposition to Barbara Ewing's brassy redhead barmaid Zena. The implied chasteness and innocence of the character is interesting: quite different from the more sophisticated figures portrayed by the studio's other leading lady Barbara Shelley. Dracula wants nothing more than to corrupt her; but Veronica Carlson is just too darn good to be corrupted.

This slightly wide-eyed aspect was transferred to Miss Carlson's portrayal of Anna Spengler in *Frankenstein Must be Destroyed* and thence to the role of Elizabeth in the uncomfortable semi-spoof *The Horror of Frankenstein* (1970). The tension in all of these arises out of the possibility that Miss Carlson will lose that quality of innocence, that the forces of evil will succeed in breaking her down. In one sense, this is a retrograde step on the part of Hammer: at a time when the women's movement was nascent, when Germaine Greer's *The Female Eunuch* was materialising in bookshops, we have a heroine who seems to be a throwback to the days of silent movie cliffhangers. Partly Carlson was there to appeal to a younger audience. At this time, the average age of the male leads in the Hammers dropped considerably as well. But it is highly likely that, quietly, Carlson was also there to appeal to the Warners executives who at that time were bank-rolling the films. It must be remembered that Americans were consistently more squeamish when it came to these films than anyone else in the world; while throughout Europe, sexier, more violent versions of the Hammers tended to get on to the screen, in the States, more cuts were made. And Veronica Carlson was exactly the sort of clean-cut white-gowned heroine calculated to appeal to this Midwest mindset – a virtuous young woman moving through a world of evil.

There was, of course, another side to this feminine empowerment at Hammer. The late 1960s were to bring changes to British rules on censorship: up until this point, the 'X' certificate meant that films were restricted to those over sixteen. But in the wake of the Lord Chamberlain's role in theatrical censorship being abolished, and the subsequent wave of nudity seen on the stage in shows such as *Oh! Calcutta!*, it was clear that John Trevelyan, Chairman of the Board of British Censors, had to address changing times. He did so by introducing a new certificate: AA, which indicated a film suitable for those of fourteen years or over. And the 'X' certificate was now redefined as films suitable for eighteen years and over. In other words, it instantly allowed far greater permissiveness.

The result of this was immediately obvious through every genre of British film save the family bank holiday efforts: comedies got bawdier, dramas more licentious, thrillers more graphically violent. And of course, the genre of horror took advantage all of these new freedoms. Which is why another abiding image of Hammer now is that of actresses running around graveyard sets with their breasts hanging out. It is not entirely a false memory: come 1970, and there was indeed a lot of bare-breasted action.

The question is: did the requirement for Ingrid Pitt or Yutte Stensgard or Madeleine Smith to whisk those nightgowns off make them every bit as exploited as the actresses right at the bottom of the market, those in the soft-porn flicks that as the 1970s wore on, increasingly came to take over suburban Odeons? Or in the rather artier porn efforts such as *Last Tango In Paris* (1972)? Or indeed actresses in Roman Polanski's *Macbeth*? Was there a single actress from the National Theatre downwards in the early 1970s who was not at some stage told by a director to pop them out?

No one is ever going to claim Camille Paglia style credentials for Hammer. But let's just, to be fair, carry out a fleeting comparison of the prominence of its female characters compared with other films of the period and indeed later. This was a period, for instance, in which the Bond girls were growing progressively dopier and more skimpily dressed. ('You seem to be showing a little more cheek than usual, Miss Case,' Blofeld purrs to Jill St John in *Diamonds are Forever* (1971)). The mini-skirted dolly was still very much with us in such dive-under-the-sofa-in-mortification efforts as *There's a Girl in My Soup* (1970). And let's say nothing of the uniquely British sub-genre of the sex comedy which by law had to feature Alfie Bass and Diana Dors for detumescent purposes after various blonde actresses playing nurses performed their sauna scene.

Well all right, let's be frank: Ingrid Pitt did spend quite a lot of time popping them out in *Countess Dracula* (1971) and *The Vampire Lovers* (1970). Practically Martine Beswick's first act after transformation from Dr Jekyll to Sister Hyde is to open up her dressing gown to take a gander at her new embonpoint. Madeleine and Mary Collinson, who took the title roles as the *Twins of Evil* (1971) were former Playboy centrefolds who lost little time in shimmying out of those Victorian stays. In the meantime, the entire premise of *Slave Girls* (1968) is the discovery of lost Amazonian women wearing leather bikinis and keen on wrestling.

There is a big 'but' here though: almost as if to make up for these outbreaks of tangy spice, women, on the whole, got much more rewarding parts in these later Hammers. No matter how much nude bathing in virgin's blood she has to do, Ingrid Pitt carries the entire film as Countess Dracula. 'Blood!'

screamed the poster with characteristic understatement. 'The more she drinks, the prettier she gets. The prettier she gets, the thirstier she gets!' Couldn't have put it better myself. Pitt's male co-stars, Nigel Green and Sandor Eles, look wispy next to her thunderously melodramatic performance. Similarly Ralph Bates is engaging in *Dr Jekyll and Sister Hyde* but not half so much as Martine Beswick who brings a genuine laugh-out-loud relish to her spree of blackly comic killing. Kate O'Mara turns in a similarly funny performance while clad in an improbably low-cut dirndl as young Victor's mistress Alys in *The Horror of Frankenstein*. This is to say nothing of Adrienne Corri's lip-smacking relish as the ringmaster of the Circus of Nights in *Vampire Circus* (1972) or indeed Valerie Leon's malevolent eye-flashing turn as the reincarnated monster in *Blood from the Mummy's Tomb* (1971).

It is true that the Hammers were never wholly regarded as completely respectable, even after they won the Queen's Award for Industry in 1968. Being a Hammer girl was not everyone's ideal career choice: former Avenger Linda Thorson turned down an offer from the studios in the early 1970s.

And Kate O'Mara also turned down a contract to do six films as 'the new Hammer leading lady'.

'I was a classical actress, done Shakespeare, everything, and I just knew that if I took it, it would make my career incredibly difficult afterwards, just in terms of limiting parts. But my then husband was pushing me to do it so I went to see Hammer management. During the course of the meeting, I told them I didn't want this leading lady contract. Sir James Carreras could not believe his ears. But I did ask them if I could be in a couple of the films and that's how I came to be performing curtseys for the benefit of the cameraman in *The Horror of Frankenstein*.

'Incidentally,' she added, laughing, 'I was too innocent to know that when I was doing those curtseys, the camera was focusing in – well, not on my face. It was hardly something they'd tell you they were doing.'

The issue of respectability stayed with many of the actresses. For instance, several years back, the intensely fashionable boutique hotel-owner Anouska Hempel was disagreeably taken aback when friends took to circulating video-taped copies of her vampish role in *The Scars of Dracula* (1970), even though they did so in a genuine spirit of fun.

But even in those early 1970s days of relaxed censorship and increased titillation, Hammer knew that it was incredibly important not to alienate its female audience. So while the gowns increasingly came off, the performances became proportionately larger. And of all the leading ladies, it was arguably Ingrid Pitt who pulled the whole thing off with the greatest gusto, especially as the (initially) middle-aged Elizabeth Barthory – *Countess Dracula* – who, having cruelly struck a chambermaid with a hairbrush and drawn blood, discovers that the splattering has had the most remarkable rejuvenating effects on her skin. Regular baths in blood follow, as do sessions of seducing Sandor Eles (prior to his regular engagements at the Crossroads motel). Her eastern European accent (Pitt was from Hungary) and her flashing-eyed cruelty lifted what was in essence a bit of a rip-off into something more diverting.

'Becoming part of Hammer films was like being welcomed into a family,' she said. 'I was very aware of it as an institution. And the Hammer publicity department went to town. "The new face of horror for the 70s!" "Queen of Horror!" "The most beautiful ghoul in the world!" I was thrilled and wallowed in it.'[10]

Similarly in *The Vampire Lovers* (1970), Pitt puts her back into it as Carmilla (disguising herself as Mircalla to home in on the breasts of her victims). She wrote about it:

> The film involved nude scenes. I'd never done the full-frontal bit
> before but I was proud of my body and not too reluctant to show it.
> Madeleine Smith, who played my second victim, had also kept her
> gear on in front of the cameras so far. She was a little more
> apprehensive but saw the relevance and agreed to get it off.
> Nevertheless, we both had reservations ... I discovered that when
> you're naked on set, everyone is terribly nice to you and looks after
> you beyond the call of duty. This is particularly the case when you are
> doing a bath scene, which I seemed to do a lot of at Hammer.[11]

Not everyone had to. Both Veronica Carlson and Kate O'Mara were rather insistent about their 'no nudity' contracts.

Incidentally, with *The Vampire Lovers*, censor John Trevelyan read the submitted script before production and warned the studio about depictions of lesbianism, pointing out that five minutes of the previous year's *The Killing of Sister George* had been excised. Hammer very politely replied that the lesbianism was not of their doing, but that of *Carmilla*'s author Sheridan le Fanu, and that it was all there to be seen on the page.[12] Thus they won again. In rehearsals, Pitt recalls, her fangs repeatedly fell down the cleavage of victim Kate O'Mara. A scene that Le Fanu inexplicably failed to get down on paper.

But Pitt's vampiric performance had a certain note of pathos too. She was allowed to demonstrate a greater emotional range, unlike many previous male vampires, and she did so with great effectiveness. More than can be said for Yutte Stensgard in the follow-up *Lust for a Vampire* (1971).

So, no, there was not a great deal here to be found that advanced the cause of feminism; unless one counts the freedom to show off massive fangs and sink them into the necks of happily submissive males. Also there was the occasional outbreak of rather chilly misogyny – the torch-bearing puritans of *Twins of Evil*, for example, stalking the countryside looking for more young women to burn at the stake. But on a very generalised balance, the Hammer films were much less exploitative of women than one might have originally supposed. Certainly when compared to other studios at the time, they were in some sense genuinely progressive.

And this leads us back to *Frankenstein Created Woman*. When we watch Peter Cushing and Thorley Walters in the sequence when the two doctors are helping the revived Christina back to health – all those deportment lessons – one now cannot help thinking of director and screen-writer Terence Fisher and Anthony Hinds, behaving like a pair of perfect old gentlemen with their fictional creation; more than happy to have this lovely bit of totty around but knowing fundamentally that she's a fine young gel and that such unworthy thoughts ought to be banished. It's a very strange and oddly rather beautiful film to watch now. Far from creating the ultimate in evil, as James Carreras's posters claimed, Frankenstein had created a poignant fable, one somehow completely divorced from the time in which it was made. And there was nothing there for Susan Denberg to complain about. She could even keep her top on.

The indignities for actresses, if they came, tended to be prompted more by the technical difficulties of making films on a threadbare budget. Thus production manager Christopher Neame, speaking of one particular challenge faced during the making of *Blood from the Mummy's Tomb* (1971), when star Valerie Leon, portraying the vengeful reincarnation of an Egyptian queen, has to perform one of the classic Hammer actress manoeuvres:

> It was a short sequence. For some reason, she had to run through a thick wood wearing a negligee over a seriously push-up bra. We could not afford the transport to go on location so somewhere had to be found on the lot. That wasn't easy as suburban houses were on three of its boundaries. There was, however, a short single line of spindly poplar trees ... by utilising a very long focus lens, it actually appeared as if we were in a wood. The camera was run at ninety-six frames per second (for a slow motion dramatic effect) and the girl came towards us. Valerie's bosom was awesome but as she ran, each breast was out of synchronisation with the other and the effect was exacerbated by the slow motion.[13]

Elsewhere, Hammer newcomer Stephanie Beacham found other bosom-related difficulties during the climax of *Dracula AD 1972* when she was required to lie on an altar in a white gown without the benefit of a bra or indeed supporting tape, the noise of which would be picked up by the microphone.[14]

Such unexpected aesthetic effects aside, certainly if an actress was to work anywhere – top on or off – then Hammer always had a reputation for being a happy studio. Even though horror was not respectable, the sheer number of craftsmen, plus the presence of rare female producers, at least gave the operation a good-humoured atmosphere. Indeed, some, like Pitt, contrived to find it all very glamorous. She recalled being picked up by limo to be taken to Elstree for *Countess Dracula*, happily omitting the less glamorous fact that the film was written in order to reuse some old sets from quite a different costume drama. No matter. Hammer treated its leading ladies properly.

Indeed, the courtesy extended to all remained a feature of the studio as, after 1967, it began to drift into difficulties. These setbacks were part financial, part creative: the world was beginning to move on and films such as *Frankenstein Created Woman,* powerful though they were, were also starting to make the studio look a little quaint. The affection that had built up among audiences and critics seemed to have had the effect of softening the nature of the horrors that the studio portrayed. Come 1968 and James Carreras would oversee what was possibly the studio's finest achievement, with no one realising that it had come at the point when the Americans were starting to withdraw their money from the British film industry as a whole, while simultaneously shifting the rules of the horror film.

Chapter Nine

THE PEAK AND THE PIT

 Popular literature is strewn with forgotten authors. Who these days has ever clapped eyes on a Sax Rohmer? Or an Alistair Maclean for that matter? Ladies – when was the last time you dipped into one of the Scottish romances of Jean Plaidy? Fading fast from view currently are Sidney Sheldon, Harold Robbins and Judith Krantz. Even authors as cracklingly good as the thriller writer Eric Ambler now barely see the light of day.

Among the very bad authors – though staggeringly popular in his day – was Dennis Wheatley, who specialised in thrillers with a satanist slant. During the late 1960s and 70s, his paperbacks were to be seen on bookshelves the length and breadth of the nation, riding as he did a wave of renewed interest in the occult. Unless one was very very susceptible to being frightened by robed rituals, ceremonies involving the repeated use of the word 'astaroth', sinister prelates, pale women with bobbed hair called Tanith and wicker baskets full of black hens, the books were grindingly waffly and didactic. In the late 1960s, though, they caught a gathering wave just as the New Age movement saw its very first flowering. The very notion of devil worship became a staple of the down-market Sunday papers, always happy to latch on to the idea of suburban ceremonies involving nudity.

One man who emphatically was not a Wheatley fan, though, was the Hammer executive Anthony Hinds. Many had suggested to him that Wheatley was surely a natural for Hammer, and that the company should be snapping up the rights to the books. But Hinds possibly saw problems beyond questions of pace and turgidness.[1] If there was one subject that really got John Trevelyan and his censors going, it was black magic and the occult. In particular, anything which saw the inversion or misuse of traditional

Christian symbols was absolutely out. Hinds was happy enough to let it be. Hammer surely had enough of its own monsters without having to conjure the Horned Beast.

But in 1968, this changed, when James Carreras bought up the rights to *The Devil Rides Out*. Dennis Wheatley himself was obviously enthusiastic and swiftly suggested that Christopher Lee – who happened to be an old friend – should be cast against type in the heroic role of the Duc du Richelieu. Lee naturally was also very happy with this idea. Indeed, after filming, he informed the members of his fan club:

> I finished *The Devil Rides Out* about two weeks ago and after five extremely unpleasant nights in the rain and the damp in the woods near Pinewood Studios, down the road from Bray, I have high hopes for this film and it will prove once and for all that I can be accepted in a completely normal role.[2]

Up to a point, of course. But *The Devil Rides Out* was to prove a tremendous high point for Hammer. Terence Fisher directed with a pace and focus and urgency that he had not matched before; American writer Richard Matheson delivered a screenplay that was a masterclass in muscular economy. And the actors, among them Lee, Paul Eddington, Leon Greene, Sarah Lawson and Patrick Mower, gave performances of unusual intensity. In Hammer films, the actors normally operated to a high standard and never allowed any sense that tongues might be in cheeks; but this time round, there seemed to be an added frisson. Certainly, Charles Gray (later to be Blofeld in *Diamonds are Forever* [1971]) stepped up to the plate to give the performance of his career as the evil Mocata, ringleader of the Satan worshippers. The film also featured a characteristically striking score from James Bernard. Lee is the Duc du Richelieu who, in the course of rescuing Patrick Mower from the influence of Mocata's devilish cult, pulls Sarah Lawson's family into the struggle; they all must face assaults from the very Angel of Death himself. Contemporary audiences recall this as being the most straightforwardly frightening Hammer film of them all.

Cracking stuff – which makes it all the sadder that *Devil* faced three rival films the same year that made it look – well, a little old-fashioned.

One of these was Roman Polanski's *Rosemary's Baby* based on the novel by Ira Levin. Once again the theme was a pernicious satanic takeover; but rather than taking place in a period world of antique cars and big country houses, this was one of the first horror films to be set unambiguously and frighteningly in the present day (in fact, it was filmed in the Dakota apartment building in

New York where John Lennon was shot in 1980). Mia Farrow is not mad about her new neighbours, nor the increasingly oppressive behaviour of her husband and the stifling atmosphere of her home, nor indeed that horrible dream about being ravished by a demon. Naturally things get worse as it slowly seems to become apparent that she is carrying the devil's child.

The film still carries a nauseous punch today. The themes of alienation, oppression and sexual neurosis had been explored before by Polanski in *Repulsion* (1965), starring Catherine Deneuve, but the excesses of that film made the effect easier to shake off; here, the quiet menace exuded by husband John Cassavetes and the normal-seeming-yet-oh-so-sinister next-door neighbours actually make one want to stop watching. When boiled down, it is all nervy melodrama: but this was the first movie to make the claustrophobic inner city an extension of the tormented imagination. The film was an enormous critical and financial success. Surprising to think now that it was funded by William Castle, a schlock purveyor who had in previous years given audiences productions such as *The Tingler* (1959), which had a gimmick of cinema seats delivering mild electric shocks; *Thirteen Ghosts* (1960), which had 'Ghost-Vision' 3-D glasses; and *The House on Haunted Hill* (1958), which featured a skeleton seeming to emerge from the very screen itself. The comparative restraint of *Rosemary's Baby*, however, shifted the entire genre into a new gear; one where horror could be seen to issue from inside one's own psyche rather than being the result of rampaging monsters or calculating psychopaths.

The second American rival – even lower budget, to the extent of being shot in black and white – was *The Night of the Living Dead* (1968); it is now one of those cinema landmarks so familiar and so oft-quoted that it is easy to forget the real charge that it initially carried. This of course was the zombie picture that went further than any horror film before in depicting dismemberment, cannibalism and suchlike and is noted particularly for the gruellingly frightening farmhouse siege scene. In the US, horror had been a teen genre; films for the kids to make out at. Thus most American attempts at horror, like the Corman Poe adaptations or, as already mentioned, the bulk of William Castle's output, were usually slightly less than serious. *Living Dead* changed the terms of engagement with gore; whereas Hammer would cut away just in the nick of time before things grew too distasteful, director George A. Romero kept the camera put. There was also an apocalyptic air to *Living Dead* – the zombie plague appears to be enveloping the world, and that, combined with the near-documentary realism of the monochrome photography, gives the film a political dimension. This of course came at the height of the anti-Vietnam war movement and almost immediately the film was being hailed as a reflection of the turbulent and revolutionary atmosphere of 1968.

The third rival was a British effort, from an even lower budget outfit than Hammer or Amicus – Tigon productions. Their 1968 effort *Witchfinder General* was so spectacularly repugnant that it is still rather difficult to watch today.

Much has been written of this film: the unusual English Civil War setting, the inspiration of the real-life witchfinder Matthew Hopkins, the uncharacteristically straight and icy central performance of Vincent Price. The film's (very) young director Michael Reeves – then twenty-three – is mourned as one of the greatest directors British cinema never had: he died as the result (so the coroner found) of an accidental sleeping pill overdose a year later. And the use of Suffolk locations, beautiful landscapes contrasting with the horror of what was taking place in and around them, is justly praised.

Lethally for Hammer, though, this film also shifted the meaning of the term 'costume horror'. For Hammer, period dress was a useful means of distancing the audience from the repercussions of gory gothic horror; the use of costume meant that the films, right from the very start, occupied a certain sort of fantasy land, brutal to be sure, but none the less a world distinctly different to the one the audience knew. *Witchfinder General* eliminated that sense of distance; in the contemporary camerawork, and in the edgy sparseness of the script and the performances, this was ninety minutes of comfortless violence. For a start, there was no supernatural element – it is horrifyingly clear from the off that Matthew Hopkins's 'witches' are very obviously no such thing, and that the young women and clerics of Suffolk are falling victim to the vile 'interrogation techniques' of a brilliant, rabble-rousing sadist.

Secondly, this is a film in which virtue is portrayed as the victim throughout. From the sickening burning of a young woman lowered face down into the flames, a whole village looking on blankly, to the final psychotic breakdown of hero Richard Marshall (Ian Ogilvy) as he turns on Hopkins with an axe and sets about chopping him to pieces, audiences are left feeling a terrible mix of nausea and gloom. It is the very opposite of escapism. Romance is a helpless, delicate thing in this pitiless, filthy world. As a vision of pure inhumanity, in fact, there is little else to match it in the history of cinema.

Witchfinder General was, by 1968, something that Hammer would have had no intention of even trying to emulate. For the writers and producers, escapism was the key. However, the very thing that both James Carreras and his son Michael seemed to crave most – acceptance by the wider and more grown-up film establishment – seemed to be within their reach.

For 1968 also saw Hammer gaining the Queen's Award for Industry, a trophy handed out to those companies perceived to have done well in export terms. This was a dream come true for 'The Colonel' – the accolade of royal recognition combined with an unbeatably good publicity opportunity.

And by golly, they milked it, as the rather startled faces of the Buckingham Palace party at Bray attest.[3] It is possible that palace courtiers had not paid full attention to the nature of Hammer's output over the course of the years. When the Lord Lieutenant was sent to Bray to present the award with Carreras and Christopher Lee in attendance, the situation was fraught with the possibility of embarrassment on both sides.

James Carreras naturally could not contain his pride. 'This company,' he announced, 'has made a very real and substantial contribution to the United Kingdom's balance of payments.' He later acknowledged: '[The award] was a marvellous thing for us, because the majority of the British film industry, up to that point, regarded us as a bit of a joke.'[4]

It's a grippingly telling point that: if Pa Carreras was hankering after a little social status, the urge burned even brighter in his son Michael, who seemed later to become a little obsessive about removing the 'stigma' from the term 'Hammer films'. Fat chance. Non-Hammer actors recall talking to friends who, rather than admit what they were doing in terms of work, would simply say: 'I'm off to spend a few days at Bray.' Even to utter the word 'Hammer' was considered highly infra dig.

On the other hand, as industry expert Bryan Forbes recalls, on the production side, Hammer was actually regarded as a more than respectable operation. 'Don't forget, they made the money,' Forbes said, 'and in this business, anyone who finds a way to turn around that sort of money of course gets respect.'

Interestingly, by 1968, the phenomenon of 'Hammer Horror' had become so pervasive that the newspapers began to take note of it as a sign of the cultural times. The *People* – a Sunday red top that specialised in scandalised stories of wife-swapping and perverted clerics – suddenly decided to become hugely concerned that so many people were going to see horror films. 'Horror at any price!' yelped the headline, with the subhead: 'Can Britain really be proud of this?'

In their fact-finding mission, the paper discovered that in the space of one week, 164 cinemas in London had shown no fewer than fifty-four horror films. Warner Pathé, who at that stage were distributing the Hammer films, gleefully disclosed that each of the studio's productions could expect to get at least two million viewers. Audience members were interviewed; the motives of the young men who attended such films with their girlfriends were fairly clear. But why were so many women so happy to go along? Didn't they find these productions beyond the pale? 'I go to horror films because I like to be frightened,' said Ruth Gillespie of Cheshire, artlessly. 'But I always go with a boyfriend. I am not particularly frightened of blood, corpses, cemeteries and that kind of thing. What frightens me is something that happens without warning.'

So back to that Queen's Award for Industry, so warmly welcomed by the Carreras clan. On the day it was given, James Carreras received – and what a *fantastic* summary of an era this is – telegrams of congratulation from the following: John Trevelyan, Earl Mountbatten and Charlie Drake.[5] It is a combination somehow beyond parody.

As a treat, the Lord Lieutenant got to witness a scene being filmed: the climax of *Dracula Has Risen from the Grave* where the Count, impaled and writhing on a giant gold crucifix, is seen to weep tears of blood. Somewhat improbably after this spectacle, the Lord Lieutenant still stuck to the text of his little speech which marked the presentation of the award. 'I know you have had great success with what are termed "horror films"', he said, 'but I was glad to learn from your chairman that the word "horror" does not include scenes of actual personal violence.'[6]

The telegram from Earl Mountbatten was not a one-off, incidentally. Somehow, under the charitable auspices of the Variety Club, James Carreras had contrived to make friends with him. The Earl was a frequent visitor to the company's Wardour Street offices, where Carreras would give him lunch accompanied with the finest vintages from the Hammer cellars.[7] It is very sad that we will never know what they discussed. Perhaps Carreras was in on the alleged 1968 coup plot to depose Harold Wilson and form a National Government with Mountbatten and newspaper tycoon Cecil King? The very notion alone is worth savouring.

Whatever the nature of these cosy lunches (and how shocked son Michael was to discover that Hammer's cellars were so lavishly stocked), the Colonel was clearly consolidating his place in what he perceived to be the heart of the establishment.

And why ever not? It is the aim of businessmen everywhere. But there was a cloud around this silver lining. This official acknowledgment, almost like a Royal Seal of Approval on Hammer films, made them somehow tamer and more domesticated. In the 1950s, their shocks and their techniques had been a new and unpredictable phenomenon, but now Hammer had, fatally, become a cosily familiar institution, fondly thought of rather than recoiled from, a thing for television comedians to make light fun of with comedy fangs. If those words 'A Hammer production' came up on screen, you would know roughly what you were in for. But of course, cosiness is the enemy of suspense.

The unrelenting bleakness and savagery of *Witchfinder General* put it far beyond the Hammer pale. The fate of the young leads at the end has echoes of the black nihilism of Jacobean revenge tragedy. Alan Bennett, reviewing the film, said that it made him come away feeling physically dirty.[8] In other words, it fulfilled the ultimate function of the horror film as discussed before: the ability to lead an audience, only half-willingly, to terrible places that they have never been before and into a world where the virtuous suffer more than the immoral.

Which leads us back to *The Devil Rides Out* in which Terence Fisher's caramel-heartedness found its fullest, truest expression. Unlike many other Hammers, the good guys, led by Lee, are in the forefront from the start; they have a belief in the innate power of goodness that gives them the confidence to fight; and even at the end, when all seems lost and Mocata is about to conduct his most terrible human sacrifice, there is a moment of hocus-pocus redemption, all fogs and soft focuses that destroys him in a stroke and underlines the indomitability of the human spirit.

Yes, there are some solid frights along the way (oh, but let's *not* count the ethereal vision of the big black man who is summoned to frighten our heroes early on – this is just one of those scenes that was clearly not meant as racist but cannot help looking that way now). In particular, the scene when Charles Gray almost succeeds in hypnotising Sarah Lawson and bringing her under his control is a fine example of tight intercutting ratcheting up the suspense: it is always worth remembering that Terence Fisher was a very fine technician. And there is the set-piece that most still seem to recall as being the peak of fear: when Paul Eddington, Patrick Mower, Sarah Lawson and Christopher Lee stand within the chalk circle in the library, attempting not to be bamboozled by the forces of darkness, including a vision of a vast tarantula.

But the film must also have seemed tremendously old-fashioned to audiences, an impression not helped by the prolific use of vintage cars which accidentally served as a reminder of the gentle comedy *Genevieve*. For all the creepiness of the night shoots (proper ones, not the 'day for night' efforts that audiences were used to) and even the evocation of the Devil himself as a shimmering, hazy goat figure, this was the first of the Hammers that in moral tones felt on the same level as the Universal pictures of the 1930s and 40s. This makes it wonderfully and easily watchable today; but it was a clear indication that Hammer had grown up – and cinema audiences on the whole had not.

It did tremendous business in the UK but, talking of another contemporaneous Hammer film, one critic noted: 'Time has stopped at Bray Studios and they're still making "B" pictures for a market that was willing to queue in the rain for Stewart Grainger and Patricia Roe.'[9] For all his hankering to be accepted as an above-the-salt studio chairman, Carreras knew this too.

And so now we can see that it is a huge shame. To take a different series of cheapo, popular films: in much the way that *Carry On Up the Khyber* is now regarded as a legitimate classic of British cinema, shining out from among the general dross of this series, *The Devil Rides Out* represents the same sort of high point for Hammer. It was a moment when director, screenwriter and actors were all in perfect agreement about the deadly earnestness of the story. Because a young family is involved, the stakes are that much higher; and Christopher Lee clearly adores every minute of being, for once, the authoritative good guy and delivers all his lines, as opposed to refusing to speak any of them at all.

This was also Terence Fisher's finest moment. It is true that many continue to hail his uncanny powers of directorial genius – there are still a great many Hammer devotees in France and his is also a regular name on film studies university circuits over here – but the truth is that Fisher himself would probably have been rather surprised at the level of attention these films have received over the years. While it is true that he had a terrific eye for colour and a genuinely exciting sense of pace and camera movement, we do have to recall that he was mainly directing scripts of the highest absurdity. Thus Francis Matthews, who suffered convulsions of laughter during production of *Dracula – Prince of Darkness* (1966):

> So there we are. My screen brother has been stabbed, my screen wife
> is being threatened by old toothy ... and I appear at the top of the
> stairs and shout 'leave her alone!' I mean, if someone with bright red
> eyes and vast pointy teeth is bearing down on your wife, that is not
> the expression you would immediately use.

No such hysteria on the set of *The Devil Rides Out*. Many actors recall that Christopher Lee was at heart a serious soul and this film meant a very great deal to him. And he has good reason to be proud. Thanks to Fisher and Lee, this is one of the Hammers that translates best for non-Hammer fans, those who normally cannot bear the films.

But the world had moved on. The studio itself, by this stage, had physically moved on. Come 1967 and the company packed up and bade farewell to Bray Studios. Despite the uniqueness of the atmosphere, and the way that the small scale meant the crew could fully focus on each production, Hammer had started to outgrow its old home. The back-to-back efforts of Rasputins and Draculas were now starting to become a little obvious even to the dopiest audience members: there are only so many times that a set can be recycled, no matter how ingeniously it was done by the designer Bernard Robinson. By the time they shot the previous year's *Frankenstein Created Woman*, that middle-European village, with its higgledy-piggledy rooftops, weird bridge over nothing in particular and naturally the village inn by the square were almost beyond a joke. Familiarity was one thing. Insane repetition was another. More space was needed. It was felt by Carreras that the films needed room to breathe. This would mean relocating to the very much larger studios at Elstree in Hertfordshire, and mucking in with all the other productions using those studios at that time, including television series such as *The Saint*.

There are some though who would cite the abandonment of Bray as marking the end of the studio's golden era – believing that within those incredibly enclosed spaces, designers and directors were inspired to heights of ingenuity that could never be replicated elsewhere. Certainly the other trappings of the place would come to be missed by the crew, with one actor recalling, misty-eyed, the Bray canteen and the fact that the cook, Mrs Thompson, prepared roasts every single day, no matter what, and 'perfect bacon sarnies' first thing in the morning when everyone had arrived by coach from West London. Another remembers the brilliance of designer Bernard Robinson, working from a shed built on to the side of Down Place, producing props and replicas and often showing fascinated actors how it was all done. 'Hammer wasn't starry at all,' said Francis Matthews. 'Everyone really did get on like a family and you would often find yourself learning about camera technique from people such as Jack Asher. Bray really had a unique atmosphere in that sense.'

The world was changing in other ways too. Since the mid-1960s, the US had become embroiled deeper and further in the Vietnam war and this was starting to have repercussions across the American economy. In the 1950s and 60s, an enormous number of American film-makers and stars had come to Britain, with the result that Borehamwood, Herts, was becoming known as 'Little Hollywood'. And it was not only Hammer films that were largely funded with dollars – the same was true of almost every other film made on British soil in that period. One actor recalls that in that sense, it was a terrific time to be working: 'There were just so many films being made and one knew that no matter what one was working on, Ingrid Bergman could have been in the studio next door.'

Vietnam began to change that. Hollywood, already hit incredibly hard by the accelerating popularity of television, was now facing a scenario in which the US government did not want to see funding going overseas. Bryan Forbes, who became managing director of Rank EMI in 1969, recalls that there was another factor: the big Hollywood studios, from MGM to Paramount, were slowly losing their autocratic bosses, the Cukors, the Thalbergs, the Selznicks, and no one was taking the place of these men at the head of what were becoming faceless corporations. Cutbacks were the new order of the day. The industry was being rationalised and taken over, as Forbes sees it, by businessmen who had no natural feel for the medium. Where once a director could get an instant decision on a pitch for a film, now each production had to go through increasingly uninspiring and uninspired committees.

So like a mighty tide receding, American dollars began to disappear from the British film industry. In 1968, the process was just beginning. By the end of the decade, it would bring all the British studios into a state of acute crisis.

Hammer was among the first to feel it. Over the last few years, through good contacts and assiduous schmoozing, James Carreras had contrived to keep the American markets very interested in Hammer, securing funding and US distribution from Universal, Columbia and Warners. The Warners/Seven Arts deal was brokered through Carreras's old friend Eliot Hyman, who had been involved on the finance side from *The Curse of Frankenstein* onward. By 1968, the climate was looking rather cooler and although Hammer still had an awesome production line, Warners was becoming a trickier customer to deal with.[10]

The previous year, for instance, had seen the adaptation of Nigel Kneale's *Quatermass and the Pit*, a quite brilliant BBC serial brought into Technicolor by Roy Ward Baker and this time starring Andrew Keir as opposed to Brian Donlevy as the titular scientist. *Quatermass* was still very fondly remembered in England and the film, the story of which contrived to merge science fiction and the occult, explaining mankind's belief in demons as the result of ancient alien intervention, did reasonable business. Warners, however, were slightly puzzled by it, not understanding the context of its television success, and the confusion was reflected in that American title *Five Million Years to Earth*.

Warners were not pleased by *The Devil Rides Out* either, although this was on the grounds that the subject of Satan worship was not altogether a proper one for a film (as if fanged creatures leaping out of coffins was). First, there was a suggestion that they thought, from the title, that it was a western. This is unlikely. In fact, the very idea of the film caused a flurry of nervousness and disquiet in the Warners offices and these views were conveyed to James Carreras. The thrust of messages coming across the Atlantic was that after *Devil*, *Quatermass* and the oddity that was *The Lost Continent*, the Americans wanted Hammer to return to its core business.[11] That, of course, meant further adventures for Dracula and Baron Frankenstein. But even with these big hitters in the pipeline, US funding was no longer quite the done deal that it used to be and Hammer, for the first time, was beginning to feel the slowly strengthening breeze of change.

1968's *Dracula Has Risen from the Grave* was pretty much the last manifestation of an untroubled, straightforward, anxiety-free Hammer production. Although it was a setback that Terence Fisher was out of commission (having been run over and injured by a bus in Richmond), Freddie Francis stepped up to the directorial plate and Aida Young found herself producing her first gothic horror. As discussed before, the film, involving some ice, a monsignor, a big cross and an angry Count, somehow managed to eke eighty-eight minutes out of a very thin and frankly illogical scenario. But owing to some lively acting from Rupert Davies, Veronica Carlson and Barbara Ewing, and some rather stylish use of colour filters from Francis, giving Lee's Count a green-and-yellow-edged hue of decay, this was one of the studio's most enjoyable films. Dracula points imperiously, young romantic leads negotiate studio-bound rooftops, priests climb a painted hill to a painted castle and – of course – those rather amazing tears of blood that Dracula sheds at the end. Next to *Witchfinder General* and *Rosemary's Baby*, it all looks puppyishly innocent; Dracula's network of evil never seems to extend much further than the village inn and even the saucy barmaid has a heart of gold and would never dream – unlike the bar-scene slatterns in *Witchfinder* – of getting her bosoms out. Perhaps knowing of the forthcoming Queen's Award, the entire studio had subconsciously put itself on best behaviour, imagining somehow that Her Majesty and Prince Phillip would be settling down to watch (there is no evidence, incidentally, that they did any such thing).

Come 1969, and another social barrier was crossed by James Carreras: the resistance to letting it all hang out was finally dropped. From then on, the very identity of Hammer was to subtly morph; but it was too little, too late at this point, when the scouring effects of recession in the film industry were beginning to bite.

Chapter Ten

PURPLE HAZE

'I believe implicitly in everything I do in terror pictures,' wrote Peter Cushing in his autobiography.

> Because I believe there is a public demand for this type
> of escapist entertainment. They are, after all, harmless
> outlets for what might otherwise be awkward tensions in
> people. I believe in the characters I play and the weird
and uncanny games they get up to. I have to believe. It is the only
way I prevent myself and my pictures being laughed out of the
cinemas. By believing what I am acting in ... I am able to give greater
credulity to the character and the picture so to strike the necessary
note of authenticity to capture the audience's true attention.[1]

Anyone who knew Cushing paid testament, first, to his sweetness of nature
and, second, to the astonishing sincerity of his acting when it came to what
he termed these 'terror pictures'. Actor John Standing recalls that when
Cushing was not filming, he was a brilliant water-colourist. Other fellow
actors remember visiting him at his home in Whitstable, Kent, and spending
afternoons 'helpless with laughter'.

A literary friend of mine recalls that Cushing was a family friend, and as
a boy, he was taken to visit the actor one day in the 1970s; my friend, at that
young age, happened to be a huge fan of Christopher Lee. Cushing picked
up on this and asked if my friend would like to speak to Lee? He dialled
Lee's telephone number, and handed the receiver over to my friend as Lee
said hello and asked him how he was. My friend was simply too nervous to
say a word. Lee kindly pressed on with more questions, making my friend
even more dumbstruck with terrified nerves. Then Lee said, with kindly
patience: 'Can you now put me back on to my friend Peter?'

One senses that this sort of thing was happening the whole time. But the point is that Cushing and Lee were to remain the firmest of friends throughout those decades. And this was a recurring feature of life at the studio itself. Kate O'Mara similarly recalls that instead of the on-set tensions that were a feature of life at many other studios, unexpected friendships were cemented at Hammer. Indeed, she and Cushing became great pals, going to the cinema together to see such productions as *Bonnie and Clyde*.

And Cushing also had a quality of loyalty that's quite difficult to imagine today. As Hammer pitched towards a new decade with an apparent darkening of heart – a purely temporary darkening, as it thankfully turned out – the actor stood firm and did not turn away from these films.

As mentioned before, the rape scene in *Frankenstein Must be Destroyed* must have been a signal to Cushing that Hammer was at that stage in danger of becoming too brutalised an operation. The truly hideous irony is that even though it was the American backers, Warners, who demanded the scene, it was in fact the American censors who cut it out when the film came to be screened in the US. But it was only the start, and the terrible thing was that James Carreras could not see a problem. The future as he saw it was looking sexier.

And it was a future that the long-term producer/writer Anthony Hinds felt that he could not quite accept. Son of Will Hinds (Hammer) and in many respects, the main founder of Hammer's gothic success, Hinds found by 1969 that his taste for it was gone.[2] Of course, he had inherited Will Hammer's wealth, and so there was no real pressing need for him by then to continue working. But on top of this – after a year spent supervising the production of a Hammer co-foray into television called *Journey into The Unknown* – he could sense what was coming to the film studio and he wanted no part of it.

Hinds said some years later:

> I did not like the change that came after I left, when it was thought that the films would have increased audience appeal by making them soft porn shows. I thought the originals were sexy enough without having to resort to tired music hall tricks ... but Carreras thought [relaxed censorship] was great. He was a showman. He told me: 'God, you can do anything now.'[3]

Carreras, as ever, was nothing if not an enthusiast. But by 1969/70, the American backing for the films was looking ever dicier. And the solution was of course to risk infuriating Christopher Lee time and again with an increased number of Dracula sequels. *Taste the Blood of Dracula* (1970) in truth contained little that would have caused the censors to gag; its evocation of an East End Victorian brothel is in fact inadvertently hilarious, not helped by the presence of Peter Sallis, and Russell Hunter as the camp brothel keeper. There was a shade more Kensington gore splattered around. Indeed, one special-effects assistant recalled an unfortunate accident involving Peter Sallis. Mike Tilley told the *Sunday Mirror*:

> There was a dramatic scene where he discovered his daughter is a vampire, She rises from the grave and plunges a stake into his heart. Peter was wearing a false chest with 'blood' pumped in with a bicycle pump so that when the stake punctured it, the blood shot all over his shirt. Unfortunately we pumped too much blood into the false chest with the result that Peter's shirt remained Persil white while the cameraman ten yards away was drenched.

Yet by this stage, the studio was popular with actors, especially those starting out, because the roles it offered were always substantial enough to be inter-esting. One such actor was Martin Jarvis, who was appearing at Bernard Miles's Mermaid Theatre when he was asked by producer Aida Young if he would like to take the part of the romantic lead in *Taste the Blood of Dracula*. For a screen debut, Jarvis realised that this would be a terrific part. However, Bernard Miles would not allow Jarvis to take time out from his stage commitment and the young actor instead got the lesser part of Jeremy. 'Although Aida Young very kindly made sure that I was paid the same amount of money as I would have been for the lead,' says Jarvis. He recalls:

> There was a lot of hilarity on set, and Peter Sasdy, a Hungarian, was a strong, enthusiastic director. Isla Blair and I had a scene where she was fanging me and it was at this time that we realised one of the big drawbacks of fang-acting. Isla had to lure me into this garden and, with those teeth in, but not showing them, had to say the line 'Kiss me, Jeremy.' Try it. It's very difficult without drooling and looking absurd. We were helpless with laughter. Christopher Lee was getting crosser and crosser and saying, 'Now look, I think you two had better leave the set until you can control yourselves.' Then came the biting itself where Isla did finally show the teeth. But in order to properly show fangs, you have to open your mouth into this enormous wide smile. That set us off all over again.

Even though Martin Jarvis was not in the brothel scene, it was none the less to prove a source of some embarrassment to him.

> Because this was my film debut, I took my mother to see it. There was no premiere of course, this film just sort of slid out, so we saw it at the Apollo Victoria. Then of course this scene flashes up with a bare-breasted girl – it probably doesn't seem like very much now, but back then ... my mother said: 'I think I preferred you in *The Forsyte Saga*.'

That aside, this was still – in relative terms – very much a buttoned-up Hammer affair. One of the last, it transpires. The other important production from that year, *Frankenstein Must be Destroyed*, had that new note of brutality in the rape scene – but other than that jarring element, it was thoughtful, well-written and nicely played. Frankenstein's scheme this time involves a brilliant scientist, Dr Brandt, who is going mad. The Baron needs his knowledge and so plans a rather drastic cure: that is, transplanting Brandt's brain into another body. On the face of it, the idea is almost altruistic. But in this entry, Frankenstein has become an icy blackmailer, coercing help from young Simon Ward and Veronica Carlson. And what is Mrs Brandt supposed to make of it all? Together, Terence Fisher and actor Freddie Jones, as post-transplant Dr Brandt, made this the most melancholic and moving of the Frankensteins, where for once we can see the full emotional consequences of the Baron's dabblings, and the impact that he has on the lives of those around him. By the end, Dr Brandt is having none of it in his new body; and having seen the murderous lengths Frankenstein is willing to go to in pursuit of knowledge, he traps the scientist in a burning house and they both perish. No subsequent Hammer would be quite so serious or sombre.

Indeed, as the decade changed and the face of cinema transformed in the wake of the classification shake-up, Hammers were going to have to evolve in new directions.

By 1969, the quest to be accepted into the establishment lost a little of its urgency for James Carreras: for that is the year that he received his knighthood from Buckingham Palace and became Sir James.

What greater accolade (save a peerage) could be bestowed on a man who had cornered a rather downmarket corner of the film industry and largely made it his own? What sweeter triumph could there be for a man whose family had largely made its wealth from cigarettes and who craved greater social acceptance? It is worth speculating whether Carreras's friend Earl Mountbatten might have had a small part to play in Carreras being recommended for this honour. Whatever the case, it came at an extraordinary time: in re-classifying 'X' films, John Trevelyan had raised the bar for increased nudity and violence in adult films and Carreras was in no doubt that extra sex and violence were exactly what was needed. And with his knighthood safely attained, he had no further anxieties about making films that were deemed acceptable in the eyes of the cinema – and wider – establishment.

To be fair, neither did anyone else. What was behind the epidemic of permissiveness that swept the British entertainment industry in the late 1960s and early 70s? Was it purely the result of middle-aged producers and

Christopher Lee looking larky with his red contact lenses in. (1970)

Red-coated toffs ride through Hammer's much-used village set for *Plague of the Zombies* (1966)

Christopher Lee welcomes Jenny Hanley and Dennis Waterman into his garishly redecorated castle in *Scars of Dracula* (1970)

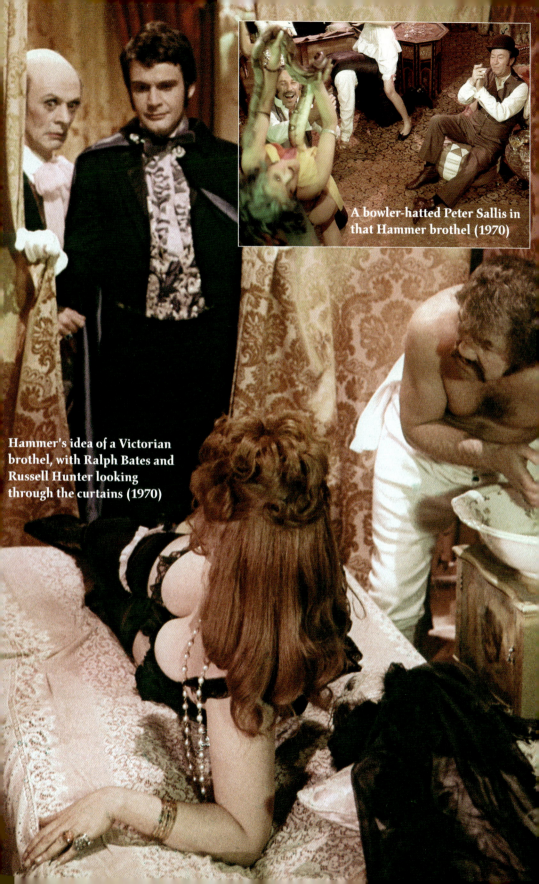

A bowler-hatted Peter Sallis in that Hammer brothel (1970)

Hammer's idea of a Victorian brothel, with Ralph Bates and Russell Hunter looking through the curtains (1970)

The quintessential Hammer inn, where strangers generally are welcome.

The finest inn landlord of them all: brilliant character actor Michael Ripper.

Some Oscar-worthy rubber bat acting in *Kiss of the Vampire* (1964)

Jennifer Daniel dashes through a (non-nocturnal) forest in a nightie in *Kiss of the Vampire* (1964)

The young cast of *Taste* take a location tea break (1970)

Isla Blair and Martin Jarvis (and horse) looking jolly on location for *Taste the Blood...* (1970)

Isla Blair — as tradition demands — about to be bitten in the middle of a wood (1970)

The Transylvanian coachman refuses to take anyone a step further. (1965)

Veronica Carlson strikes a tasteful pose by a grave in a nightie (1968)

directors getting overheated by the perceived permissiveness of youth, and simply attempting to join in the free for all? Or was there a genuine widespread public appetite for more and more tit and bum, and more and more gore? No matter how tasteless those years are now judged to be, it is difficult to believe that the latter could have been the case.

But look at what was happening to film generally: *Soldier Blue*; *Straw Dogs*; *Bonnie and Clyde*; a Norman Wisdom sex comedy – and no, we can't go blaming the background noise of the Vietnam war for that. (Nor indeed the social repercussions of cabinet minister Barbara Castle and the perceived union-baiting of her 'In Place of Strife' measures.) Nor the cynicism of slippery old Harold Wilson. Nor the economic consequences of the 1967 devaluation crisis which haunted his increasingly beleaguered government.

Television, some might say, was indirectly to blame – the advent in 1969 of colour television was a further blow to an ailing British film industry. With colour television, the last novelty of the widescreen, that of Technicolor, was wiped out. And it is certainly true that by this stage, with over ninety per cent of British households having access to a set and firmly staying in of an evening to watch it, it is easy to see how film producers and cinema managers alike would have been panicked into doing anything they could think of to lure the punters back.

Changing demographics, too, one might say – in the sense that a new young generation of film-goers needed films that would speak to them directly, and that the bead-wearing supposedly bed-hopping young people of 1969 were concerned to see everything hanging out. It might be, in a charitable view, that older film-makers were desperately trying to get the measure of a youth that they signally failed to understand, like a well-meaning dad putting on a *Top of the Pops* compilation album at a party.

But no. There are some episodes in film history that can only reasonably be attributed to the salivating efforts of claret-nosed, grey-haired, pot-bellied men, aroused at the prospect of making films with more flesh.

Flesh came in the form of *Countess Dracula* and *The Vampire Lovers*; meanwhile, a younger, fresher-faced cast was assembled for the almost compulsory *The Horror of Frankenstein* (1970). It was here, for one film only, that Peter Cushing had to relinquish the role of the Baron – not through choice, but because the script was a rerun of *The Curse of Frankenstein*, casting the Baron once again as a young man. So it was that publicity pictures were taken of Cushing shaking hands with his long-haired successor Ralph Bates, who was now pretty much the golden boy of Hammer.

In the meantime, the departure of Hinds led to a creative as well as an executive gap within the studio and it was at this point that Sir James Carreras suddenly found his workload increasing rather dramatically; it was he who had to make decisions on all the films that would go into production.[4]

But Carreras knew that with the departure of Hinds, the studio needed a little creative stability and so it was that he managed – at some cost – to lure screenwriter Jimmy Sangster back from the US where he had been engaged in lucrative television projects. But writing was not enough for Sangster in this case – he needed a bigger draw than that to bring him back. And so Carreras offered him the chance to direct *The Horror of Frankenstein* as well.

Sangster certainly had a jolly time doing so, but it was one of the few times that Hammer really badly slipped not only in terms of tone but also in production values. The body-builder Dave Prowse, almost omnipresent on 1970s screens, would have exuded more menace as the Green Cross Code Man than under the half-hearted monster make-up – a hugely unconvincing square-headed effort – that was contrived for him. Kate O'Mara, Veronica Carlson and Ralph Bates come at it all with some enjoyment and gusto but one never knows if one is actually supposed to be laughing, or whether indeed the comedy was intentional at all – fairly lethal for something that is in essence a spoof.

These days, Kate O'Mara is slightly more forgiving of the whole thing, even though, some thirty-seven years on, she has yet to actually see the film. Indeed, she relates how she was staying in a hotel one night and fell asleep with the television on. She awoke in the small hours, looked at the screen and recognised the set of Castle Frankenstein. Then she realised that her character Alys was going to walk on at any second – and she leaped up to turn the television off. But, that said ...

> I had the sense, that even though there was more sex and violence –
> and at the time, I was really getting some quite dodgy offers –
> Hammer were playing a slightly different game. There was that sense
> of a silent conspiracy between the producers and the audience, that
> both sides knew that nothing really terrible was ever going to happen.
> Hammer was a serious operation, yes. And both Sir James and
> Michael Carreras were both very gung-ho. But on that film, there was
> more of a sense of humour coming in, more black comedy.

Miss O'Mara is to be excused, not being a Hammer aficionado herself, for not knowing that there had been quite enough dry humour in the films as it was and that 'Horror' tipped the balance just too far even for Hammer. Just one year previously in *Frankenstein Must be Destroyed*, Cushing was on top of his form as the Baron, solemnly telling unwilling assistant Simon Ward not to 'invoke the name of the Almighty – he'll be cross enough as it is.'

But what would get the pulses of those hip young things racing? 1970 brought yet another Dracula sequel, just minutes after the last. *The Scars of Dracula* was the film of which producer Aida Young said: 'It was the beginning of the end and everyone knew it.'[5] She wasn't quite right about this; there were still some excellent, inventive and exciting entries to come from the studio as the 1970s progressed. But *Scars* was an unfortunate blip.

Quite aside from the anorexically thin plot – Dracula kills Christopher Matthews, then Dennis Waterman and Jenny Hanley go to the castle to look for him and have to take on the Count themselves – the film actually looked different, and this was true of *The Horror of Frankenstein* as well.

The sets weren't right – they gave the impression that Dracula lived in a branch of the Angus Steak House. The make-up, as Lee has said, was all wrong, making the Count look like an etiolated Uncle Monty. And even the quality of the celluloid seemed different. The fact was that veteran Hammer set designer Bernard Robinson had died. His absence makes one realise just how vital his role really was. On top of this, Jack Asher had long stepped down from the role of cinematographer. It is said in some quarters that Hammer could not afford him any more – not because of his wage packet, but because of the time-consuming lengths that he went to to get everything just right. By the time *The Scars of Dracula* came to be produced, the joins, which had never previously shown, were disconcertingly on display. We cut from the young leads dashing through a sunlit forest straight to a darkened studio and cardboard battlements, the floor wreathed with the sort of mist seen most usually in BBC light entertainment shows.

And those young leads! Actually, it is not the fault of the youthful Dennis Waterman (as a matter of interest, his agent told me that he would be altogether too busy to discuss the subject of Hammer for this book and I suppose if I had starred in such a stinker, I'd be reluctant to discuss it too). In fact, he and Jenny Hanley do their best to give the thing some oomph. But what can one do in the face of manservant Patrick Troughton sailing over the top and Dracula apparently wearing Biba make-up?

Not to mention Anouska Hempel as vampire lady Tania. Again, this is in no way Hempel's fault, but the role itself is so very bad as to be ironically iconic. Tania is there near the beginning of the film, purple-gowned, eyebrows painted on, eyes wide and goggling in simulation of hypnotic eroticism. Tania would appear to be Dracula's live-in girlfriend, welcoming young protagonist Christopher Matthews into the Angus Steak House baronial hall, complete with crystal drinks cabinet. Matthews is shown to bed – there is a touch of the Radisson Edwardian about his room – and back in the hall, Dracula and his lady friend indulge in a saucy bite. But then, inexplicably, Tania scoots off to Matthews's room, lures him into bed and seduces him. In the early hours, Dracula bursts in and stabs Tania to death in a rage. Matthews is thrown out of bed and is seen to be sporting – unusual, this, for the late Victorian age – a pair of tight scarlet briefs.

Poor Christopher Lee! What was anyone to make of this unmotivated bilge? By the time Dennis Waterman and Jenny Hanley turn up even they look wan with embarrassment. When Lee hands Waterman a goblet of wine from that crystal cocktail cabinet, it is almost as if the two cannot meet each other's eyes, so awkward has the whole thing become. The only saving grace is Waterman's never-heard-since posh accent.

It was a further sign that the studio had no idea how to address the younger generation they were attempting to lure in.

By this stage also, the question of funding and distribution was becoming increasingly precarious. Warners were pulling out,[6] just as American money was haemorrhaging from the British film industry as a whole. And as for American distribution – if Hammer could not guarantee that they would get on to those screens, then the funding would become even patchier. A deal with American International Pictures was to follow, but it was short-lived. The studio tried mummies, lesbians, everything. The only thing was to deal with the younger generation on their own terms.

There is a film made in 1972 – one of a crop of exquisitely bad British films released that year – called *Father Dear Father* starring Patrick Cargill and based on a TV sitcom about a divorced middle-aged man and his two teenaged daughters. The opening scene features Cargill's very posh house being used for a teenage party. The pop music playing on the turntable is an electric guitar version of Saint Saëns. Dancing involves moving the hips very slightly to the right, then to the left. An ornament gets slightly broken. By curious coincidence, the first post-credits scene of *Dracula AD 1972* features almost identical action, except that the one in *Father Dear Father* has greater dramatic tension.

What Hammer seemed to be saying to its loyal audience was: 'Hey – these colourless long-haired loon-panted Herberts are what we think *you* are.' Again, this is not the fault of the actors. Indeed, special commendations for top performances in trying circumstances go to Stephanie Beacham as Van Helsing's daughter and Michael Coles as the amusingly lugubrious police inspector trying to keep up with the kooky neck-biting action.

I just have to say at this point – hand held high – that *AD 1972* is one of my favourite Hammers. This preference can't be explained, it just is, that's all. Against all odds, it's an insanely cheering (and hypnotically watchable) production. Not because it's 'so bad, it's good' – but because, I suppose, that no matter how illogical and naff it all is, there is tremendously good humour running throughout it. Plus also a sigh-inducing nostalgia for the days when the King's Road wasn't a super-glitzy high street for impossibly rich people, but a faintly tatty parade for gormless teenagers. Plus, the narrative just seems to work. Crushed velvet aesthetics aside, you do, slightly against your will, genuinely want to know what is going to happen. And it's funny.

In theory, there was no reason why the old Count shouldn't work in the present day and in this he did manage to confine his activities to a ruined church, which at least allowed him to preserve a little dignity. Perhaps the ceaselessly skew-angled camerawork militated against it. Plus the Hammond Organ/squealy saxophone score. 'The Count is back with an eye for London's hotpants – and a taste for everything!' yelped the artless poster. The film should be preserved by English Heritage or at the very least donated to the Victoria and Albert museum. And by golly, those purple-lit eighty-four minutes scoot by. But again, with contemporary audiences, the effect was disastrous. They saw it as neither proper horror nor pop comedy; they couldn't really see what it was supposed to be. Having said that, the film made enough money to justify just one more crack of the Count's whip a year later.

We might be tempted to state that these films, in all their uncertainty of tone, reflected the general tenor of the early 1970s. Were these years expected to be continuing the spirit of the 1960s? Or was everything due to crash? And Britain then was an even weirder hybrid than it had been throughout the previous decade. Left-wing agitprop and maxi-skirts jostled in close proximity to the slightly flared pinstripe suits of the rapacious property developers. The Conservatives under Edward Heath were in, as indeed were cravats and tie-dyed T-shirts. The Vietnam war was dragging bloodily on and had seeped its way right into the very core of American culture. Britain, heavily unionised, was experiencing further industrial unrest, and would see a very great deal more as the decade progressed. The cost of living rose inexorably. It was an ugly, shabby country. From the black, soot-encrusted buildings standing in litter-strewn city centres, to the relentless awfulness of the food (who remembers that restaurant chain The Golden Egg?), to the proliferation of grey pre-cast concrete council blocks and office skyscrapers, to the ubiquitous crackle of purple and brown synthetic fibres, this was not a good time to be a delicate aesthete. In cultural terms, it is little wonder that Hammer was up a gum tree; when the most popular comedians on television were Benny Hill and Dick Emery and when the most talked-about film was the pompous pornography of *Last Tango In Paris* (1972), how could one gauge what the fast-evaporating cinema audiences really wanted?

And for most of the British film industry, the game was almost up. The Yanks had gone home; Rank, once the towering titan, was foundering desperately and had gone into business with EMI. It was around this time that the ever-canny Sir James Carreras started reeling in a few of those old contacts and managed to strike up a deal with EMI for six new Hammer films in 1970.

Among them was the Carmilla sequel *Lust for a Vampire*; the thoughtful title was a suggestion from Rank/EMI chairman (and temporary Hammer business partner) Bernard Delfont.[7]

In fact, this and the other EMI funded Hammer efforts were a matter of some bemusement to the young managing director of Rank EMI, Bryan Forbes. While Forbes was producing successful family films such as *The Railway Children* (1970) and *The Tales of Beatrix Potter* (1971), there was this diametrically opposed activity going on on the other side of Elstree, under an incredibly byzantine budget arrangement whereby EMI got its investment back only when three of these Hammer productions were deemed to have gone into profit. 'It wasn't ideal,' said Forbes. 'And it's not really my genre. But they were turning them out and there is certainly a skill to making horror films. It's not something that I could have done.'

But *Lust for a Vampire* was a perfect indicator of the fraying reality behind Hammer's ever-confident and permissive facade. Not that Carreras let this show. The press excitedly got hold of the idea that *Lust* would feature an actress getting out of a bath with what used to be known as a 'full-frontal' view. Carreras was insouciant. 'It's cheaper,' he said, 'because we don't have to pay for a towel.'[8]

Ingrid Pitt was unavailable for this one, starring as she was in *Countess Dracula*. And Terence Fisher was unavailable for directing purposes, having been in another traffic accident. Also poor Peter Cushing could not be involved, as he was grieving for his beloved wife Helen. So this time novice Yutte Stensgard took the Pitt role as Carmilla and Jimmy Sangster, who had not learned his lesson after *The Horror of Frankenstein*, elected to direct again. And the ever-obliging Ralph Bates stepped into Cushing's shoes.

This is one of the very few Hammers that is simply unwatchable. It is not just a question of the galumphing script (thank you so much, the improbably named Tudor Gates), the worse-than-cardboard set design or the frankly weird acting. It is that as a whole, the film is entirely purposeless, failing either to frighten or titillate. It does nothing. It is a void. And you will never ever be able to reclaim the eighty-four minutes spent watching it, so don't. This, by the way, was pretty much the judgement on the film made at the studio too. And it was clear to Sir James that things could not go on like this, otherwise Hammer would simply dissolve, like the Count.

Now, the studio had already lost the services of Anthony Hinds as a screenwriter. In 1970, he also resigned from the board of the studio. See how quickly the *Lust for a Vampire* debacle followed. In his absence, and at this delicate stage for the British film industry, Sir James found himself buried under a stream of job applications from would-be writers and producers – for the simple reason that Hammer was now one of the very few companies that was still left making films. The tatty old Carmilla cycle had been pitched by freelance producer Harry Fine, who had promised that it would 'always be in good taste';[9] classier acts such as Brian Clemens and Albert Fennell of *Avengers* fame were also at Carreras's door. Indeed, Clemens seemed a little sharper about the formula, declaring that the only necessary ingredients for Hammer success were: 'Blood, boobs, and a good title.'[10] But Carreras needed another pair of eyes. Someone who could offer alternative judgements. Someone who could help him divine the viability – and relative tastefulness – of a production.

And so, in December 1970, the call went out for the prodigal son to come home. Sir James wanted his son Michael to rejoin him, to see Hammer through these tricky times. He offered his freelance son the title of Executive Producer. Michael chewed this over – and then turned it down.[11]

Sir James was not at all happy about being defied by his son in this fashion and there was a short stand-off between them, both behaving equally implacably. Then a little while later, Sir James gave in. Michael became Managing Director of Hammer, finally guaranteeing him a loud say in the future of the company. Meanwhile, the accountant Roy Skeggs was appointed Production Supervisor. Carreras senior remained the ebullient beaming optimist chairman but had things already gone too far?

'One other factor in the downward spiral of the industry,' said Kate O'Mara who, like many other actors, found that particular period very trying, 'is that for some reason, the notion of pure escapism went out of the window. And increasing levels of sex and violence – violence is bad enough but the combination is a really unhealthy one – made it even harder to get the idea of escapism back.'

Not that this appearance of a harder heart seemed to have got through to the young audience. Indeed, there were occasions when Michael Carreras found the devoted Hammer fan-base a little younger than he would have thought. For instance, he was once forwarded this letter, which had been addressed to 'Count Dracula Castle, Transylvania, Romania,' and which the post office larkily sent on to Hammer in Wardour Street. It read: 'Dear Count Dracula, would you please vampirise my sister because she is a pest and always pinching my books and things. Yours sincerely, John. PS she doesn't leave her window open so you will have to find another way in.'

For the more regular teenage audience, Hammer had made a bit of an effort to swing, but had crucially left it about five or six years too late. We will give the company credit for one real-life youth craze in the early 1970s though. It involved Highgate Cemetery, in North London, used as a location for *Taste the Blood of Dracula*. The episode is evidence, if evidence is needed, that Hammer's idea of vampires had thoroughly percolated British society.

Highgate, by that stage, was a sorry ruin, a once breathtaking Victorian necropolis, vast and rambling, with streets of tombs cut into the hillside and bordered with thick foliage, it had long-since been closed up and was neglected. In the early 1970s, it became the target for occultist thrill-seekers, not unlike those groovily portrayed in *Dracula AD 1972*. An urban myth began, not too long after the Dracula film, that the cemetery was haunted by a black-garbed, white-faced vampire. Two local women, with flats overlooking the cemetery, claimed to have been bitten in the neck. So, having dropped tabs and swigged Skol, these thrillseekers shimmied over the walls of the old cemetery and, in a haze, set about vampire hunting.

It might just have seemed like jolly nocturnal japes – except tombs were broken into and defiled and occult paraphernalia was scattered about the place. This cemetery invasion became a semi-frequent occurrence – and it all came to a head one summer night when swarms of proto-vampire hunters climbed into the vast cemetery and larked about in those crescents of tombs before what used to be termed 'the fuzz' turned up. Indeed, the fuzz presented itself in force and arrests were made. Go on to the web and you will still find voluble eccentrics protesting the truth of the Highgate Vampire to this day. But a black-garbed, white-faced vampire? Now where could such an idea have come from? As a tribute to the all-conquering pervasiveness of Hammer films at that time, it is possibly a little inappropriate. But it is a good illustration none the less. Vampires were by now as much a part of British life as sliced white bread and Morecambe and Wise. So in a sense, the quality of the films by this stage did not matter so much; the films themselves had become woven into the fabric of the nation's culture – potent pop cultural icons. This perhaps is why audiences, feeling increasingly familiar with them, did not bother to go and see them.

Poor old Hammer. The truth was that as the 1970s dawned, the entire British film industry was in the same sorry state. EMI/Rank was riven with internal disputes; production costs were rising inexorably, thanks to the march of inflation; the Americans in the shape of Warners and MGM had all but buggered off. And here we were left with high streets still stubbornly filled with ABCs and Odeons, which couldn't keep showing the same films for weeks on end. The notion of cinema being entertainment for the family had somehow died off as well; at this time, it was reckoned that about sixty per cent of films released carried an adult 'X' certificate, which generally meant more and more nudity and increasingly harrowing violence. What disturbed reality had led to this cinematic breakdown? And in the midst of the Swedish soft porn double-bills that were increasingly becoming the staple of suburban Odeons, what possible direction could Hammer Films take in order to safeguard its future?

Chapter Eleven

COMIC
MISUNDERSTANDINGS

No book focusing on the Hammer phenomenon could reasonably leave out the most gothically awful productions that the studio made. So far as I am aware, in fact, no other scholar of film has felt strong enough to tackle this section of the oeuvre. But someone has to do it. For these films give us a horribly, dazzlingly clear sense of what was happening to Hammer in the early 1970s and, indeed, what was becoming of British popular culture.

The three words *On the Buses* are by themselves sufficient to make many of a certain age get up abruptly and leave the room. This ITV programme widened the parameters of broad comedy to an extent never previously imagined. Here is the basic scenario: it is the story of a randy bus driver, his clippie, his sister and brother-in-law and the bus inspector. Reg Varney was the lead, Stan Butler, and played the role as though he imagined he was a) under thirty and b) in some way attractive. The truth was very different. His sister Olive, a whinging harridan with pebble-lensed glasses, remains a uniquely memorable portrait of what the scriptwriter considered early 1970s womanhood. The inspector, called Blakey, can now be seen in *Last of the Summer Wine* and you give thanks that the actor concerned, Stephen Lewis, at last has found a job that won't lead to half the population actively detesting him. If one was an apologist, one might say that *On the Buses* blended the sauce and innuendo of the Carry On films with an unprecedentedly earthy approach to working-class life. One might. One might also have found it tolerable in chunks of twenty-five-minute episodes. But when Hammer bought up the rights to the series, under the auspices of James Carreras, grateful audiences – and yes, let's get this clear, audiences were genuinely grateful – were served up three ninety-minute slabs of the thing.

And to give you an idea of what British cinema in 1971 was like: the first entry, *On the Buses,* was the highest grossing domestic film of that year.

So, here on the big screen, we have the randy driver and clippie, young women in negligees in pebble-dashed houses, the dowdy avenues of outer London, the randy driver's oily hair and prop bus stops that don't even begin to make the first concession to realism. The screenplay entirely revolves around loud people hurling witless insults at each other while Blakey shakes his fist and falls off the bus's rear platform. It is gob-stoppingly mortifying. And it makes any one of the Carry On films look like Richard Brinsley Sheridan.

Here was the new Executive Producer Roy Skeggs's first day in the sunshine. It was not one that he relished in the slightest and he recalled it later:

> James Carreras called me in to his office and said: 'This film is being made for pennies, so I want you to produce it.' I said 'Do you mind if I don't? I can't stand the thing on television.' He said 'Produce it or go,' and pointed at the door. So I produced it. We made it for £97,000 and it took £1.4 million in its first six weeks alone.[1]

Naturally that 'ker-ching!' resonated with a message for Hammer – and indeed, young Skeggs. The film obviously was the opposite side of the coin to the horrors and, obviously, the film was too successful not to have sequels. Two were to follow, the quality diminishing as they went. There might be a few anthropologists who protest the worth of these films as social and cultural documents but it simply won't do. And Doris Hare, playing Reg Varney's mother, should have known better. One interesting note: there appears to be quite a large amount of wondrously downmarket product placement going on in the films, chiefly for the holiday camp company Pontins, advertisements for which feature prominently on the sides of the buses. The third film in the series is actually largely set in such a camp. The profits generated should have been able to resuscitate the entire British film industry. They evaporated like water in the desert sun. But once again, Hammer had kicked off a trend.

Between 1971 and 1974, it was almost impossible to go to the cinema and not see something that you'd already seen on the television, and usually made by companies even cheaper than Hammer. We were given *Steptoe and Son*; *Steptoe and Son Ride Again*; *Up Pompeii*; *Up the Chastity Belt*; *Up the Front*; *Love thy Neighbour*; *Ooh, You are Awful*; *Are You Being Served?*; *The Best of the Benny Hill Show*. Hammer investigated more comedy possibilities: they made an adaptation of the flat-sharing sitcom *Man About the House*, rather a witty show with Richard O' Sullivan and Paula Wilcox which was a very great deal less offensive than *On the Buses*. They also ventured into black comedy with a farce set in a funeral parlour, entitled *That's Your Funeral!* with Bill Fraser which was neither crude nor funny, just plodding, and which featured yet more of those drab outer-London pebble-dashed avenues.

For an explanation of this attempt at branching out, we must look not just to Sir James Carreras, but also to son Michael.

This was not, perhaps, the easiest time for Michael. Particularly when we consider that, in 1973, he was still unaware that behind the scenes, his old father James was in talks with outfits such as Studio Film Laboratories to sell Hammer altogether. According to Denis Meikle, when Michael found out, he and fellow board member Brian Lawrence went to the venture capital arm of ICI in a bid to make a buyout. It is said that, at this point, Sir James and Lady C. were on a world cruise; on his return, it was made clear to him that Michael had succeeded in his buyout and it was time for Sir James to properly bow out of the day-to-day operation.[2]

Again, according to Meikle, there was one request from old Sir James: that he be allowed to retain his company chauffeur-driven Rolls Royce. This was the first his son had heard that Hammer owned such a thing.[3]

'Up until that point, of course, the company had been run as a family business,' Michael said in a later interview. 'Now although family businesses are a wonderful way of life, I don't think they exist today in the same way that they did.'[4]

By this stage, the Americans had cleared off altogether, and things were starting to look apocalyptic on Wardour Street. *On the Buses* was never going to win the Palme d'Or at Cannes but for a short period, it kept the werewolf from the door.

British comedy in the 1970s was no laughing matter and we cannot merely blame Hammer. We must also take a final look at the series that seemed to mirror Hammer's own progress through the years: the Carry Ons. In the early 1970s, like the Hammers, they remained remarkably prolific, apparently levitating above the economic quagmire that was sucking in all other companies. And the series saw a couple of high points, like *Carry On Henry* which ingeniously cast Sid James as Henry VIII and Kenneth Williams as Cardinal Wolsey. But the production values had fallen off a cliff and the films just looked tattier and tattier. Could there be any cheaper effort than a ninety-minute film set entirely in a caravan park (*Carry On Behind*, [1974])? Yes, *Carry On England* (1975), set in a WW2 army training camp which happened to be mixed sex. Strange to think now that such films were even reviewed in the serious newspapers. But they were. What else was there?

The question leads us reluctantly, and fleetingly, to the 'Confessions of ...' series of sex comedies. Where would a portrait of 1970s popular culture be without a simian Robin Askwith, successively a window cleaner, photographer and driving instructor, climbing through windows and falling into bubble-baths with naked ladies?

We mustn't make the mistake of thinking that Hammer was incapable of sophistication. Indeed, one of their efforts, now a little neglected, from a few years back, speaks of an entirely different, if slightly camp, sensibility. In 1967, the studio bought up the rights to the trendy black comedy *The Anniversary* and installed Bette Davis – over for a return match following the success of *The Nanny* (1965) – in the lead role. Complete with different eye-patches as accessories, she portrayed an appalling matriarch determined to control the sex lives of her sons, and the piece involved such shockingly fashionable themes as transvestitism. As with most shocking things from the 1960s, it does not travel especially well now but at least at the time the production could be seen as an unusual meld of queasy comedy and psychological suspense. Despite a barn-stormingly unpleasant performance from Davis (and how odd now to think of her to be working for a two-and-sixpence effort like Hammer), this glossy Technicolor effort talks more to its own time.

Compare and contrast the scene just four years later in 1971: Stan Butler having a little slap and tickle on the upper deck with a tasty bird while the passengers wait in the queue below was pretty much the quintessential image of early 1970s British cinema. Dumb, dowdy, depressing – that's who we all were. And who were Hammer to buck the trend?

Chapter Twelve

CREATIVE SPURTS

One of Michael Carreras's most endearing traits at Hammer was his continued insistence to the press that the films had finally lost what he termed 'their stigma'. 'Yes, all the big names come to us,' he told the *Sunday Telegraph* in 1972. 'There is no stigma now in being in a Hammer film.'[1]

Well, we'll leave that one hanging in the air for the moment. The younger Carreras had also inherited his father's knack for amplifying the studio's continued and remarkable success story. In 1971, *Variety* breathlessly reported:

> Slump there may be here but Hammer Productions is going like a one-company British film industry. It has delivered five films this year, with two shooting in London and three scheduled to roll pre-Christmas ... these are all distribution commitments – mostly with EMI and Rank ... (the company has) continued Tiffany identification in the horror realm ... it's keeping to the basic gothic line it knows best but a certain storyline evolution is being fostered, the old stable spook stuff being played down in favour of psychological suspense. Nudity is also an au courant element.

You could say that again. And the 'psychological suspense' that the reporter referred to involved such well-meaning efforts as *Demons of the Mind* (1972) and *Fear in the Night* (1972), which were all perfectly good in their own way but, to be honest, never half so memorable or entertaining as those Hammers which stuck to the 'basic gothic line'. The thrillers, it's true, were getting some interesting actors, including Patrick Magee, Judy Geeson and the effortlessly creepy young Shane Briant. But this, remember, was an era when there were simply no other films to be in. Much lower down the scale than Hammer, Tigon was making *The Beast in the Cellar* with Flora Robson. She is reported to have met Laurence Olivier one day on the train up from Brighton and told him of the script, in a state of some distress. Olivier is said to have told her that in these straitened times, everyone had to appear in whatever they could.[2]

So against this rather dreadful backdrop of tits, bums, increasing industrial unrest and the lights going out at 10.30 p.m., it is surprising to note that in this period, Hammer, on occasion, perked up quite a bit in creative terms.

In fact, several of their films produced between the years 1971 and 1974 now deserve to be ranked among their very best. And no, this is not an exercise in deliberately provocative revisionism. There were some startling ruby gems in that grim beige 1970s dust.

Let's take them in reverse order. First, a round of applause for *Hands of the Ripper* (1971) starring Eric Porter and young Angharad Rees. The premise, very simply, is that a troubled girl, Anna, finds herself, at moments of stress, inhabited by the spirit of her late father. This would be vexing enough by itself; but as it happens, her father was Jack the Ripper. Indeed, we see in a prologue the dreadful moment when toddler Rees witnesses her mother being slaughtered by her father. Angharad Rees's murderous outbursts – including one spectacularly flinch-worthy effort involving hatpins stuck into eyes – are accompanied with some visual stimulus, usually the flickering light of jewellery. And it was all slightly more violent than previous Hammers had been.

But that was balanced with a slightly more subtle than usual script, partic- ularly in the depiction of protagonist Dr John Pritchard (Porter) whose approach towards Anna's mental illness, and his general treatment of her, is ambiguous. Also, the film recovered a little of Hammer's old visual stylishness, notably for its evocation of turn-of-the-century London, and particularly in the film's climax, set in the Whispering Gallery of St Paul's Cathedral, where sticky ends are met. There was a faintly more serious and – dare it be said – grown-up tone to the entire enterprise. Naturally, for the purposes of posters and publicity, Rees's character was said to be possessed by the ghost of the Ripper – it was a Hammer film, after all – but it's quite clear that the film would work equally well as a straight, non-supernatural psychological thriller. In other words, rather than just yet another Dracula sequel, the studio really was looking for new ways to frighten audiences without always having recourse to mechanical bats. And as a new twist on an old frightener, *Ripper* also has the pleasing feeling of being utterly unpredictable. A shame, then, that this marked the final effort for the company of producer Aida Young; tir- ing of being sidelined in favour of producers who seemed to have walked in off the street, like Harry Fine of *The Vampire Lovers*, she resigned and left for a full-time executive position with EMI.[3]

In film terms, also well worth a bow, but for rather different reasons, is 1971's *Dr Jekyll and Sister Hyde*, which followed *Ripper* into the cinemas some months later. It was slightly unfortunate – and telling, in that there were now so many executives running around and not talking to each other – that this should also feature a new approach to the old Ripper story. But that is only one almost incidental element of this perverse and amusing film.

Young Ralph Bates is Dr Jekyll, and he is quite a long way from the goody-two-shoes idealist as portrayed over the ages by Frederic March, Spencer Tracey and others too numerous to mention. He's after the elixir of youth, or some such, and his old friend Utterson (Gerald Sim) is tickled as opposed to horrified. But then Jekyll gulps down the fateful fluid – the glass beaker, at least, remains a constant in this respect – and when Jekyll stands and stares into the mirror, he has become a she (see reference to dressing gowns and breasts in Chapter Eight). The music score at this point leaps into a simulation of a beauty pageant theme; Miss Hyde (Martine Beswick) finds some suitable attire and heads off into the London streets where, it seems, she must murder prostitutes in order to find more of the gland that secretes the vital fluid (or something). Into this mix (and it is not too long before old Gerald Sim, flirted with by Miss Hyde, comes a horrible cropper at the point of a letter-opener), two other elements are thrown in: Burke and Hare, who strictly speaking are surely a century late. But that doesn't seem to matter too much. The whole thing has that sort of feckless enthusiasm.

As it might well have done, because it was produced (and written) by Brian Clemens and Albert Fennell, the men who had made TV's *The Avengers* such a success in the US in the late 1960s, only to have the US then pull the rug out from under them in 1969. Hammer seemed a perfectly reasonable port of call for their expertise; and Brian Clemens found himself walking up the stairs of Hammer House in Wardour Street in order to pitch this new twist to James Carreras.

Carreras, it seems, made humming and hah-ing noises, and asked Clemens to give him a little while to consider the suggestion. He did so. Returning a day later, Clemens arrived at the office to discover that Carreras had already had the poster for the film mocked up. This, of course, was the sign that Clemens was to go ahead. Indeed, in Hammer terms, it meant the film was practically half-made.[4]

Unusually for a Hammer film, there was much in Clemens's script that was deliberately jokey, particularly in the dialogue between Jekyll, Burke and Hare, and in the scenes featuring a highly amused looking Martine Beswick. And it suited; the audiences still got their frightening shots of gore (this time splashes of blood hitting a street poster concerning the crimes, ironically enough, of Jack the Ripper). But they were also allowed in on the joke that the actors seemed to be having.

It is not, let us be honest, a great work of philosophy; and indeed, when it came to questions of gender ambiguity, the comedy *Some Like It Hot* was a very great deal more multi-layered. But like *Ripper, Sister Hyde* represented a proper attempt to engage with a young and notably more sophisticated audience than before (and they would have been a very great deal more sophisticated than those who queued to see *On the Buses*). There were no insults, intended or otherwise, aimed at the auditorium. As Hammer's 1970s charmer of choice, Ralph Bates kept his tongue out of his cheek as far as possible. And Martine Beswick, with her often random murderous impulses, made one of the more diverting and straightforwardly funny female characters in any horror film thus far.

Critics at the time were not convinced by the attempt at Elstree to convey a period atmosphere, but it had worked in *Ripper* so it was a case of win some, lose some.

One other entry from that time could have made it to the 'very good' list were it not for two blows which the production received. The film – *Blood from the Mummy's Tomb* (1971) – was, for Hammer, a subtle and oblique re-imagining of the whole rotting bandages sub-genre, and was based on Bram Stoker's *The Jewel of the Seven Stars*. In the film, a reincarnated Egyptian princess (who has had her hand amputated) is the focus of the action, here played by the statuesque Valerie Leon. He-who-meddles-with-her-tomb-with-consequences-we-can-guess-at was supposed to be Peter Cushing; but two days into shooting, his wife Helen, from whom he was inseparable, died after an illness. At this very short notice, Andrew Keir – who had been such a good Quatermass in 1967 – was prevailed upon to step in.[5] And he did so very ably, but just wasn't quite the same as Cushing.

Blow number two was the death of the director, a man called Seth Holt, who had previously been responsible for so many of Hammer's black and white psychological thrillers. He died of a heart attack. Hammer apparently saw to it that he got seen off in style. His funeral now sounds a masterpiece of bad taste. According to the actor James Villiers, quoted by Hearn and Barnes:

> Hammer lent out one of the original hearses from one of their many
> films with the plumed horses and the fine carriage with the black
> drapings and silver trappings used in every single Dracula film ever
> made and we followed along behind this marvellous hearse and we
> buried the old bean.[6]

But Hammer was also a professional outfit to its fingertips and saw no reason why the film could not be rescued – a substantial part of it had been shot already. Michael Carreras decided to step in and finish it all off, working from Seth Holt's notes. Unfortunately, there were none.[7] And there was one other small, macabrely funny setback, according to production associate

Christopher Neame, manifesting itself in the hiccup attacks that Holt experienced. 'Those hiccups,' Neame wrote, 'could be heard on the rushes that were left after his death.'[8]

There were other setbacks Carreras encountered with the footage, including an oblique style that was never entirely explained, but the show had to go on, the film was sewn together and completed; oddly enough (and others may disagree), it now seems to work rather well. It feels rather different to any other Hammer and has its longeurs but that is not to say that it doesn't have its interest – and we say a loud 'huzzah' for Hammer at last introducing the element so beloved of previous generations of horror fans, that of the disembodied crawling hand, long separated from its reincarnated Princess owner. And of course, instead of an old stuntman wrapped in muddy bandages, we have instead the spectacle of Valerie Leon running through a spinney in the regulation negligee. Once again, it made a change and you cannot blame Hammer for trying.

But *Blood* is a film it is only possible to enjoy with some reservations. Much more straightforwardly entertaining – give or take a scene or two of high dubiousness – was the 1972 effort *Vampire Circus*.

Once again, a new screenwriter, producer and director stepped up to the plate for this one. The script was by Judson Kinberg, Wilbur Stark was the producer and Robert Young, an old *Avengers* stalwart, was the man behind the camera.

At first sight, in the first few minutes, the signs are not good, for we have a rerun of the usual Hammer paraphernalia of counts and castles – and this time with the added nastiness of a child being involved, and indeed a new count, named Mitterhouse, clearly an intended lookalike for Christopher Lee. The villagers fetch the burning torches, the castle goes up ... but once we have got past the prologue, things look up rather dramatically.

The village concerned is in Serbia and we are now one year on. The countryside around is riven with the plague and under a curfew. Into this tired and frightened atmosphere comes the carnival: a carnival calling itself the Circus of Nights, led by an enthusiastic Adrienne Corri. Naturally, the villagers – among whom are Laurence Payne and our dear old favourite Thorley Walters as the burgomaster – are slowly bewitched. The circus, as its name suggests, gives evening performances, and these largely comprise weird transformations – panther into handsome man (and take a bow once more, Anthony Higgins!), large bats into beautiful acrobats ... there is also a sinister strongman and dwarf and quite the most sinister hall of mirrors seen in the cinema thus far. It only takes one performance for the circus to get under the skins of the spectators.

But the village finds that its young are being targeted by nameless evil – as in a scene where two boys find the hall of mirrors is a mesmeric gateway to another world into which they are lured by two young acrobats, preparatory to being bitten. And the circus, with its panther vampires and bat vampires, soon throws off its not tremendously elaborate disguise – they are all there to avenge and resurrect vile old Count Mitterhouse.

But the story doesn't matter so much as the hypnotic set-pieces: one performer's strikingly erotic dance routine with a green-painted jungle lady; the transformation shots, particularly those of the bats becoming acrobats, filmed in hazy slow motion; and the scene in which the film's young protagonists are trapped by two attractive vampires in the beautifully painted chapel of an eastern European church (incidentally, one of those vampires was played by Lalla Ward who is now Mrs Richard Dawkins). When one considers the state of the British film industry at the time – and remember, this would have gone out almost contemporaneously with *Father Dear Father* – it seems a rare example of poetry made for peanuts.

Of course, it doesn't look like the most expensive film ever made, and how could it? In the outside world, inflation was rising and so were production costs. Also the main circus set always ends up being over-lit which is not so much a question of cost as craftsmanship. And, without wishing to sound nitpicky, the climactic scenes in Mitterhouse's crypt, featuring unusually absurd blobs of ersatz blood, simply won't do.

But to balance these small niggles, there is much else that is straightforwardly beguiling. Once again, we have a dominating female character, in the shape of Adrienne Corri. The dark fairy-tale feel of the screenplay is something that seems to pre-date the stories of Angela Carter by several years, particularly in the focus on sensuality, and the beast within the handsome male. Anthony Higgins plays that aspect up to the hilt, even though in a few scenes it is clear that he is having some difficulty with his fang-acting – those particular canines seem to be rather more obtrusive than usual. And the visual touches, like the shine of the panther's eyes glimpsed on the darkness of a forest road, are, considering their cheapness, remarkably arresting.

It is no surprise to learn that the innovative Robert Young found himself clashing with the production office over this film, chiefly because of the amount of time he seemed to be taking to get it all done. Time, for Hammer, was nothing but money. And it was as a result of some of these clashes of approach that several even more startling transformation sequences were left unshot.[9]

And where had all this sprung from? Apparently it had all been a terrific spot from the studio's script-reader Nadja Regin, who had this to say about the screenplay: '*Vampire Circus* introduces an element of beauty, colour, magic and excitement into an ambience of sickness, fear and death.'[10] Despite the vampiric scenes involving children, which possibly seem more flinch-worthy now as a result of a sensitive climate – such considerations may not have occurred to audiences in 1972 – and despite the prologue and climax, in which an astoundingly naff Milk Tray Man pretends to be a vampire Count, this is one of Hammer's most fascinating efforts. If only it had been made during the studio's golden age of cinematography, it might be better remembered now.

Vampire Circus didn't really do tremendous box-office business back in 1972 either. Naturally, by this point, American distribution of any sort was a very sore point for Hammer. And perhaps it wasn't just a question of the domestic cinema market faltering generally; the posters emphasised fangs rather than fairy tale. It could simply be that audiences were becoming vampired out.

The film deserved better. And along with the other films mentioned here, it suggests that while it looks as if the old gothic formula might be running out of steam at the end of the 1960s, the studio was charging into the 1970s with new ideas and a real sense of evolution.

This also brings us back to the question of what a Hammer film really is and indeed whether there was any such thing as a consistent Hammer sensibility. For all the films mentioned here seem at first sight to be as different from *The Kiss of the Vampire* or *The Revenge of Frankenstein* as they could be. When one also removes the elements of Christopher Lee, of Peter Cushing, of director Terence Fisher, of composer James Bernard, are we not left with something that is Hammer in name only?

No, for even if the films were now self-consciously a little funnier than they were before – an entirely reasonable progression after the granite-faced approach of the 1960s – some things didn't change. First, there was still a belief that a period setting was, on the whole, a better thing for a fantasy; monsters of any description were easier to accept, it was clearly felt, with some measure of distance. Second, and related to this, was the otherworldly presentation of sex, especially in *Vampire Circus* and *Dr Jekyll and Sister Hyde*; but sex in Hammer could never have been described as a straightforward business. And the studio executives (with the possible exception of James Carreras) would argue that, unlike the efforts put out by rivals, nudity was never used gratuitously. And, all right, if it was, then at least it was never explored at the expense of an actress's essential dignity.

And in one thing Hammer still stood pre-eminent in what was (admittedly) rather a dodgy market: its consistent imagery. The fangs, the frocks, the blazing log fires in castle interiors, the fogbound studio streets of old London town, the fancy waistcoats and, please, let us not forget those quite essential woodlands, brightly sunlit for every midnight scene. Even the scores, which were now only occasionally composed by James Bernard, at least attempted to follow his template when composed by others, like David Whitaker: the pulsating percussion, the dramatic horns, the use of carefully built-up recurring themes. Though it has to be said that one disappointment of Hammer as it moved into the 1970s was not merely a decline in the quality of the cinematography but also that something weird happens not to the music itself, but to the sound reproduction – tinnier, flatter, less multi-dimensional. This was true for some reason of all British soundtracks. They get washed out and end up having a strange elevator quality. Nevertheless, a Hammer score remained a genuinely distinctive, instantly recognisable thing.

It's difficult to overstate just how pervasive the entire idea of Hammer had become throughout British popular culture by the mid-1970s. Comedians like Dave Allen would base entire sketches around Dracula fangs, coffins and capes. There were pop songs such as the reissued 1960s hit 'Monster Mash' ('it was a graveyard smash'). Added to this, the Hammer films were now starting to be shown on television. Audiences were being reminded, after many years, of the exploits of the younger Peter Cushing and Christopher Lee. With the studio still cranking them out at a rate of knots, it is little wonder that Hammer continued to give the impression that it was an unstoppable British success story. Only Amicus seemed able to come anywhere near its output, and even Amicus by the early 1970s was beginning to look a little threadbare. Indeed, after *Tales from the Crypt* (1972), which had contrived to star Ralph Richardson, Joan Collins and Peter Cushing in the same film – a stellar line-up that the world was destined never to see again – that company's output declined sharply. Entries such as *Vault of Horror* are now only notable for the interest in increasingly unlikely cameos such as the young Tom Baker as a mad artist, not long after he had played mad monk Rasputin.

By 1973, it was not merely the old British film industry that was in a state of outright crisis; the entire nation was. Indeed, the recession was worldwide. But Britain's predicament had been amplified by the policies of Tory chancellor Anthony Barber, which inadvertently stoked inflation just at the point when the OPEC oil crisis had already set it climbing. In the meantime, the country had, the previous year, been through an immensely damaging strike by miners; the result had been power cuts, with electricity often being switched off around 10.30 p.m. The knock-on effect throughout industry was seismic, both in terms of productivity and also in terms of labour relations. The management/worker dichotomy was widening: slick-haired pinstriped capitalists versus long-haired sideburn-sporting pseudo-communists. Those at least were the views that both sides held of each other. 1973 brought another miners' strike that in turn led to the Three Day Week. There were shortages of items such as sugar and lavatory paper. It was, now that one thinks about it, an amazingly appalling time. How had it ever come to that? Throughout the 1950s and 60s, Britain had lost its empire, piece by piece, and the national consciousness seemed to be resigned to a future of slow decline. But actually this decline was steep and seemingly terminal, a nosedive from which the country could never be rescued.

Against this backdrop, Hammer House in Wardour Street remained defiantly and almost bumptiously in business, although Michael Carreras by that stage must have seen that the battle was going to be lost.

For one thing, the company did not own quite as much as it was widely presumed that it did. When, in 1973, Carreras and Brian Lawrence bought the company out, one of the first things Michael found was that some of the films were no longer to be found in the Hammer crypt. They were elsewhere, in the vaults of American film companies like Warners and Universal, which had originally backed them.[11]

Then there was the troubled question of ever-spiralling production costs, an issue affecting not just film but television too. The price of fuel, plus the increasingly rigid rulings of union members concerning who could do what and under what circumstances people could be hired or dismissed were fast proving to be lethal to any creative endeavours. How anyone got anything made at this time is something of a mystery.

The third thing was the decreasing allure of cinema itself. Once one had fought through all the adaptations of television comedies and crime shows (like *The Sweeney* and *Callan*), the screen no longer offered much that was genuinely original. And what there was was often either repulsive or depressing or both: witness *Ten Rillington Place* with Richard Attenborough as the slum-dwelling killer Reginald Christie; and Kubrick's *A Clockwork Orange*, the 'ultra-violence' of which needs no rehearsal here. There were some developments in the cinema business itself. As George Perry observes in *The Great British Picture Show*: 'Suburban cinemas of the post-war years continued to close at a high rate but while many sites were being turned into supermarkets, office blocks and service stations, many sites were rebuilt, opening later as 'twinned' or 'tripled' complexes.'[12] In other words, the screens and auditoriums were getting smaller; and many of the larger unaltered cinemas were instead redeveloped into bingo halls. Today some have moved on into fresher lives: a nightclub in Uxbridge in the still recognisable shell of the old 'Roxy'; a grotesquely vast pub on the Holloway Road which once, many years ago, would have played Hammer double-bills.

It really is to the credit of Michael Carreras that he fought on against a slopping, brackish tide of pessimism and powerlessness. And indeed

Hammer came good twice more, giving audiences in 1973 and 1974 last hurrahs from both Peter Cushing and Christopher Lee before trying to adapt to life in an altogether darker, more difficult world. The company would start to sink into the quagmire (together, it has to be said, with many others). But even in the face of an utterly hopeless situation – plus a death blow to the old style of Hammer Horror from America – Michael showed great resourcefulness and indeed inventiveness in producing new ideas that might still keep the show on the road.

Chapter Thirteen

WHO HAS DONE THIS THING?

 In the early 1970s it might have seemed that the Hammer veterans had largely dispersed. But the close of 1972 saw something of a vintage Hammer reunion, with most of the old hands making a comeback. First and foremost was Peter Cushing, returning to his defining role of Baron Frankenstein. Handling the script for this new horror was old Anthony Hinds. Behind the camera was Terence Fisher. And providing the score was James Bernard.

In many senses, this should have been one of the ultimate Hammer Frankensteins, especially after the dismal spoof effort of a couple of years previously. All the elements were in place, including the gruesome main setting of a Victorian lunatic asylum, the most fitting home for the obsessive Baron and his necromantic work. Also present were the classic ingredients of a sceptical, handsome young sidekick (Shane Briant, still slightly more creepy than you would expect most conventional young leading men to be) and a pretty lady for the monster to turn its attentions to (Madeleine Smith – playing the pretty lady, not the monster). It could have been the veterans' last hurrah; sadly, it turned out to be more of a dying croak.

Poor old Peter Cushing. Never a beefy chap to begin with, this time round he looked terribly emaciated, skin as translucent as muslin. The addition of a curled wig did not seem to help matters. Of course, as mentioned, Cushing had lost his wife Helen a year previously. They had been exceptionally close and this was no ordinary period of mourning. The effect that grief has had on him is all too evident, even though Cushing approaches the part with his customary brisk professionalism.

He had always been loyal to Hammer, probably in recognition of the fact that the studio had opened up his career and given him worldwide recognition in a way that few other jobs could have done. By 1972, his name was synonymous with the part of Frankenstein, and an invaluable asset to any horror film. Indeed, on the brief occasions when he had worked for people other than Hammer, he had selected some real mustard-gas stinkers to appear in. For instance, 1967 brought a film that, inexplicably, gained a reputation for being striking and good. It really was neither of those things. It was called *The Blood Beast Terror*, it was directed by Vernon Sewell and it largely concerned people in Victorian England being killed by what later turns out to be a giant moth. When it is not a moth, it is Wanda Ventham, and her efforts with the part – she is after all a very good actress – are heroic. The same goes for Peter Cushing's scientist hero. But neither can hope to save the film, made on a budget even more minuscule than those allocated to Hammer productions. Occasionally it still gets shown on television. Don't go near it. It is not even amusing.

Cushing's seeming inability to differentiate between good scripts and rubbish heaps continued into the 1970s, but after the death of his wife there was more a tragic sense that it really didn't matter to the old actor any more, that he couldn't see the point in any of it, good or bad. He had taken the role as the puritan witch-hunter in *Twins of Evil* (1971) even though it was obvious that the film would suck. 'I knew the only way to keep going was to keep busy,' said Cushing. 'It didn't matter what they offered – I just kept working. It was the only thing that saved my reason.'[1]

It is very sad to think of this serious – and fundamentally rather brilliant – actor carrying on in roles that were mostly appreciated by loon-panted tank-top sporting Herberts out for a laugh on a Friday night.

But Baron Frankenstein was his, completely his, and we can see that it must have been in some ways a relief to be reunited with old Anthony Hinds and Terence Fisher, the three of them having been together for that original *Curse of Frankenstein* in 1957. But from the very start, it was clear that this new film was not going to be the glorious swansong that it should have been.

The title was typically rumbustious: *Frankenstein and the Monster from Hell*. There is an element there of telling it like it is. The first real setback was that the budget was so very obviously, miserably low. The thing looks as though it was filmed in some dark corner of the Elstree back lot in about one and a half days. The other setback, once again, is the monster. These creatures were never really Hammer's strong point and this one is pretty much one of the worst – a hulking, hairy, vaguely simian figure, with scarred facial make-up so atrociously bad you could take it to a toddlers' tea party and see not an eyebrow raised.

Frankenstein, as ever, is in pursuit of constructing the perfect creature, but the twist this time is that he wants the brute – with its innate and terribly human love of weepy violin music – to mate with Madeleine Smith. Finally, thank the lord, the beast is torn to pieces by the inmates of the ayslum and another of Frankenstein's dreams bites the dust, with the Baron vowing to try again another day.

But the whole thing is subdued and listless – the murky greens and browns of the set design are depressing and there is a feeling that we are simply tracking over old ground. It has been said that by this stage, Terence Fisher, after his two road accidents, had lost his confidence;[2] he was also having problems with his eyes (and interestingly, eyes and blindness are a recurring leitmotif in ... *from Hell*). The film certainly lacks the pace and verve that marks his earlier work.

To make things worse, the film was not actually released until two years later. Thankfully, Cushing was set to make two more Hammer Horror appearances and this time as good old Van Helsing. But in the meantime, ... *from Hell* does not make a satisfactory finale to the series that had, after all, originally catapulted the studio into such a prominent position.

Around that time, critic Harry Ringel wrote an unkind though amusing summary of Terence Fisher's career: 'Like his Frankenstein, he has worked resolutely, without critical encouragement, under the most compromising circumstances. His mistakes noisily roam the countryside; his best films dead within a cultural vacuum.'[3]

Happily that is no longer true. Fisher's films, in the end, escaped that vacuum and took on a new undead life. Learned cinephile books have been written, lectures delivered, retrospectives screened and discussed. The ebullient screenwriter Jimmy Sangster recalled attending a retrospective in the mid-1990s himself.

> I was at a film festival in Nancy, France. And they screened the French version [of *Dracula*]. Needless to say, I didn't understand much of it, French not being a strong point with me. Added to this, the print was old and scratched. However, after the screening, a couple of young people who couldn't even have been born when we made the movie came up to me and said it was a masterpiece. I kid you not. Their very words. OK, so it was a pretty good movie. The sets were great and Christopher Lee was very good, even if he hasn't stopped bitching about the part ever since. But masterpiece! Come on![4]

Well, the couple weren't alone. That original Dracula still gets wheeled out in art houses the world over. The New York Metropolitan Arts Centre recently screened it, praising the innovative use of colour.

By way of contrast, one film that we rarely see at art house retrospectives is Christopher Lee's final outing as the Count, although contrary to what the actor has said, it was by no means a car crash. Indeed, the intervening years have lent it a great deal of charm. For *The Satanic Rites of Dracula* (1973), the studio decided to keep the Count in contemporary London.

The opening titles show us a montage of familiar London landmarks, including the Tower of London and Trafalgar Square, with the image of Dracula's shadow slowly looming over them. These images are accompanied with an action-adventure saxophoney score, composed by the man who would later go on to provide the music for TV's *Kojak*. The scenario is very 1973: police are investigating some naff nude black-magic rituals, which are naturally secretly attended by government ministers, members of the judiciary and other bowler-hatted establishment figures. But there is also an Avengerish plot going on, involving the discovery of a virus lethal to humanity. Who the devil can be behind all these shenanigans? Time to call in Lorrimer Van Helsing, grandson of the original (Peter Cushing on rather more sprightly form) and his Sloaney sophisticated daughter, as played by Joanna Lumley. Van Helsing soon gets to the bottom of it all – a shadowy property developer calling himself D.D. Denham, operating out of the top of one the soulless office skyscrapers that were shooting up all over London at that time. But this Denham is in fact none other than – mwooarh-hah-hah! – Count Dracula. And as Joanna Lumley gets caught up in a cellar full of naked vampire ladies at a big country house, and then finds herself the chief attraction in the climactic black-magic ritual, complete with red plush curtains, it transpires that Dracula plans to infect the whole of humanity with the sinister virus and render it undead. Thankfully Van Helsing intervenes, Dracula flees the big country house, runs into a hawthorn bush to which, it seems, he is allergic – and Van Helsing stakes him.

Other quaint attractions in the film include: heavies wearing sheepskin coats; Michael Coles' amusingly lugubrious inspector from *AD 1972*; car chases through the as-yet ungentrified streets of Notting Hill and North Kensington; and all the while the wonderfully un-gothic score, squealing and tooting away, tom-toms in the background. In other words, it is almost indecently entertaining.

The screenplay was by Don Houghton, who had provided all the kooky, way-out hip happenings of *AD 1972*. He had previously specialised in writing some of Jon Pertwee's tougher *Dr Who* adventures. A young director called Alan Gibson, who had crammed *AD 1972* with as many 360-degree fisheye lens pans as he could, once more took the helm.

And though he patently hated every second of it, Christopher Lee was professional to his very vampiric talons, turning in a boomingly authoritative final performance as the Count. Indeed, thanks to the script, he came off very much better than on some other recent occasions.

But dear, oh dear, he was having absolutely none of it behind the scenes. The film, to Lee, represented the absolute nadir. Once more, he did it purely out of loyalty to Hammer, but unfortunately he could not disguise his contempt at a special press conference held to publicise the film.

The working title had been *Dracula is Dead and Well and Living in London* which admittedly did not strike quite the right note. Lee announced to the assembled journalists that he found the script 'fatuous' and 'inane'. He later said: 'I reached my irrevocable full stop. That last film was a parody – unintentionally so. Dracula was a mixture of Dr No and Howard Hughes. [The critic] Margaret Hinxman said that now we know who owns that white elephant of property speculation, Centre Point.'[5]

But exactly. That is precisely what makes the film so watchable now. The idea that Dracula, in the modern world, should choose to make a living out of property development is a splendidly satirical idea. And actually it didn't detract from the power of the character – Lee was too good an actor for that to happen. Also it was an intriguing effort on the part of (by this stage) poor beleaguered Hammer to move away from the now staid conventions of costume horror and instead focus the drama on a world that would have been highly recognisable to the audience.

This, after all, was the era of the rapacious property developers, from Harry Hyams to Slater Walker, who were changing the face of London, filling it with grey, chilly monoliths, the most famous of which, Centre Point, remained empty for many years. Meanwhile, the popular perception of politicians and judges was of a class mired in secret sleaze and corruption. Under every pinstriped suit, or so the widely held view had it, beat the heart of a pervert. And it was a neat trick to combine that theme with the *News of the World's* favourite topic of covert black-magic covens. The fact was that the 1970s audiences were very much more cynical about their betters than previous generations had been. Hammer was simply trying to capture that mood.

But the pre-publicity for the film was accompanied with a torrent of barely tepid reviews. The critics, it seemed, were now pretty cynical about Hammer. The audiences didn't seem all that thrilled either. For what now seems a cheerful experiment in updating a myth was simply too much of a dislocation: Hammer meant castles on hills, and coffins, and inns and horses. Not people in flares in Ford Cortinas.

Later that year came the real fightback from America, threatening to burn that old Hammer castle to the ground. It was a film that, in its unflinching gratuitousness, absolute sincerity and production values that Hammer could never afford, changed the face of horror every bit as much as Hammer had when it first seized the high ground back in 1957. That film was *The Exorcist*.

Here was a film where, for the first time in many years, the word of mouth was that it was almost too frightening to watch. Levitations, vomiting, the voice of James Earl Jones, priests being hurled out of windows ... its reputation grew fantastically quickly and made a quite enormous success out of a film that many people were actually too nervous to go and see.

There were reports in Britain of people in the cinema audience fainting, or being sick, or having the heebie-jeebies on the way home. There were fast-circulating urban myths about real-life outbreaks of demonic possession, and of a curse on the film's production. The film's demonic reputation lasted for years – in the 1980s, it was banned on home video. It was never shown on television. Only come the 1990s did everyone relax slightly and realise, finally, that *The Exorcist* was, to use that great old phrase, 'only a movie'.

Back in 1973, it changed the entire focus of horror, rewrote all the ground rules. Hammer had consistently made the source of evil, be it vampire or monster, a corporeal being, a breathing thing. Evil was depicted as something you could confront and, possibly, defeat. For the first time, *The Exorcist* told a stark tale of a girl possessed by demonic forces and portrayed the terrifying notion of the evil within; a malevolent force that could strike anywhere, seize anyone, in the most banal of settings. It also seemed incredibly apposite at a time when America was going through an unprecedented crisis of confidence sparked by the Watergate saga, which came in the immediate wake of the painful and prolonged south-east Asian conflict. As corruption could exist within the previously unimpeachable White House, so evil could exist in the most ordinary of suburban homes.

The Exorcist proved that horror did not need to have cloaks or fangs or even blobs of ersatz blood to make girls leap into the laps of their boyfriends down at the Odeon. It was the way forward. And it was a lesson that Hammer Films was going to learn shockingly quickly.

Christopher Lee never seemed to regret hanging up that scarlet silk-lined cloak for good. Around that time, he told author John Brosnan: 'In the [Bram Stoker] book, Dracula hardly ever stops talking. I think he should say something in these films, though when he does speak, it has to be something worth saying.'[6] Something better, indeed, than 'Who has done this thing?' and 'The cross – remove it!'

His very good friend Peter Cushing was in agreement when it came to Lee's character. At the time he told Brosnan: 'Christopher doesn't want to keep playing the sort of Dracula films he has been playing. *Dracula in the Dark; Dracula Meets Frankenstein; Search the House for Dracula.* All he has to do as Dracula is stand in a corner, show his fangs and hiss.'[7]

But before we feel too much sympathy for Lee, we should note that 1973 brought a happier development in career terms. To be sure, it was another horror film, but one cut of quite a new and unusual cloth, and one which has gained critical momentum since. *The Wicker Man*, scripted by Anthony Schaffer, was a tale of paganism on a remote Hebridean island; Lee was Lord Summerisle, chief promulgator of nudity and sun worship. The script was intelligent (in its own absurd way) and gave Lee the part he had thirsted for all those years: a villain who did have something worth saying. It was released in a double-bill with *Don't Look Now*, having been slashed to a running time of eighty-four minutes (so important, that eighty-four minutes!). Then the film was forgotten, buried. But like Dracula, it later found a new lease of life, first as a cult classic, then as a genuine bona-fide classic, given the ultimate accolade of a very bad Hollywood remake in 2006. *The Wicker Man* also provided another pointer for Hammer and Michael Carreras about the future of horror.

Another non-Hammer effort from 1973, *Theatre of Blood*, made the monster human: Vincent Price is a ham Shakespearean actor who, after a failed suicide bid, exacts vengeance on the critics who drove him to it, killing them off by methods used in Shakespeare's plays. It reeled in an extraordinary cast, from Diana Rigg to Jack Hawkins to Diana Dors. Especially memorable was Robert Morley being killed off by being force-fed his two beloved poodles. It is remembered now as a camp classic, if a sometimes jarringly unpleasant one. But Hammer, on the whole, did not do camp; it most certainly would not have been a convincing way forward for the company. It was altogether too protective of its beloved monsters.

By this stage, the end of 1973, the future of British film altogether was looking rather dicey. Soft porn involving Swedish nurses was practically the only growth area. Horror, itself another rather dodgy genre, had always previously been a banker. But had the cinema-going public moved on? It is almost bathetic to note that a few weeks after the sensational, blockbusting release of *The Exorcist, Frankenstein and the Monster from Hell* finally limped on to British screens. A crueller comparison between the old and the new way of doing things could not really be found and ... *from Hell* vanished from view shortly afterwards. It rarely made it on to television either. Just as well really for it is not a film that any of its participants would want to be remembered for. Even James Bernard's score sounded manically depressed.

Chapter Fourteen

THE GRISLY

DENOUEMENT

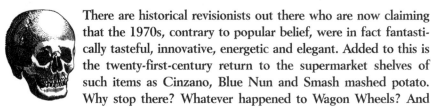

There are historical revisionists out there who are now claiming that the 1970s, contrary to popular belief, were in fact fantastically tasteful, innovative, energetic and elegant. Added to this is the twenty-first-century return to the supermarket shelves of such items as Cinzano, Blue Nun and Smash mashed potato. Why stop there? Whatever happened to Wagon Wheels? And why isn't there an Arctic Roll on our foldaway dining tables every single night?

In addition to this re-imagining of the recent past, there are those who would claim that of all the stylish years in the 1970s, 1974 was up there among the coolest.

But it wasn't. It really wasn't.

My seven-year-old self is going to come forward and take a bow here. That's the one, living in unselfconscious suburban bliss in Crystal Palace, south London. It's Saturday and mum is going to the hairdressers, called Barberella. Quite good, that pun. In fact, I've only just got it, over thirty years on. Anyway, to alleviate the boredom, I am allowed to buy a comic from the newsagent next door. And what does my eye alight upon?

It is a brand new comic from Marvel, long-time purveyors of *The Hulk* and *Spiderman* and *The Fantastic Four*. But this one features a rather more unusual form of superhero. He has a widow's peak and a cape with a sort of crescent-shaped collar. The title of this publication – and this surely cannot be a false memory – is *Dracula Lives*.

I'm struggling, really struggling, to remember what it was ever about, except that Marvel had contrived to turn Dracula into the misunderstood anti-hero. Could that be right? Actually no. Occasionally he would join forces with humanity to see off bigger devilish threats but, on the whole, it was

Dracula vs. a team of vampire hunters. Oh, and the Count now had a daughter called Lilith. Soon I was having this excellent comic delivered along with the newspapers. I remember my father's eyebrows knitting as he caught sight of it one morning. But this was the same man who had, that same year, allowed me to stay up for the first twenty minutes of an ITV screening of *The Evil of Frankenstein*. Now, Dracula as a character was out of copyright and the Marvel version was not interlinked with Hammer's own saga. But it is not difficult to see the inspiration that Christopher Lee may have provided.

Anyway, that I think was as good an illustration as any of how far Hammer's efforts had seeped into the national consciousness. To have your monster made the star of a children's comic is one of the most extraordinary endorsements you can have.

It went further in 1976 with a monthly magazine aimed at the teenage market called *House of Hammer*, again with the full-hearted endorsement of the studio. The centrepiece of each issue would be a comic strip adaptation of one of the Hammer Horrors, from *The Gorgon* to *Brides of Dracula*. Remember, children, that this was the age just prior to video, when you couldn't see films on demand as you can now. You had to wait for them to come on telly or see productions transmogrify into a different form altogether. The magazine also featured reviews and previews of all the current horror films, together with some splendidly unpleasant stills. This enterprise managed to keep going until 1978.

And this was in addition to all the other Dracula-related fun available to the young. Including Dracula figurines that you could daub with luminous paint so they would glow in the dark in your bedroom. And Peter Powell kites in the shape of vampire bats with Dracula faces on them. And joke plastic fangs, which always made the mouth fill with saliva and could not be taken out without an accompanying waterfall of drool. You could even get coffin-shaped piggy banks – the idea was that you put the penny on a certain spot and a white skeleton hand would emerge from beneath a tiny fold of cloth and snatch it. The macabre imagery of Hammer was all over the high street.

But by 1974, Hammer itself was fading fast. Michael Carreras knew very well that as far as gothic costume horror was concerned, the game was up. Others thought otherwise. Thus Peter Cushing, talking of plans for the studio's final vampire epic: 'Michael Carreras thought that twenty years of that kind of film was enough,' the actor said. 'But of course it was like people wanting a box of chocolates still to have their favourite assortment in it; they didn't want anything new out of the Hammer stable.'[1]

All very well, but where was the money for a new box of chocolates to come from? In 1974 it came from the Hong Kong film-makers the Shaw Brothers who had a novel suggestion to put to Carreras. The result was *The Legend of the Seven Golden Vampires*.

Even over the distance of all these years, this is a film that still has the power to make one shake one's head in admiring disbelief at its sheer insanity. It is off its head. The unique selling point this time round is that it's Dracula – with kung fu! Given the then vogue for all sorts of martial arts, sparked by Bruce Lee and *Enter the Dragon* and continued on television with David Carradine, it had an undeniable appeal as an idea. What puts the brass hat of utter beguiling madness on it is the period setting.

So once more, and for the final time, enter Peter Cushing as Van Helsing, the real one this time, not the grandson. He's in China. As indeed is Dracula who has contrived to take the form of a Chinese monk. Because it is a film that is best watched when one is very, very drunk, the rest is a sort of eerie and rather colourful blur. There is a blonde woman; there are creepily-masked vampires on horseback, filmed through an unsettling gauze; there are great pools of livid reds and greens everywhere; Van Helsing gets to fight and run about just as much as he did in 1958 but this time he is helped by people who have kung fu moves; and then, at the very end, Van Helsing has the Chinese monk trapped ... and the monk turns back into Dracula. Except it's not! It's nowhere near! Instead of Christopher Lee, it's someone called John Forbes-Robertson. They have given him the hair and the clothes but it looks like someone pretending to be Dracula in a comedy sketch. Van Helsing doesn't look tremendously convinced either. But he stakes him, anyway, and Dracula dissolves for the final time in a Hammer film. As well as the iconic silky cloak lining, we have one bonus shot of the vampire's eyeball popping out, which after a few pints, is something we can all do without.

It sounds execrable but in fact it isn't. That's not to say that it is good either. Thus a review in *Melody Maker* magazine:

> Perhaps the worst film I have ever seen. The part of Christopher Lee is played by a gent called John Forbes-Robertson who looks like an old queen whose make-up has run ... the part of Peter Cushing is played, rather reluctantly, by Peter Cushing ... the part of a pair of big tits with a Swedish accent is played by Julie Ege ... why do otherwise intelligent people pay money to see this garbage? I don't know. That's why I'm going to see it again next week.[2]

It's a classic of something, although it is difficult to say quite what. And actually it did rather well in Britain. As the hit song of that same year went, 'Everybody was kung fu fighting ...'

But it was also a bit of a dead end. After you have had shaolin warrior vampires kicking and punching their way around, where do you go? On top of this, more pertinently, where does one go when the studio no longer has the funds to do anything?

As already mentioned, Hammer did manage to squeeze out an adaptation of the television sitcom *Man About the House*. But generally, as with the rest of the British film industry, from Rank to EMI, things were looking very thin indeed. More and more cinema screens were closing, making the transformation into bingo halls. And the awful thing was that they weren't mourned.

In 1975, even though the stake was firmly in the studio's heart, it still writhed around a bit, clawing the air, and the result was a return to Dennis Wheatley with *To the Devil a Daughter*. The film is almost too unpleasant and humourless to watch. Nastassja Kinski (creepily, just fifteen years of age then) plays a young nun who is targeted by the forces of darkness. Christopher Lee is the satanic priest, Richard Widmark is the American who has been brought in in the hope that the film will do some business in the US, and Denholm Elliott is the man looking agonised while holding a naff 1970s Trimphone receiver. It was a film beset with horrendous production difficulties, script changes, outbreaks of ill-temper from Widmark; and yet, rather surprisingly, it did reasonably well in British cinemas.

Doing reasonably well butters no parsnips, however, and the effort involved in securing financing for films was, in those increasingly stagflationary days, a Sisyphean task. And yet Michael Carreras pushed on, determinedly – one might say with a level of bonkers optimism. He wrote to the then notorious director Ken Russell. As well as an Oscar-winning adaptation of *Women in Love* (1969), Russell had directed *The Devils* (1972) which not only featured nuns cavorting naked, but Oliver Reed being burnt at the stake, his flesh seeming to sear and pop in the flames. In other words, Russell was never one for holding back, when it came to either horror or sex.

Carreras wanted him for a project entitled 'Vlad the Impaler'. Vlad Tepes was a mediaeval Romanian nobleman who, as well as holding back the Turkish hordes in eastern Europe, was also noted for his amazing brutality – the legend had it that entire fields would be filled with victims impaled upon sharpened stakes, slowly and agonisingly slipping down the wood. And of course, he is widely credited as having been the original inspiration for the figure of Count Dracula. So it was quite natural for Hammer to turn to this figure of distant legend as a means of propagating the vampire cycle.

But having received Carreras's letter, Ken Russell ruefully wrote back:

> In your letter, you say you feel it time the horror film becomes
> respectable. In my opinion, it always has been and to my mind, Vlad
> is no exception. All the potentially sexy scenes are downright coy!
> What I have always felt is that most horror movies rely on gratuitous

sadism instead of spine-chilling invention. And once again, Vlad backs up my theory: the blood bath at the end is as unnecessary as it is obnoxious. I would like to make a horror film with you – a real one.[3]

Russell never did – although it is worth digressing briefly to illustrate how, just over ten years later, he made two rather wonderful homages to Hammer. The first was *Gothic* (1986), which told the story of the weekend at the Villa Diodati in 1816 when Mary Shelley was inspired to write *Frankenstein*. Russell turns it into a horror film psychodrama, with Gabriel Byrne's Byron summoning unholy forces, Julian Sands' Shelley seeing nightmare figures in the barn and Natasha Richardson's Mary haunted by Freudian bad dreams involving priapic walking suits of armour. In invoking the thunderstorm and the big house, Russell was tipping his hat to Hammer while outlining a rather more modish view of horror as psychotherapy. Two years later came *The Lair of the White Worm* which was an even more straightforward tribute to the studio, even down to the opening titles in gothic script, picked out in bright red against shots of green grass. In this, an adaptation of a Bram Stoker story, a very young Hugh Grant (and what are the bets he has had this film buried in some secret vault?) investigates mysterious bitings, a strange reptile skull found at an archaeological dig, and a beautiful woman (Amanda Donohoe) who not only has a swaying, snake-like walk but actually turns into a penis-biting cobra woman when the moon is full. Nothing coy about the sex there, Ken! But he would probably argue that Hammer were thinking it, if never actually showing it. Anyway, the point is that for one brief moment, Ken Russell returned the horror movie to the environs of big houses and woodland settings. Clearly where it should have been all along.

Ken Russell was not the only arty director to have used the Hammer template as a launching pad: in 1973, and 1974, the American artist Andy Warhol stepped forward to tip his own hat to the studio with two imaginative reworkings of Frankenstein and Dracula. *Flesh for Frankenstein* (1973) was produced by Warhol, directed by Paul Morrisey and starred Udo Kier. It was very gory but intended both as a black comedy and a satire on the bourgeoisie, if you will.

The follow-up, *Blood for Dracula* (1974), seemed a rather more thought-out, wry affair. Once more produced by Warhol, with the same production team headed by director Paul Morrisey, this told the story of an exhausted Dracula travelling from Transylvania to Italy in the hope that a Catholic country could offer him a better class of victim than the cynical youth-thronged Communist Eastern Europe. In Italy he meets a man who is keen to marry his daughters off to wealthy men – as a member of the stricken bourgeoisie in the middle of a stagflationary economic crisis, he badly needs the old money that Dracula represents. If Hammer were always keen to portray its monsters in terms of sublimated class conflict, it took Warhol and his associates to bring the economic consequences of vampirism to the surface. Together, naturally, with lashings of blood.

It would be wrong, incidentally, to omit any mention of the kitschiest homage ever paid to Hammer Horror; it may not be art, but it is now sure as hell cult. 1972 saw the release of an American production called *Blacula*. As the title suggests, this was a prime slab of platform-booted blaxploitation, but one that gave us the screen's first black vampire in the shape of William Marshall. He plays the part of Mamawulde who is vampirised by a racist Count Dracula in 1780 and imprisoned within a coffin; when that coffin is purchased in the present day by two gay antique dealers, Blacula is awoken and goes off in search of the reincarnation of his lost love. It sounds mortifying, but actually the element of the film that appeared to cause most offence at the time was the depiction of the gay antique dealers. And it did sufficiently well to merit two sequels. Recently, it was cited in a Gnarls Berkeley video, as well as several episodes of *The Simpsons*. And all of this, from Warhol to Harlem, goes to show just how flexible that old Hammer iconography was.

Closer to home, in 1975, Michael Carreras may have been a little hurt to see key members of the Hammer family jumping ship and joining a putative Hammer competitor called Tyburn Films. This was set up by Kevin Francis, the son of veteran Hammer director Freddie Francis, who succeeded in employing the services of his father for two horror films: *Legend of the Werewolf* (1974) and *The Ghoul* (1975). Providing the scripts for these Tyburn horrors was none other than John Elder aka Anthony Hinds. Behind the make-up chair was Hammer's old monster man Roy Ashton. And in front of Tyburn's cameras stood Peter Cushing and, in *The Ghoul*, Veronica Carlson. It must have seemed like a slap-up reunion, if it hadn't been for the absence of the Carreras clan. Tyburn was based at Pinewood. These two films are very rarely seen now but in fact, they weren't too bad. *Legend* was a roundabout re-telling of *The Curse of the Werewolf*, with David Rentoul as a young man brought up by wolves, who falls in love with a prostitute in nineteenth-century Paris and gets hairy with her paying customers. Peter Cushing is a comedy pathologist and Ron Moody was in there too, as a comedy zookeeper. Then came *The Ghoul* which advanced the period setting a little to the 1920s and featured a secluded, mist-enshrouded house in Cornwall, John Hurt as a sinister gardener, Veronica Carlson, playing, as *Melody Maker* might put it, the pair of big tits, stranded travellers, eastern mysticism and a monster in the attic. There were high hopes that Tyburn might somehow inherit the torch of horror from Hammer. It was not to be. After *The Ghoul*, that was it.

And Hammer itself was slowly sinking beneath those grim waves of recession although it is worth bearing in mind that come 1975, there were no British films in production at either Elstree or Pinewood. Oh, but how Michael Carreras held on!

He had an idea that the studio should branch out into the recording industry, putting out Hammer horror stories on LPs, acted out by the usual bunch. He had the notion of releasing the films' soundtracks on records.[4] Someone suggested a TV series made on videotape, for the purposes of holding down production costs; the only reason this notion failed in the mid-1970s was that the original Hammer films were still being shown, during summer, on a weekly basis on BBC2. Carreras noted beadily that the Carry On team, also at the fag end of film investment, had taken instead to the theatres with an enormously successful show called *Carry On Christmas*, featuring all the favourites, but on stage. And so there was the suggestion that Hammer should follow suit, heading into theatre with a gothic horror show. The idea was not received with universal enthusiasm.[5]

One of British cinema's éminences grises, Bryan Forbes, whose slightly scratchy dealings with Hammer in the early 1970s when he was the managing director of EMI have been described, found himself being approached in the mid-1970s to help rescue the old concern in cinematic terms. An expert scriptwriter, the screenplay he wrote was for an epic production called 'Nessie', which would dramatise the Loch Ness Monster and be a sort of cross between King Kong and Jaws. 'It was a sort of horror in that it was a monster movie,' he recalled. Forbes wrote a very detailed screenplay, one involving underwater ruins and oil rigs in the Indian ocean getting wrecked. And there was a suggestion that David Frost wanted to get involved, with his company Paradine. 'But it disappeared,' said Forbes. 'Just disappeared without trace, really.' Forbes still has the script, and production sketches and, as with many of the great 'what-ifs' of cinema, you do find yourself wondering if it could ever have given the company a new lease of life, or whether the studio was now inextricably intertwined with gothic.

Carreras gave it another shot, this time with a project called 'Vampirella'; a concoction in which the lead character, fanged as the title would suggest, is in fact the heroine, a kung-fu fighting Avenger kind of vampire in a spoofy battle against aliens.[6] Given that *The Rocky Horror Picture Show* had opened in 1975, it is more than possible that the musical was an influence on the project. Again, it's impossible to say how the film might have done if only Carreras had ever found the financing for it. A great gobbling turkey? Or a cult hit on the lines of *Dracula AD 1972*?

Cruelly, 1976 brought another blockbuster American horror, and this one filmed on Hammer's home turf in London. *The Omen* – which, as you recall, involved Gregory Peck as the US ambassador to Britain accidentally adopting Satan's firstborn – continued the American obsession with insidious and unsuspected corruption within. When it came to President Nixon and Watergate, they very clearly had still to get over it. But it enjoyed the sort of glossy budget that would have made Michael Carreras sit down and weep. There were hangings, decapitations, impalings and devil dogs. And there was our old friend Patrick Troughton as a priest, a shade more restrained in this, and ending up with a church lightning rod jammed through him. And once again, no period costumes, no faux country accents, no sudden and jarring switches from location to studio. *The Omen* put the seal on the horror film as a contemporary genre speaking to contemporary unease.

As the 1970s ground on, so the House of Hammer continued to decay, stone by stone. Indeed, Carreras and co. were obliged to give up the Wardour Street offices of Hammer House itself and move into less convenient accommodation at Pinewood. And yet, and yet ... this is where we see the difference between the grey world of blank corporatism and the altogether more eccentric face of the family business. By this point, there are few of us who would not merely have thrown in the towel, but actually hurled it out of the window. But Michael Carreras had inherited the Hammer mantle (actually, Sir James was still alive – he lived until 1990 – he had simply retired) and he had family pride. Enrique Carreras had kicked it all off with William Hinds; James Carreras had run with it, giving the world a new byword for horror; and Michael could not bear to see it all grinding to a halt with him, despite the fact that he must have seen that the entire British film industry was in the same stricken state. It was in no way his fault.

There was one last shot, one last attempt to galvanise the whole enterprise. The idea was for a remake of the 1930s Hitchcock classic *The Lady Vanishes*. At one point, the name of George Segal was mooted for the lead – naturally an American would give the film a much better chance in the States.[7] One is somehow reminded of those first Hammer Quatermass films with Brian Donlevy there for the purposes of US distribution. The two American leads that they eventually got were Elliot Gould and Cybil Shepherd, with those great stalwarts Arthur Lowe and Herbert Lom batting for Britain. There was location filming in Austria – imagine, after all those years, actually going to middle Europe for real, rather than clip-clopping through those Pinewood spinneys! Added to this, the film seemed to come in the midst of a revival for period adventure – around that time we also saw remakes of *The Thirty Nine Steps* (with Robert Powell) and *The Riddle of the Sands* (with Simon Ward), which in themselves were probably reactions against the all-conquering futurism of *Star Wars* (1977) which had taken over the world from the very moment it opened.

And you know, *The Lady Vanishes* really wasn't bad. Gould and Shepherd may not have been Robert Donat and Margaret Lockwood but it was engaging and funny and Gould got to hang on the outside of the moving train and it was all good-humoured and thoroughly fine family entertainment. A Hammer film with a child-friendly 'A' certificate. In many ways, it was a summary of what Michael Carreras was clearly about. Like his father, he wanted as many people as possible to see the films made under his aegis. Unlike his father, he just didn't want those films to be gothic horrors.

The film opened and belly-flopped. The assorted bankers and investors who had been propping Hammer up finally shook their heads. The gig was up. Michael Carreras shrugged and resigned.[8] The stake was driven through the company's heart. It writhed, it wheezed and then it turned to dust.

But as with any good Hammer creation, that was by no means the end of the story. It was to find one last late flowering in a different medium; and indeed the old films themselves were to find fresh life when seen through the eyes of a new generation of upcoming film directors who, like everyone else, had been raised on these colourful horrors. The films may have ceased production but the studio's undead life was about to begin.

Chapter Fifteen

FROM BEYOND THE GRAVE

 For those of a certain age, one particular television series would have been not only their first taste of Hammer but indeed their first taste of horror altogether. So it is not surprising that *The Hammer House of Horror* anthology series made for ITV in 1980 is so fondly remembered. There were thirteen one-hour long episodes, each telling a different story, each with a different cast and director. The idea was that it would be the same old Hammer, but simply twisted around for a modern TV audience.

Perhaps you were one of those who breathlessly watched the moody opening titles, featuring what was certainly a house, though not looking much like any previous Hammer house, with a light in a window being extinguished by a camp silhouette. Perhaps you felt your heart start to thump at the title music, a lazy eight-note affair with one of those twirly *Rentaghost* flute effects at the end. If either of the above is true, then I put it to you that you were a wuss, even if you were six years old. For those of us brought up on the real thing, this pallid TV version was milk and water stuff.

It is not that the scripts weren't inventive. We all remember the one with Ingrid Pitt and the vampire eagle and the one with the creepy African statue called 'Charlie Boy'; some of us recall the episode with Denholm Elliott trapped in a recurring dream, part of which involved the most unrealistic telephone box prop ever committed to celluloid. And let's not leave out that one where Nicholas Ball and family move into an ordinary-looking suburban house and blood starts gushing out of the pipes, ruining an otherwise enjoyable child's birthday party. That one was called 'The House that Bled to Death' and in general conversation seems to have been the one that inspired the most nightmares in the young.

No, the fault didn't lie with producer Roy Skeggs or his fine intentions: this was, over the space of thirteen weeks, a genuinely spirited effort to keep the entire notion of Hammer – quality purveyors of quality horror – alive and kicking. They even managed to get Peter Cushing for one episode, 'The Silent Scream'. The series faced two problems: ITV, having just emerged from a year-long strike which had kept it off the air, was still punch-drunk and all over the place and never quite knew what to do with the series. As a result, it was transmitted at all sorts of different times across the network (unlike, say, *Coronation Street* which would go out at the same time everywhere so people knew when it would be on); this instantly weakened *Hammer House*'s ratings. The second problem was expectations: because vintage Hammer films were still so prominent on the television, routinely filling either Friday or Saturday night horror slots, so the TV series caused some bafflement over the absence of a) fangs, b) low-cut gowns and c) castles. It was never really entirely certain what the series was supposed to be.

Also, in cinematic terms, the horror genre had been developing rather fast. 1977 saw the British release of the still-notorious *Texas Chainsaw Massacre*. Like *The Exorcist* before it, there were awed anecdotal accounts of audiences projectile-vomiting at this black inversion of a Scooby Doo story, where the traveller van and its goofy contingent of teenagers lands up stranded in the badlands of the Midwest at Ed Gein's place and the guy in the scary leather mask is not the janitor but an inbred serial killer who dismembers his victims with power tools and turns their flesh into home decorations. A friend of my mother's, an amused and highly cynical PR, went to see it for a dare in Notting Hill Gate and returned swearing that she had seen people being sick into specially provided bags.

Then in 1978 came the John Carpenter classic *Halloween*. This was the first film to bring horror to the suburbs. As everyone must undoubtedly be aware, this story involved babysitter Jamie Lee Curtis being terrorised by an escaped loony, with even the picket fences and wisteria hedges of American suburbia acquiring a level of deep menace. And again, it changed the ground rules of horror, just as Hammer had done twenty years previously. This could be seen most notably in the climax: in the old days, when a monster was defeated, that was that; the audience could breathe a sigh of relief. But this particular chap, no matter how often he was stabbed, shot and fell out of windows, just wouldn't stay down. The audience was allowed no let-up right until the very, very end. One might say that this had been Hammer's game too; but Carpenter did not allow the reassuring distance of the supernatural in period costume.

One of Michael Carreras's other spin-off ideas came to fruition around this time: 1980 saw the grand opening of a new London attraction called the Palladium Cellars located, as the name suggested, round the back of the famous theatre. The notion was a sort of cross between Madame Tussauds and the London Dungeon. Instead of waxworks, there were animatronic figures. The most impressive was a tableau from *The Curse of the Werewolf*; the Oliver Reed lycanthrope is found holding the bars in its green-lit cell. As visitors walked past, the werewolf suddenly sprang to mechanical life, growling and shaking the bars. It was a good fright. There were other tableaux such as a Dracula arrangement, something based on the Vincent Price horror *Theatre of Blood* and, slightly puzzlingly, a mock-up of a futuristic spaceship corridor.

The notion had novelty, and it managed to get itself a great deal of publicity, especially on television, but it was not destined to work. The exhibition was just slightly too obscure, slightly too difficult to find and slightly too expensive to get into. Those few visitors sometimes found that they had the place to themselves, which had the effect of making the animatronic werewolf slightly more unnerving.

Hammer returned for one more television series in 1984 but, in order to guarantee an American sale, had to drop the word 'horror' from the title; the television executives felt it was too much. So instead we had the *Hammer House of Mystery and Suspense*. This batch of thirteen stories wasn't altogether bad – Susan George made a very fine heroine getting trapped in a nightmare behind the Iron Curtain in 'Czech Mate'. But they weren't Hammer. In Britain, some of these dramas went out after 11 p.m. on Monday nights, possibly to lower audiences than *Newsnight*.

Moreover, by now we were well into the age of the 'video nasty'. Home video was finally becoming a widespread phenomenon (yes, children, there was a time Before Video when there were only *three* TV channels) with films available for sale or rental, and among the early delights on offer were items such as *Cannibal Holocaust, Nightmares in a Damaged Brain, I Spit on Your Grave* and *Driller Killer*. How the *Daily Mail* howled, and it was quite right to do so. Horror had always been the delinquent of the film world; but this was borstal sociopath territory, marked with a grinding nihilism. One might now look back and detect a post-punk sensibility – civilised values disintegrating into anarchy and violence in a world seemingly teetering on the brink of nuclear armageddon. Febrile times, the early 1980s, especially in Britain, where Margaret Thatcher had begun the process of dismantling Britain's old industrial base, unemployment was rocketing and, in economic terms, many people now felt themselves to be looking into an abyss.

In screen terms, things were not much more reassuring in the cinemas: the age of the 'slasher' horror was upon us, as exemplified by *Friday The 13th* (1980) and its innumerable sequels. The supernatural had been almost wholly banished in favour of the lone psycho, masked, inexorable, impossible to reason with and seemingly indestructible. Countless American screen teenagers were hacked, stabbed and gouged, in woods, in campsites, in barns, in fairgrounds. Joe Dante's *The Howling* (1980) and John Landis's *American Werewolf in London* (1981) brought a transfusion of modernism to the lycanthropy genre. Stanley Kubrick introduced the mannered style of art house with his adaptation of Stephen King's *The Shining* (1980), as well as, in one scene, a literal flood of Kensington gore, more than poor old Hammer could ever have rustled up. David Cronenberg initiated the sub-genre of 'body horror' with *Scanners* (1980). In other words, the horror film was once more thriving. The truth is that it nearly always does. But it had taken on a completely radical, new – and Americanised – form.

Then, around 1981/2, the first Hammers tentatively made their way on to VHS, available at rental shops. How very sweet they suddenly seemed. For the studio to have gone back into production at that point – even if it could have done – would already have been an exercise in nostalgia.

So was that it then? It certainly seemed so. Throughout the 1980s, Hammer maintained an office, the company under the control of Roy Skeggs. Increasingly the films were featuring in art-house festivals. They were still shown regularly on television. The VHS video market started to expand further, and it now became possible for fans to own earlier, rarer Hammer Horrors. Every now and then, the newspapers – all largely in favour of dear old Hammer – would occasionally report that the studio was rising from the grave, going back into production, preparing some fresh shockers for a new generation. Projects were in and out of development. But nothing ever came of it.

But come the 1990s, it became clear that the films were not entirely dead, that they did in fact live on in another form. For a number of top American directors started to make plain the formative influence that those Hammers had had on them.

Martin Scorsese, as we have seen, was happy to speak up for the merits of *Frankenstein Created Woman* (1967) and its metaphysics. It was said that Steven Spielberg had long been a Hammer fan. Meanwhile George Lucas tipped his hat to Hammer by casting Peter Cushing as the villain Grand Moff Tarkin in the original *Star Wars* (1977) – Cushing once said that the name made him sound like something that lived in a wardrobe[1] – and Christopher Lee as the satanic Count Dooku (now what does that name conjure?) in *Attack of the Clones* (2003).

John Carpenter, who by the end of the 1980s had pretty much established himself as the genre's leading director (as well as *Halloween*, we had had

The Fog [1980] and *The Thing* [1982] amongst others), at last came forward to declare the debt that he felt he owed to Hammer. His 1988 production *Prince of Darkness*, featuring Donald Pleasance heading up a team of scientists who make an ancient and terrible discovery in the crypt of a church, was a virtual remake of *Quatermass and the Pit*. A few years later, he wrote of the key Hammers and of the director that inspired him.

> Terence Fisher's first horror film, *The Curse of Frankenstein*, has haunted me from 1957 until this moment, The films were graphic, by the standards of the late 1950s and 60s – but they were also visually elegant and crafted with authority and passion and their creator was an artist ... [Fisher had] an absolute commitment to storytelling, to style and point of view – he took his stories and characters seriously ...
>   Anybody who has made a horror picture since 1957 has been influenced by Terence Fisher. He changed the rules and set the standard. I was especially motivated by *Dracula*, one of the five best horror movies of all time ... when I consider doing a horror picture, I think of that final confrontation between Dracula and Van Helsing.[2]

Bravo! Equally cheering for Hammer-heads was Tim Burton's 1999 production of *Sleepy Hollow* which was a full-throated Hammer Horror in all but name. Johnny Depp, as Ichabod Crane, faces not only a demonic headless horseman but also a Hammer landscape of green woods and red blood, deserted villages and mist-wreathed studio scenes. Plus Christopher Lee as a judge, there to give us all the final wink that this tale of serial decapitations and a small huddled community going in fear is Burton's great homage to both a studio and a style.

When interviewed on the subject on the net by America's Cranky Critic, Burton had this to say about the films that he had so enjoyed as a child, watching saucer-eyed in Saturday matinees: 'A lot of the Hammer Horrors are those kinds of films where the images burn into your consciousness,' he said. 'They were like fairy tales. They were so strong. What they were so good at was bringing back that beautiful lurid horror movie.' He also hugely enjoyed casting Lee. 'You're sitting with Dracula,' Burton said. 'It's so intense!'[3]

Talking of intensity, the Hammer films also retain a very large and loyal base of fans. Actors who appeared in the films are regularly flown over to the States for conventions, where they are put up in five-star hotels and sell signed photographs of themselves to eager disciples.

Some of the Hammer film prints – those original lengths of celluloid – are now in rather aged condition; but a new digital age, free of celluloid, is poised to give these and other vintage films another shot of undead action. At the moment, it is relatively rare to be able to see a Hammer on the big screen, simply because prints are few and sometimes just not good enough for large projection. Once the prints have been cleaned up and digitised, however, the possibilities suddenly open up like never before.

Director and screenwriter Bryan Forbes has been considering this new digital future and how it will change the face of the multiplexes. 'Once a film has been digitised, the costs of screening it plummet,' he said.

> And for the multiplexes, this opens up amazing daytime possibilities –
> at the moment, their daytime audiences are practically zero and they
> are forced to play these same films currently out on release.
> Digitisation holds up the possibility of specially themed afternoon
> showings, say, when old films can be screened to an amazing level of
> quality, for very low amounts of money. There are whole new
> audiences out there to be lured in.

And this very much goes for Hammer too. The current owners of the company have plans to digitise all the films, thus making them widely available to any film festival or cinema that feels that it may want a Hammer season. There is no question that there will be an audience.

Each generation gets the horror films it deserves; and as Hammer Horror, on its fiftieth anniversary, settles securely into the landscape of British cinema, in its own unique aesthetic niche, we can judge a little more closely what sort of generation these films entertained. Outwardly more sophisticated than their 1940s predecessors about matters such as sex, certainly, but actually inwardly gauche; outwardly stronger-stomached when it came to the portrayal of violence where the good guys don't always necessarily win, but inwardly still yearning for the happy ending.

But there was more to it than this: like the Ealing comedies, Hammer Studios bequeathed an entire world to us; a genuinely appealing fantasy land where black horses are endlessly charging up and down wooded lakeside roads; where the inns are full and boisterous only until the point when someone comes in and mentions a certain word; where the distance implied on screen up the mountain to the painted castle is always covered in minutes by the protagonists; and where vampires, re-animated corpses, mummies and other assorted monsters rarely waste any time hanging around in the shadows, preferring the shock of high-key lighting. But for all the brutality, the outbreaks of moral ugliness and the crazy sexism, it's a rather romantic-looking world now. And as the years pass, its innocence will – unusually – grow.

Just as many of the Ealing comedies invited audiences into a relationship of delighted complicity with the anarchistic spirits that populated their films, from *Passport to Pimlico* (1949) to *The Lavender Hill Mob* (1951), so

Hammer sought to elicit sympathy for its comely young protagonists, always at the mercy of corrupted and decaying authority. It has been suggested by cultural historians such as Dominic Sandbrook that Hammer reflected a prevailing fear of technological advance; with all due respect, this is not the case at all. None of Baron Frankenstein's alchemical instruments ever pose a threat in themselves; rather, the tension in these narratives arises from the shape of the invented societies that they depict, which are backward, grotesquely top-heavy, still in many ways mediaeval structures, dominated by autocratic nobility but also administered by implacable local bureaucrats and thin-lipped police chiefs with scant regard for civil liberties. In some cases, we might argue that the general, loose idea was to invoke images of the British aristocracy, and the mandarin class beneath it, and the way that it still held a certain sway. But it would be daft to suggest that Hammer's social constructs resembled Britain's in any realistic way, or indeed any of the other countries where the films had such a devoted following. Rather, Hammer were playing on something older, more atavistic: the tremendously simple idea that an inexperienced young man and woman, with the help of a wise older person, can stand up to, and defeat, the most terrifying, evil personifications of abusive power. That's what you all paid your two and sixpence for. That is why Hammer had such genuinely international appeal. And that's why the films remain so very enjoyable today.

If the films tell us anything at all about the times in which they were made, then they tell us that it was a less cynical period; that at the cheaper end of the film scale, both producers and audiences were engaged in an amusing act of silent conspiracy, where the producers pretended to make scary films, and the audiences pretended to find them frightening. The Hammers were macabre and often tense but it is difficult to imagine now that they ever caused anyone a sleepless night.

We look back with great fondness on both Sir James Carreras and son Michael; two men who understood that films, primarily, had to be entertaining and make the audiences leave the cinema with a smile. The purity of their ambition – regardless of any financial motivation – is something to be applauded loudly today.

We also tip our hats to the designer Bernard Robinson and the composer James Bernard, who invested these make-believe landscapes of inns and turrets, these tales of tombs and corpses, with such overwhelming sincerity that the illusion rarely wavered.

A good Hammer film defies academic critical dissection; what on earth would be the point of such an exercise? Christopher Lee raising the hem of his cloak as he lowers his fangs into the neck of a barmaid in a wood; Peter Cushing pulling a face of intense concentration as, off camera, he removes the top of someone's head with a saw. Back in the 1960s and 70s, Hammers became known among showbiz correspondents and critics as 'screamies' and 'girl meets ghoul' pictures. Plain fun, in other words. An analysis of Terence Fisher's use of montage may be interesting to film students but it is ultimately not going to add to anyone's enjoyment.

When we watch a Hammer film today we are experiencing something pretty similar to the original audiences, except that we now tend to watch on DVD. One is not in the darkness with one's partner, in a tobacco-fumed auditorium, nestling in a slightly sticky plush seat, with the people around you either whispering incessantly or rustling about in bags of Fruit Gums. But we still have that momentary catch of breath, as James Bernard's music pulses out, and the words 'A Hammer Film Production' materialise on screen.

Will we ever see their like again? It currently seems unlikely – but then one can never be sure. Even the most unlikely and old-fashioned seeming things can make breathtaking comebacks. Who could have foretold that the BBC would have such monster hits in the resurrections of *Doctor Who* and *Robin Hood*? In the 1970s, who could ever have known that George Lucas's insanely nostalgic *Star Wars* would take over the world?

And there are rumours. There are always rumours. The actress Kate O'Mara was recently at a signing event in Milton Keynes, autographing, as it happens, that notorious 'nighties and coffin' publicity still from *The Vampire Lovers* (1970). As well as being impressed that there were still so many Hammer fans out there, she was also told that there were plans afoot to go into production again. 'It couldn't be done the same way as it was,' she said. 'You couldn't really go back to that. But it's still an interesting idea.'

If it is the case that a fresh lease of life looms, Hammer's owners are currently being coy. But it is interesting. Is there any possibility that following the current extremes of 'ordeal horror', audiences will once more yearn for something a little more stylised and romantic?

It is perfectly conceivable that in a few years' time, as digital techniques make film production all the cheaper, and as tastes become more and more niche, catered to by technologies that favour the esoteric, that someone – not necessarily Hammer – will decide that what horror needs is a return to gothic castles, big fangs, low-cut gowns and mist-enshrouded graveyards. They may decide that the only way such an enterprise could work would be to play it absolutely straight, to make it as believable as they can. They may even decide on a certain level of taste and restraint when it comes to matters of violence and sex.

Hmm. All right. Probably not for a while yet. But let's not forget Baron Frankenstein in his final Hammer outing, pledging that at some point, he will 'begin again'. Who can say absolutely that he won't?

NOTES

Chapter Two

1. From *Time* magazine, 1959.
2. *British Cinema of the 1950s – The Decline of Deference*, Sue Harper and Vincent Porter (Oxford University Press, 2003).
3. Ibid.
4. *Best of British: Cinema and Society 1930–1970*, Richards and Aldgate (Basil Blackwell, 1983).
5. *Films and Filming*, July 1964.
6. *Transatlantic Crossings*, Sarah Street (Continuum Publishing, 2003).
7. *Never Had it So Good*, Dominic Sandbrook (Little, Brown, 2006).
8. *The Hammer Story*, Marcus Hearn and Alan Barnes (Titan, 1997).
9. *Do You Want it Good or on Tuesday? – The Autobiography of Jimmy Sangster* (Midnight Marquee Press, 1997).
10. Ibid.
11. *The Peter Cushing Companion*, David Miller (Reynolds and Hearn, 2000).
12. Hearn and Barnes (1997).

Chapter Three

1. James Carreras, interviewed in *Variety* magazine, May 1958.
2. Hearn and Barnes (1997).
3. Sangster interviewed in the *Sunday Telegraph*, 1997.
4. Ibid.
5. Street (2003).
6. Ibid.
7. James Carreras, interviewed in *Variety* magazine, 1959.
8. Interview with Christopher Lee by Francis Wyndham in the *Observer* newspaper colour supplement, 1964.
9. *English Gothic – A Century of British Horror Cinema*, Jonathan Rigby (Reynolds and Hearn, 2000).
10. *Tall, Dark and Gruesome*, Christopher Lee (W.H. Allen, 1977).
11. Ibid.
12. Ibid.
13. Ibid.
14. Ibid.
15. Michael Carreras interviewed by John Brosnan in *The Horror People* (MacDonald and Jane's, 1976).
16. Terence Fisher interviewed by Brosnan (1976).

Chapter Four
1. Review in *Encounter* magazine, 1960.
2. Hearn and Barnes (1997).
3. *A History of Horrors*, Denis Meikle (Scarecrow Press, 1996).
4. Michael Carreras interviewed in *House of Horror* edited by Jack Hunter (Creation Books, 2000).
5. Rigby (2000).
6. Meikle (1996).
7. Ibid.
8. Margaret Robinson interviewed cited in Harper and Porter (2003)
9. Cited in *Caligari's Children*, S.S. Prawer (DeCapo, 1978).
10. Hearn and Barnes (1997).
11. *Hammer, House of Horror*, Howard Maxford, (Batsford, 1996).
12. James Carreras interviewed in *Uneasy Dreams: Golden Age of Horror*, Gary A. Smith (McFarland, 2000).
13. Hearn and Barnes (1997).
14. Sangster (1997).
15. Hearn and Barnes (1997).
16. Maxford (1996).
17. Hearn and Barnes (1997).
18. Ibid.
19. James Carreras interviewed in the *Observer*, 1963.
20. Meikle (1996).
21. Hearn and Barnes (1997).

Chapter Five
1. Meikle (1996).
2. Hearn and Barnes (1997).
3. Meikle (1996).
4. Hearn and Barnes (1997).
5. Interview with Jacqueline Pearce in *The Times*, 2006.
6. *Sixties British Cinema*, Robert Murphy (BFI Publishing, 1992).
7. Ibid.
8. Ibid.
9. Meikle (1996).
10. Ibid.

Chapter Six
1. James Carreras interviewed in the *Evening News*, 1966.
2. Meikle (1996).
3. Hearn and Barnes (1997).
4. Brosnan (1976).

Chapter Seven
1. Michael Carreras in a publicity interview for *She*, 1965.
2. Hearn and Barnes (1997).
3. Maxford (1996).
4. Hearn and Barnes (1997).
5. Rigby (2000)

6. Murphy (1992).
7. Maxford (1996).
8. Brosnan (1976).

Chapter Eight

1. *The Heritage of Horror – English Gothic Cinema 1946–72*, David Pirie (Gordon Fraser, 1973).
2. Anthony Hinds, quoted in Murphy (1992).
3. British Film Institute programme notes, 1987.
4. Pirie (1973).
5. Brosnan (1976).
6. Hearn and Barnes (1997).
7. Meikle (1996).
8. Interviewed on-set for *Dracula AD 1972* in the *Daily Mirror*, November 1971.
9. From Veronica Carlson's sleeve-note introduction to *The Hammer Frankenstein Film Music Collection* (GDI Records, 2000).
10. *Life's a Scream*, Ingrid Pitt (Heinemann, 1996).
11. Ibid.
12. Meikle (1996).
13. *Rungs on a Ladder – Hammer Seen through a Soft Gauze Lens*, Christopher Neame (Langham MD, 2003).
14. Hearn and Barnes (1997).

Chapter Nine

1. Hearn and Barnes (1997).
2. Ibid.
3. As featured in various national newspapers, 1968.
4. Brosnan (1976).
5. Hearn and Barnes (1997).
6. Ibid.
7. Meikle (1996).
8. Alan Bennett writing in *The Listener*, 1968.
9. Murphy (1992).
10. Meikle (1996).
11. Maxford (1996)

Chapter Ten

1. *Peter Cushing – An Autobiography* (Weidenfeld and Nicolson, 1986).
2. Meikle (1996).
3. Ibid.
4. Rigby (2000).
5. Smith (2000).
6. Maxford (1996).
7. As noted in *The Sunday Times*, 1970.
8. James Carreras interviewed in *The Sunday Times*, 1970.
9. Harry Fine interviewed in *Variety* magazine, 1970 .
10. Brian Clemens quoted by Michael Pye in *The Sunday Times*, 1972.
11. Michael Carreras interviewed in Hunter (2000).

Chapter Eleven
1. Meikle (1996).
2. Ibid.
3. Ibid.
4. Michael Carreras interviewed by Steve Swire in Hearn and Barnes (1997).

Chapter Twelve
1. Michael Carreras interviewed for the arts pages of the *Sunday Telegraph*, 1972.
2. *Shepperton Babylon*, Matthew Sweet (Faber and Faber, 2005)
3. Rigby (2000).
4. Hearn and Barnes (1997).
5. Neame (2003).
6. Hearn and Barnes (1997).
7. Meikle (1996).
8. Neame (2003).
9. Rigby (2000)
10. Hearn and Barnes (1997).
11. Meikle (1996).
12. *The Great British Picture Show*, George Perry (Hart Davis/MacGibbon, 1974).

Chapter Thirteen
1. Peter Cushing interviewed in the *Radio Times*, 1972, quoted in Miller (2000).
2. Brosnan (1976).
3. Murphy (1992).
4. Sangster (1997).
5. Lee (1997).
6. Lee interviewed by Brosnan (1976).
7. Cushing (1986).

Chapter Fourteen
1. Miller (2000).
2. Hearn and Barnes (1997).
3. Ibid.
4. Maxford (1996).
5. Meikle (1996).
6. Maxford (1996).
7. Hearn and Barnes (1997).
8. Rigby (2000).

Chapter Fifteen
1. Peter Cushing interviewed in the *Evening News*, 1980.
2. John Carpenter interviewed in *Charm of Evil – The Life and Films of Terence Fisher*, Winston Dixon (Scarecrow Press, 1991).
3. Tim Burton as interviewed on crankycritic.com.

FILMS

1935
Polly's Two Fathers
The Public Life of Henry the Ninth

1936
The Mystery of the Marie Celeste
The Bank Messenger Mystery
The Song of Freedom

1937
Sporting Love

1946
Candy's Calendar
Cornish Holiday
Crime Reporter
Old Father Thames

1947
Bred to Stay
Death in High Heels
Material Evidence
Skiffy Goes to Sea
We Do Believe in Ghosts

1948
Dick Barton, Special Agent
It's a Dog's Life
River Patrol
Tale of a City
The Dark Road
Who Killed Van Loon?

1949
Celia
Dick Barton Strikes Back
Doctor Morelle – The Case of the
    Missing Heiress

Fight for Life
Fight to the Finish
Foiled Again!
Jack of Diamonds
Plan for Revenge
Sudden Death
The Adventures of Dick Barton
The Fiendish Experiment
The Poison Dart
The Smugglers' Cove
The Tower of Terror
The Wail of Fear
The World at Stake
Trapped in the Snake House
Yellow Peril

1950
Dick Barton at Bay
Meet Simon Cherry
Monkey Manners
Room to Let
Someone at the Door
The Adventures of PC 49
The Lady Craved Excitement
The Man in Black
What the Butler Saw

1951
A Case for PC 49
Chase Me Charlie!
Cloudburst
Keep Fit with Yoga
The Black Widow
The Dark Light
The Rossitor Case
The Vicar of Bray
To Have and to Hold

1952
Death of an Angel
Never Look Back
Queer Fish
Stolen Face
The Lady in the Fog
The Last Page
Whispering Smith Hits London
Wings of Danger

1953
Four Sided Triangle
Mantrap
River Ships
Sky Traders
Spaceways
The Flanagan Boy
The Gambler and the Lady
The Saint's Return

1954
Blood Orange
Face the Music
Five Days
Life with the Lyons
Mask of Dust
Men of Sherwood Forest
The House Across the Lake
The Mirror and Markheim
The Stranger Came Home
Thirty Six Hours

1955
Break in the Circle
Murder by Proxy
The Quatermass X-Periment
The Glass Cage
The Lyons in Paris
The Noble Art
The Right Person
Third Person Risk

1956
A Man on the Beach
An Idea for Ben
Barbara's Boyfriend
Chaos in the Rockery
Copenhagen

Dick Turpin – Highwayman
Dinner for Mr Hemmingway
Just for You
Moving in
The Round Up
Women Without Men
X – The Unknown

1957
Clean Sweep
Quatermass II
The Abominable Snowmen
The Curse of Frankenstein
The Steel Bayonet

1958
A Man with a Dog
Dracula
Murder at Site 3
Sunshine Holiday
Camp on Blood Island
The Enchanted Island
The Revenge of Frankenstein
The Snorkel
Up the Creek
Further up the Creek

1959
Danger List
Day of Grace
Don't Panic Chaps!
I Only Arsked!
Operation Universe
Ten Seconds to Hell
The Hound of the Baskervilles
The Man Who Could Cheat Death
The Mummy
The Ugly Duckling
Ticket to Happiness
Yesterday's Enemy

1960
The Brides of Dracula
Hell Is a City
Never Take Sweets From a Stranger
O'Hara's Holiday
Sands of the Desert
The Stranglers of Bombay

Sword of Sherwood Forest
The Two Faces of Dr Jekyll
Visa to Canton

1961
A Taste of Fear
A Weekend with Lulu
Highway Holiday
The Curse of the Werewolf
The Full Treatment
The Shadow of the Cat
The Terror of the Tongs
Watch it, Sailor

1962
Captain Clegg
Land of the Leprachauns
Sportsman's Pledge
The Phantom of the Opera
The Pirates of Blood River

1963
Cash On Demand
Maniac
The Damned
The Scarlet Blade

1964
Nightmare
Paranoiac
The Curse of the Mummy's Tomb
The Devil Ship Pirates
The Evil of Frankenstein
The Gorgon
The Kiss of the Vampire
The Old Dark House

1965
Fanatic
Hysteria
She
The Brigand of Kandahar
The Nanny
The Secrets of Blood Island

1966
Dracula – Prince of Darkness
One Million Years BC
Rasputin the Mad Monk

The Plague of the Zombies
The Reptile
The Witches

1967
Frankenstein Created Woman
Quatermass and the Pit
The Mummy's Shroud
The Viking Queen

1968
A Challenge for Robin Hood
Do Me a Favour, Kill Me
Dracula Has Risen from the Grave
Eve
Jane Brown's Body
Matakitas Is Coming
Miss Belle
One on an Island
Paper Dolls
Slave Girls
Somewhere in a Crowd
The Anniversary
The Beckoning Fair One
The Devil Rides Out
The Girl of My Dreams
The Indian Spirit Guide
The Lost Continent
The New People
The Vengeance of She

1969
A Stranger in the Family
Frankenstein Must be Destroyed
Moon Zero Two
Poor Butterfly
The Killing Bottle
The Last Visitor
The Madison Equation
Wolfshead

1970
Crescendo
Taste the Blood of Dracula
The Horror of Frankenstein
The Scars of Dracula
The Vampire Lovers
When Dinosaurs Ruled the Earth

1971
Blood from the Mummy's Tomb
Countess Dracula
Creatures the World Forgot
Dr Jekyll and Sister Hyde
Lust for a Vampire
On the Buses
Hands of the Ripper
Twins of Evil

1972
Demons of the Mind
Dracula AD 1972
Fear in the Night
Mutiny on the Buses
Straight on till Morning
Vampire Circus

1973
Holiday on the Buses

Love Thy Neighbour
Man at the Top
Nearest and Dearest
That's Your Funeral!
The Satanic Rites of Dracula

1974
Captain Kronos – Vampire Hunter
Frankenstein and the Monster from Hell
Man About the House
Shatter
The Legend of the Seven Golden Vampires

1975
To the Devil a Daughter

1979
The Lady Vanishes

TELEVISION

1980 – *The Hammer House of Horror* (13 episodes, broadcast on ITV)

1984 – *The Hammer House of Mystery and Suspense* (13 feature-length episodes, broadcast on ITV)

WEBSITES

Naturally the internet is bristling with sites devoted to horror films, and there are a few devoted to Hammer in particular, not the least of which is the one maintained by the studio's current owners.

www.hammerfilms.com The official site for the studio, now partly hosted by myspace

www.unofficialhammerfilms.com Enthusiastic fan site, with all the latest news and events

www.pittofhorror.com The website of actress Ingrid Pitt, with news and also her own version of the Hammer story

www.christopherleeweb.com Christopher Lee's main website, with news of all of his latest projects, both acting and musical

www.petercushing.co.uk Website produced by the utterly devoted Peter Cushing Association, with history, essays and pictures

Index